Handy returned

D0182008

Phone 1-309

755 - 0720

Bird Walk Through the Bible

by Virginia C. Holmgren

DOVER PUBLICATIONS, INC.

New York

To all those who have gone
a-birding with me, especially
My Mother
who led me on many a bird walk
and taught me to look with
seeing eyes at the beauty of
earth, sea, and sky and all living,
growing things in God's wide world

Published in Canada by General Publishing Company, Ltd.,
30 Lesmill Road, Don Mills, Toronto, Ontario.
Published in the United Kingdom by Constable and Company,
Ltd., 10 Orange Street, London WC2H 7EG.

This Dover edition, first published in 1988, is an unabridged,
slightly corrected republication of the work first published by
The Seabury Press, New York, 1972.

Manufactured in the United States of America
Dover Publications, Inc., 31 East 2nd Street, Mineola, N.Y.
11501

Library of Congress Cataloging-in-Publication Data

Holmgren, Virginia C.
　　Bird walk through the Bible / by Virginia C. Holmgren.
　　　　p.　　cm.
　　Reprint. Originally published: New York : Seabury Press,
c1972.
　　Bibliography: p.
　　ISBN 0-486-25566-2 (pbk.)
　　1. Birds in the Bible.　　I. Title.
[BS664.H64　1988]
598.2933—dc19　　　　　　　　　　　　87-27013
　　　　　　　　　　　　　　　　　　　　　　CIP

CONTENTS

TO THE READER

Why look at Bible birds? Why look at birds of any kind? The second question has been tossed at me many times over more than a half century of birding. During the last dozen years when I have been writing about birds for *Northwest Magazine* in Sunday edition of Portland's *The Oregonian,* there have been two more questions: How did you get started? Why do you keep looking?

The "how" of starting is easily told—I was born a bird-watcher. My mother kept binoculars and bird guide on the hall table, ready for instant use whether a chirp called us from front door or back, and I learned the names of birds almost as soon as I learned my own.

Explaining why I'm still fascinated is easy, too—there's always more to learn. I am deeply grateful to David Bernstein, who has shared his knowledge of Hebrew texts, and to all the many authors who have written about birds and to Portland's Multnomah County Library (and especially to librarians Betty Johnson and Ellen Byrnes) and to many other libraries and librarians across the country whose books have enriched the hours.

In sum, my answers go like this:

When people shrug and say, "Why look at birds?"
I first of all feel sad they have to ask.
To look with wonder at the world God made
Is mankind's birthright—ours alone to claim.
The beasts have eyes, but not the inward look.
Even the soaring eagle, keenest eyed,
That sees the scampering rabbit far below
Has not the gift of wonder for the way

That motionless fur blends with the fading grass
And leaves no target for his hunter's gaze.

Only our wondering brings our wider world:
A robin at his worm hunt on the lawn—is its head cocked
    to listen, or to look?
A hummingbird in ballerina twirl—how does a bird fly
    backward, anyway?
And why are robin nests of grass and mud, while hum-
    mingbirds choose moss and spider webs?
Why do a pheasant hen and all her chicks come dressed
    in blending browns and dappled tones, while pheas-
    ant cocks flaunt battle-flag array?
And why do pheasants court with fantailed dance, while
    sparrows only know to hop and chirp like Jack-Be-
    Nimbles in a nursery rhyme?
The chickadee must hammer a seed's shell; the house
    finch simply turns it round and round, shucks off
    the hull and swallows down the meat. Why is the
    same food eaten different ways, with different beaks,
    each suited for its task?
How can mere feathered forms make migrant flight each
    spring and autumn through uncharted skies? Or
    should we say "uncharted" only to our own dim
    sight, but surely marked for theirs, we know not
    how?

The more we look, the more we find to learn. But all the
    looking, all the written lore, do not tell how the
    birds read sun and stars, know when and where to
    go on migrant wing, how best to fuel their bodies for
    far flight. Their mystery's still unsolved, unless we
    say it's done by God's great hand—which leaves it
    mystery still. . . .
Why look at birds?
    Now that's a question children and wise folk never
    have to ask.
    Children and wise folk say, "Let me look, too!"

PART ONE

Bible Birdlore

one

ASK THE BIRDS

Birds were everywhere in the mild and sun-warmed lands of ancient Bible times. This small crescent of earth between the Euphrates River and the Mediterranean Sea held hills and valleys, forests, mountains, seashores, marshes, lush grasslands and untouched wilderness, with food and shelter for birds of every sort.

Many birds stayed within these boundaries the year around, nesting in lowland thicket or on high mountain crag, in wilderness or dooryard as suited their different ways. Others came only on migration journey, following this curving arrow of earth as if it were a blaze mark directing them to the safer roundabout land route instead of the hazardous open-sea crossing.

Many of the migrants lingered only a few hours or a few days, just long enough to rest and feed and gain new strength before winging on to whatever farther land their heritage bound them. But for others this was the place where birds of their kind had come each summer or winter for untold ages. Twice each year the Holy Land was shadowed with these migrant wings, and the repeated pattern of these passing flights—coming each spring with the lengthening days and again each autumn with the longer, colder nights—could not possibly have gone unnoticed by the people of Bible times. The out-of-doors was their familiar world, and they used the signs of nature for hourglass, calendar, and weather chart.

Many of these people were shepherds, raising their tents to make a home wherever the grass grew greenest. To them especially the birds were part of every day's learning, for people who live on the land must know which birds are foe and which are friend and which can be welcome food. Even the children were taught to tell at a glance which wide-winged shape belonged to harmless pelican or stork and which was hawk or eagle about to swoop down and seize some newborn lamb from the ewe's side. Birds could be hunted for food in those days of simple homemade weapons without any danger of killing off an entire species, and the shepherd lad who knew where dove and partridge roosted and how the quail and ducks hid their nests could find his supper afield as quickly as a city boy could fetch it from the market stalls.

Then, too, the people of these wandering tribes came to look on birds and animals as neighbors and friends, and they whistled back at robin or wren just the way that city-folk waved and called to each other when they passed on the street. When a roving herdsman's family returned to a brook where they had camped before and heard the same kingfisher's rattling cry, the same trill from lark or blackbird, the familiar sounds surely must have seemed a friendly "Welcome home!"

Even city-folk can be lonely and so come to think of chirping sparrows and swallows as their friends. And the ravens, kites, and vultures that came daily to snatch up the garbage tossed onto streets and dungheaps must have been welcomed, too, for the good service they gave without any need for payment. Everyone knew birds of some kind, and from the smallest shepherd boy to the women gathering at the well, the priests in the temple and the king in his palace garden, they all learned something of bird ways, even without really trying.

In city and country, people passed on these small bits of birdlore almost unaware. "As gentle as a dove," they might say. Or, "as black as a raven." Such comparisons seem old-fashioned now, but they were bright and new and full of meaning in Bible lands long ago when poets and preachers, kings, historians, and prophets first put them into song, sermon, parable, and proverb—certain that all who read or listened would know the birds, too, and understand.

Picturesque phrases of bird imagery or realistic comments on bird ways can be found in 273 Bible passages. And the tally goes over 300 if you include all the verses that tell of the bird-winged cherubim and of the people and places with bird names. To make up this total of true birdlore there are 203 passages from the Old Testament, 47 from the New Testament, and 23 from later Hebrew writings called the Apocrypha. These Apocryphal Books were not part of the Jewish Holy Scripture, for the rabbis considered them wise, but not sacred. Protestant Bibles included them at first, then omitted them or put them apart in a separate section. Catholic Bibles still include them. So the number of birdlore passages you will follow as signposts marking the trail for Bible bird walk, depends on which Bible you use.

But whatever Bible provides the lines, you will find many reminders of birdlore you already know. Thousands of years, thousands of miles lie between us now and the time and place in which the Bible birdlore lines were written, but the call of the dove, the shape and color of a raven's wings, the power-flight of the eagle, and the small size of sparrows have not changed. If we can try to know birds as the people of Bible times did, it will seem as if we are back there with them, looking through their eyes, becoming a part of their world, finding new and clearer meaning in many Bible lines.

Before we can begin this adventure we have to understand that scholars do not all agree on the kinds of birds named by each word or phrase in Old Testament Hebrew or New Testament Greek. Consequently, the list of Bible birds may change with each translation you consult, especially for the Old Testament. Indeed, a few Hebrew words thought to be bird names by some translators are not counted as birds of any kind in other texts. But there are 60 Hebrew words in the canonical books of the Old Testament that are interpreted as "bird words" in at least one reputable version, each one a name for birds in general, or for some recognizable group—such as hawks—or for an individual kind. The New Testament repeats nine of these words and adds one more, while the Apocryphal Books repeat 11 and make one possible addition for a total of 62 bird words in the original texts, and there are a dozen words more for young birds, nests, wings, feathers, and flight.

But the total of Bible birds soon goes beyond this original summary when you begin to list all the English bird names in the various traditional texts approved in the past by Catholic, Greek Orthodox, Jewish, and Protestant churches and in the newer versions prepared by churchmen or independent scholars. No two texts seem to agree on all 62 entries, although when you put some of the variant translations side by side, you discover that the same bird was being listed after all— just recorded by a different English name.

Birds can collect an amazing number of names, nicknames, folk names, book names over the years. Even today, when the *Check-list* published by the American Ornithologists' Union gives each North American species just one official label, most of the common varieties still have their aliases in different sections of the continent. A good many of us still go on talking about hoot owls and bullbats and yellowhammers, even if these old labels aren't on the official list, and some Bible translators have been equally unconcerned about using the one right name that the ornithologists have published. And since so many of these unofficial names are in daily use, there's a good chance that you'll know some of these Bible birds by still a different name from any of the variations chosen so far by the translators.

You will know Bible birds by some name if you know the birds of our own continent, for every bird named in Bible text—except the ostrich and the mythical phoenix—if not exactly like some North American bird is close enough in looks

and habits to illustrate the same passage. A bird walk to see
and know the birds of the Bible can begin in your own backyard! You can match every birdlore Bible passage with a scene
you yourself will find as you take up the Bible bird trail.

Whatever translation you use for this walk, you will begin by reading some of the world's oldest written birdlore—
certainly the oldest still in continuous use—for the first five
books of the Bible are the ancient Holy Law of the Hebrews,
called the Torah. The boldly angled characters of its archaic
script have been translated into more languages than any
other book, and so people the world around have read this
first birdlore passage of Genesis 1:20–22:*

And God said, Let the waters bring forth abundantly the moving
creature that hath life, and fowl that may fly above the earth in
the open firmament of heaven. And God created . . . every
winged fowl after his kind: and God saw that it was good. And
God blessed them, saying, Be fruitful and multiply, and fill the
waters in the seas, and let fowl multiply in the earth.

Such is the wording of the world's best-known English
Protestant Bible, the King James, or Authorized, Version,
published in 1611. Almost identical wording is used in the
old Douay Version of the English Catholic Bible, written
about the same time. Like most books of those days, these
texts used *fowl* rather than *birds* when all kinds and sizes are
intended, in keeping with the older Anglo-Saxon custom. But
bird was sometimes given this broad meaning, too, although
the scholars who did the translating of the King James Bible
had been ordered to use the wording of the older translation
already established for church use, and so they often kept
phrases that were already old-fashioned, even in 1611. As a
result they included some bird names that hardly anyone rec-
ognizes now—one of the good reasons why we want to make
up our list of Bible birds from several versions. The New
English Bible of 1970 has a number of quite different birds.

* All biblical quotations are from the King James Version unless other-
wise indicated.

So does the Catholic New American Bible of 1970, and we especially want to read the new translations by Jewish scholars, the beautifully written Torah (1962) and the books of Ruth, Esther, Song of Songs, Ecclesiastes, Lamentations, and Jonah (published as *The Five Megilloth and the Book of Jonah*) as we prepare our way on Bible bird walk.

You might say that Job first suggested this walk—or at least told us why looking at birds was worthwhile:

But ask now the beasts and they shall teach thee, and the fowls of the air and they shall tell thee . . . that the hand of the Lord hath wrought this . . . (Job 12:7–9).

In other words, look at birds to know that there was indeed a God, a Creator. Whether he made the world and its wonders in six short days like our own or in the immeasurable day-span marked for God's reckoning in Psalm 90 can be put aside here for a united faith that he was here at the beginning to set it all in motion, and the more we learn of birds, the more certain we are of a Creator's guiding hand.

Each kind of bird has a different form, a different role in keeping nature in balance between supply and need, between prey and predator. Each has its enemies, but each also has its means of defense, even against man, so that all have both challenge and fair chance in a world where everything must be a part of the whole.

Some eat weed seeds, satisfying their own hunger as they check the overwhelming spread of thistle, dandelion, and dock. Many scatter pollen and fruit seeds so that new food crops will flourish another season. Some eat insects that destroy crops or carry sickness, and others feed on fast-multiplying rats, mice, and snakes. The birds of prey take whatever birds or small animals are easiest to catch—the old and weak, the sick, the crippled, the stupid—and thus only the stronger and healthier ones are left to raise young. When some healthy animal falls victim, it is only part of the way in which the balance is kept even, with no one species multiplying beyond fair measure. Scavenger birds keep the final score, cleansing the earth of a lion's half-eaten kill, of the rotting carcass of whatever bird or beast dies unburied, of all sorts of filth strewn about by careless or unthinking people—thereby saving both man and beast from the full penalty in disease and death that untended carrion would surely bring. And there are birds to match each of the many different kinds of places that the world contains. Some live in meadows, others in mountain or marsh, seashore or forest; there are birds for both tropics and tundra, wilderness and city streets. Each is fitted in wing, beak, feet, and body for the kind of place it calls home and the kind of food it eats; but if the food becomes scarce or the place changes—by earthquake or flood or man's ever spreading encroachment—then the bird must change, too, or perish.

Some birds have been able to make the needed changes. Pigeons that once nested only on rocky seacoasts and riverbanks now make themselves at home on skyscraper window-sills, bridges, and railroad stations. Birds that once followed the bison to feed on its body ticks and the insects stirred up by moving hoofs have left the prairies for the barnyards and are now called cowbirds. Finches on the barren Galapagos Islands have learned to pick up a thorn and pry out the insects from narrow crevices in tree bark that their blunt beaks could not fit into, yet their well-fed cousins elsewhere have never learned this trick—or ever needed to—and both the changing and the original pattern are part of the wonder that birdwatching reveals.

The woodpecker is not named in any Bible passage, but it can surely show us what wonders God can work. Many trees are alive in the woods today because these birds got rid of wood-boring insects before the insects could get rid of the trees. No other kind of bird is so well equipped to pry insect eggs and larvae from tree-trunk crevices, for it not only has a beak like a chisel and a head that moves like an electric hammer, but it also has built-in shock absorbers coiled inside its skull that save it from the constant headaches that such a life of pounding would surely bring about without this protection.

Look in wonder, too, at the way of the whip-poor-will. Its small nubbin of a beak could not pry anything out of anywhere, but it does have other remarkable equipment—hinged jaws that can open wider than the painted grin on a circus clown. And its mouth is fringed with sticky whiskers besides, making a perfect insect trap. So—mouth wide agape—it flies through the air with the greatest of ease, scooping in a hundred mosquitoes for a mere snack. Nighthawks, swifts, and swallows dine on the wing, too, and they also have wide mouths to keep open as they go. Look at the way any bird feeds and you will see that each bill is a perfect tool for the task, whether it is digging out seeds from a fir cone's tiny crevices or probing slimy ooze for tasty morsels, delving into anthills, sipping nectar from flowers, or cracking hard shells on seeds and nuts.

Job surely meant for us to look at the different kinds of feet, too, for proof of a Creator's guidance. The typical woodpecker's stout toes—two forward and two to the rear—cling expertly to an upright trunk, but they do not allow their owner to strut and scratch like a rooster or perch like a wren. Perching birds like the wren have three toes forward and one behind for a good grip on branch or twig, plus tendons that give them an automatic leg-locking device that keeps them from falling off a perch even when sound asleep. Birds that scratch for daily weed and worm have sturdy toe structure suited for such labor. Herons, egrets, and other marsh birds have the long legs and widespread toes that carry them through deep water and slippery mud. Swimmers like the ducks have webbed feet that make good paddles, while diving birds not only have webbed or lobed toes, but can also displace their body weight at will to swim beneath the waves or ride the crests.

The differences in bird sizes is another cause for marvel. Acrobatic chickadees can swing underneath small twigs to get at aphids and plant lice. Tiny warblers can feed in slender

treetop branches that would never hold a woodpecker's
weight. From the smallest hummingbird that barely equals
one-tenth of an ounce on up to the male ostrich of some 200
to 300 pounds, each bird has the right size, the right structure
to take a different part.

Each bird has the right plumage, too. "Featherweight"
has become our symbol for anything insignificant or of the
smallest importance, but feathers have more marvels per
ounce than anything else in nature. They may be heat-proof
for birds on the equator, freeze-proof for those of the coldest
regions, water-repellent for swimmers, even noiseless for birds
that hunt in the silence of the night, and their camouflage
coloring can make a motionless bird all but invisible against
matching background. Hen birds and new-hatched young are
usually the ones to have this imitative coloring, while cock
birds who have to win their mates with bold display have
gleam and glitter and glowing colors, finery of such handsome
array that feathers have been prized for royal raiment from
earliest times and used also as symbols of whatever god or
spirit was held most sacred. Surely, the seeking of feather
trophies was among mankind's earliest reasons for wanting to
watch birds and learn their ways—perhaps even more important at times than the taking of birds for food.

To kill for food has been man's right ever since the days
of the Great Flood when God first told Noah to take whatever living creature he needed. Before that time only plants
had been intended for food (Genesis 1:26, 30), but now both
men and beasts became flesh-eaters. There was a high price
placed on this new privilege, for the voice of the Lord rang
out with dire warning in Genesis 9:2–4:

And the fear of you and the dread of you shall be upon every
beast of the earth, and upon every fowl of the air, upon all that
moveth upon the earth, and upon all the fishes of the sea; into
your hand are they delivered. Every moving thing that liveth shall
be meat for you; even as the green herb have I given you all
things. But the flesh with the life thereof, shall ye not eat.

But the Lord also held out the promise that the fear and dread might be overcome in time, for in the later days the prophet Hosea foretold a covenant of peace and an era when all creatures could lie down together without fear (2:18). And Isaiah 11:1–9 foretold also that the birth of a Holy Child would bring about this Peaceable Kingdom, and all of us who make friends with the birds, bring them to feed and nest in our own yards, hope that somehow we have a small share in helping to bring about this miracle so sadly needed now in this age of violence and destruction when so many of the wonders from God's hand have already vanished forever, and so many more are threatened with extinction.

Those of the Christian faith have still added reason to make friends with birds and learn their ways, for Jesus himself asked us to do so in order that we might come to a closer understanding of the ways of God. "Behold the fowls of the air," reads the simple directive in Matthew 6:26, and from the earliest Gospel centuries on through the Middle Ages, many Christians who tried to pattern their own lives by Christ's words accepted this passage as another commandment, the gateway by which they might come to the throne of God.

To follow it they felt the need to withdraw from the hurly-burly life of city or castle and retreat to woods or desert, adopt the lonely way of the hermit. The fourth century saw the beginning of this hermitage withdrawal, with Paul of Thebes leading the way and St. Anthony setting the keynote, saying that his book was "the nature of created things" in which he read the word of God. But not till the sixth century was well underway did any of these hermitage retreats become known as a haven for birds and small woodland creatures, the first wildlife sanctuaries. Visitors who came on pilgrimage, hoping for words of comfort or wisdom, spread the news, telling in wide-eyed wonder how some holy man lived only on wild fruits and greens and grains, like the birds themselves, sharing every meal with these feathered companions who had become as tame and trusting as chickens, eating from the hermit's hand, perching on his shoulder, even obeying his

soft-spoken command to go or come, sing or be silent. Such
camaraderie seemed a miracle, open witness to the Lord's
blessing, and so the hermits won their sainthood from the
awed hearts of the people themselves, for "saint" simply
meant "true Christian" in those days, without any thought of
needing official church sanction that might or might not be
granted in later times.

Some of the travelers who went home from hermit pilgrimage embroidered their stories a bit, as tale-tellers of all
kinds have always done, so that some of the ancient legends
of the birdlore saints are no longer believed. But others had
so many witnesses and such straightforward testimony that
they cannot be doubted; there seems no question that birds
were always welcomed and protected around the abbey at
Iona in the Scottish Hebrides founded by Irish-born St. Columba, who died in 597. Many birds also came in trust and
friendship to the various Irish monasteries founded by Molua,
once a herdsboy of County Limerick, who even as a child had
vowed never to harm any woodland creature. Visitors became
accustomed to hearing a happy chorus of birdsong following
Molua wherever he walked, but no bird chirped or twittered
about the abbey on the day he died in 608, and those who
gathered there for the burial said it was as if the birds, too,
were silent in grief for a dear friend.

A seventh-century sanctuary for sea birds seems to have
been kept at St. Bee's Head on the Cumberland coast, named
for Bega, the Christian daughter of an Irish king. She had
fled there, so the story went, to escape marrying the worldly
king of Norway, coming alone in a small boat over rough seas.
No house or town was near but fishermen soon told of seeing
gulls and gannets and other sea birds circling to drop fish at
her feet—her only food in this lonely place—and this seemed
so much like the Bible story of the ravens feeding Elijah that
her saintliness was accepted at once. Soon young women were
coming from far and near to ask guidance and her small hermit cell had perforce to become enlarged for a nunnery. No
trace of this building remains, and the tradition of sanctuary
for the sea birds vanished also.

But in this same century a refuge was founded that still survives, the oldest enduring bird sanctuary on record—St. Cuthbert's hermitage on the island of Farne off Britain's Northumberland coast. Cuthbert not only gave all birds and animals his own pledge of peace, but he required all visitors at Farne to observe this same truce. From the first day he came there in 676, all birds and animals were made welcome, but his favorites were the otters and seals, the gannets and eiders, with the eiders held dearest of all and still called "St. Cuthbert's birds" by Northumbrian countryfolk. It was his custom to stand in the surf as he prayed, and many visitors told of seeing him there, with gulls and gannets circling overhead, the eiders riding the waves nearby and the otters coming to rub lovingly against his feet. The anniversary of his death—March 20, 687—became a time for Farne pilgrimage in later years, and many who came there and saw the eiders still nesting under his bed went home with a pledge to keep St. Cuthbert's peace in their own gardens.

English pilgrims of this seventh century also gave the title of saint to Milburga, daughter of King Merewald of Mercia, who called to the migrant waterfowl each autumn, bidding them to come down and eat the grain she spread beside her cloister rather than the crops in nearby fields. The Lady Werburga at Ely and Hilda at Whitby were also known for their kinship with the birds in these years, and so was the Benedictine monk who would go down in English history as the Venerable Bede. Another among those who loved birds because they loved the Lord was Guthlac of Crowlands, who died in 714 and was celebrated in verse by Cynewulf, first of the great Anglo-Saxon poets. "The one hero of our time," Cynewulf paid tribute, and added lines that in modern English would read:

> Triumphant came he [Guthlac] to the hill!;
> And many living things did bless his coming.
> With bursting chorus and with other signs
> The wild birds of the hill made known their joy
> Because this well-loved friend had now returned.

Oft had he given them food
When hungry, even starving, they had come
Straight to his hand and from it ate their fill.
Bright was the glorious plain and his new home;
Sweet the birds sang; earth blossomed forth;
Cuckoos heralded the year. . . .*

Thus did the poet add the cuckoo to the list of crows, jackdaws, and ravens that were Guthlac's other companions and gave his hermitage its name, and this line is also the earliest written record in English of the springtime bird migration that marks the changing seasons. Swallows are among spring's messengers, too, and they were often seen gathering about the hermit's head, perching on his arm or shoulder, twittering away at him as if in question and answer. Once when a visitor marveled at such actions, Guthlac gave simple, earnest reply that reaches into the very heart's core of this era: "Know you not that he who hath led his life according to the will of God, to him will the wild beasts and the wild birds draw the more near?" † To him, and to many another in these years, the answer to that question was as plain as the sum of two plus two, as much a part of a Christian's dedication as praise and prayer.

The ninth century added the name of Meinrad of Zurich to the roster of birdlore saints, one of several who chose the text from Luke 12:24 and therefore spent many hours watching the ravens, feeding them, getting to know their ways. Friend of ravens, too, was Godric of Finchale in England, but Bartholomew of Farne, who came to Cuthbert's old sanctuary in mid-twelfth century, chose the cormorants, the birds whose name means "ravens of the sea."

The years that saw the twelfth century end and the thirteenth century begin marked the last cycle of the era of birdlore saints but also its greatest moments. Now came Hugh

---

* Adapted by Virginia C. Holmgren from "Song of Guthlac" in Israel Gollancz, *Exeter Book* (London, 1895), lines 732–38.
  † *The Hermits,* Charles Kingsley (Macmillan, 1890; Clay of London, 1868).

of Burgundy, brought to England by Henry II and soon called
Hugh of Stow. Visitors to his house there told in amazement
how a great wild whooper swan followed him about like a
dog, sleeping beside his bed at night, caressing his hand with
gentle beak but hissing in fury at any stranger who came too
near. Taming a wild whooper thus was almost unheard of,
for this species has none of the more biddable nature of the
mute swans kept in parks and zoos, and seeing the great bird
at Hugh's side set many pilgrims gasping in awe and wonder.
The two stand together still in the carved stone of St. Mary's
tower at Oxford, and on St. Hugh's Day—November 17—
there are often wild swans flying overhead on southbound
journey to give added reminder of a man and his mark and
a measure of the times.

Last of all came the man most widely remembered,
Francis of Assisi, who preached to the birds and called them
sister and brother. He also did more than anyone else to start
the custom of feeding the birds each Christmastime, and he
even asked the city officials to pass a law requiring all house-
holders to feed the birds and animals at this time of rejoicing
for the birth of Jesus. All birds were dear to him, but the sky-
larks were his favorites—partly because they seemed to be
dressed as he and his followers were in brown robes and
peaked hoods, partly because they sang with the same ecstasy
he felt in his own soul when he poured forth a song of praise
to the Lord. When he died in the year 1226 those who walked
beside his bier told of hearing the larks singing in the sky
overhead in lyric crescendo, and they could not help but
think of an angel chorus for Heaven's opening gates.

The next centuries seemed to bustle along with little
time for hermit retreat, and the new bird sanctuaries that
came into being were no longer linked to Bible lines. Still,
the words of Jesus—and the words of Job—come to mind
now and again when we make even city backyards into something of the sort of refuge that all the birdlore saints strove
to build. We watch a robin nesting on a windowsill, see the
swallows coming unerringly to their old nest box on almost

the very day when they came the year before, hear the contented chirping of sparrows as they glean the Christmas crumbs—and know that feeling the presence and the power of a Creator is not the least of a birdwatcher's joys.

Best of all, no one is ever too young or too old to start birdwatching. No one can ever learn so much, not even in a lifetime of watching, that there is no more to learn. Whether we roam the far yonder seeking vanishing whooping crane and curlew, or watch from a garden window, there is always something new to discover, something dear and familiar we are glad to see again.

In the words of the writer of Proverbs 20:12: "The hearing ear, and the seeing eye, the Lord hath made even both of them."

two

FOR EACH A NAME

If you have ever looked skyward on a March day at the bands of shorebirds winging overhead with plaintive piper's chant . . . or rejoiced at the first returning swallows, the first sad-sweet cooing of the doves . . . and then as you looked and listened found yourself repeating the Scripture lines about the "time of the singing of birds" or about the crane, dove, and swallow that "know the time of their coming," then your bird walk with the Bible has already begun.

But instead of chance remembering of lines and matching bird, you are ready now to make a special search—start out with a Bible verse in mind and a bird guide in hand (see p. 213 for suggested guide books), for of course you will need to identify each bird by name. Adam named all birds—and all other living things—Genesis declares, but as languages multiplied on earth, so did the names by which birds were known. When men traveled out beyond their own valleys, they were often amazed to hear strange names for the birds they knew so well and they began to wonder how such naming was done.

The first bird names were often color words, marking whatever hue caught the eye as the flitting figures darted past. When people began to notice that the little "yellow birds,"

for example, came only in summer, the name might change
to "summer yellow bird." But so many birds came year round
in varying tones of brown that something besides a color word
was needed, and so people began naming birds by what they
did—woodpecker, creeper; or by where they lived—marsh
hen, sanderling; or by syllables that imitated song or chirp.

One bird seemed to say the same two syllables over and
over so plainly that its name is almost the same in every language. We say *cuckoo*, while the French make it *cou-cou*, the
Dutch *koek-koek*, the German *kuck-kuck*, the Japanese
kak-ko, the Russians *kukushka*—and anyone who knew any
of these words would surely know what bird is meant by the
Hebrew *kuk-yah*.

Sandpipers are named by both voice and habitat. Certain
sea birds that dangle their legs over the water as they search
for fish look so much as if they were trying to walk on the
waves that they were once called "runners-on-the-sea" or "pit-
terals." But as the story of Christ and his disciples spread
abroad, the birds reminded everyone of Peter trying to walk
on Lake Galilee and so the birds became "little Peters"—the
petrels. The very smallest of these were seen so far from shore
that Italian sailors in the old days thought they must surely
be in the special care of the Mother of Christ—the dear
mother, as they called her, *Mata Cara*. When English sailors
heard the phrase they changed it into "Mother Carey's chickens" and both these names are still heard in America today,
their original coining usually a mystery, even to people who
have used them a lifetime.

Quite a few bird names used in England somehow became
applied to a different bird when the colonists brought the old
words to America, and so the names used by British Bible
scholars often lead American readers to picture a completely
different species. In British speech, for example, *buzzard* is
an old word held over from the ancient sport of falconry—
a tongue-worn contraction of Latin *aves tardes*, slow birds—
and used to tag certain kinds of slow-flying hawks, the soarers
that lack the dashing plunge that gave falconry its zest. But

American colonists used it only for the still slower vultures, and *buzzard* still means a vulture to all American readers and a hawk to the British. For additional reader confusion, "black vulture" is both the folk name of several Old World species, and also the official name of a completely different American species never seen in Old World lands. "Screech owl" is also an Old World folk label for one species, the American official label for another.

Consequently, it would seem a point of good scholarship for translators in either England or America to avoid these ambiguous labels and use others that would have the same meaning in all English-speaking lands. Folk names such as "hoot owl" that aren't official names anywhere should also be avoided for the sake of clarity—but there they are in more than one Bible translation. To straighten out the tangle and make one list for our Bible bird walk, we have started anew with the original bird words in Hebrew and Greek, then sought to identify each one with the proper label in scientific Latin—the unique and universal name that has been assigned to each individual kind of bird and each related group so that they can be recognized in every land, no matter how many other names and nicknames have been added in everyday speech.

Latin labeling of birds, beasts, and plants began in the Middle Ages when Latin was the only language used by European scholars, both for teaching and for writing. Even in the lower schools a pupil was supposed to start learning Latin as soon as he got past the ABC's, and all classes in the upper schools were conducted in Latin. Naturally all the textbooks were written in Latin, too, but this didn't make learning bird names as easy as you might think, for each scholar was free to name each bird as he pleased, choose his own labels for classification, decide for himself how each group should be named and recognized—whether by similar feet or beak or habit.

The only way out of this confusion was for all animal and bird namers to use just one system. But each expert was so set in his own way that this did not come about until the very late date of 1889, when the first International Congress of Zoologists met in Paris and at last agreed that all lists would now follow the system of classifying and naming devised more than a century before by the great Swedish classifier Carl Linnaeus. Linnaeus had revised his own system several times, but the tenth edition of his book *Systema Naturae,* published in 1758, was the one that zoologists now agreed to follow. So 1758 became "Year One" for official naming, and both botanists and geologists agreed with zoologists in adopting the Linnaean system of using a two-word Latin label for each individual kind—called a *species.* Any new discoveries, or any species that Linnaeus had placed in the wrong category, could be named by whoever first published a correct description. Also, new groups could be named by the same careful analysis and approved by the Congress, but the groups and names chosen by Linnaeus in 1758 were the basic list.

Linnaeus had used certain old terms of classification, such as dividing the "Realm" of nature into its three "Kingdoms" of Animals, Plants, and Minerals. But he coined new group terms, too, and made precise definitions for the old ones that everyone now would follow. For the first time in history there was just one key to sort out the names and classifications that had been piling up in all the world's lands and languages.

"Classification" means subdividing—separating the members of some general category into groups according to some further likeness. To begin his classification of the Animal Kingdom, Linnaeus subdivided it into the groups of beasts, birds, reptilians, fish, insects, and wormlike things— each one of which he called a "Class."

Next he divided each Class into groups he called Orders, and each Order into subdivisions he called Genera—the plural of the Latin word *genus,* meaning "kind." Each member of a Genus was called a Species, meaning an individual plant or animal like no other.

These terms are still in use, but later scientists have added another midway step, subdividing each Order into Families, and each Family into the Genera and Species. So now to classify a bird—the house sparrow, for instance—you would say that it is in *Class Aves* (Latin for "birds"), *Order Passeriformes* (perching birds), *Family Ploceidae* (the weavers), *Genus Passer* (sparrows), and *Species domesticus.*

Since the two-word Latin label for official use is made up of the name of the genus—written first and with a capital —and the name of the species, the scientific name for the house sparrow is *Passer domesticus,* and it will always be just that on any bird list in any language, no matter how varied the local names and nicknames may be. Sometimes a third Latin word is added to show that this is a subspecies, differing only slightly in size or color or geographical range, but those first two Latin names, the Latin binomial, make the basic identification. The binomial is the key that will tell us whether any bird of Bible lands is also seen in our own country, and comparing the names of genus and family and order will tell us the closest cousins.

Sometimes the name of the genus is the same as the specific name, usually because it is the most common or most typical or largest member. *Bubo bubo,* for instance, is the largest owl of the Old World, well known in Bible lands. To see if it flies here, too, look for *Bubo* in the index of your bird guide. No *Bubo bubo* is listed, but there is *Bubo virginianus,* an owl of the same genus, which you can use as stand-in, knowing its habits and habitat and hooting voice will be much the same.

When you can't find an American bird of the same genus, look for one of the same family. All family labels end in *-idae* for easy recognition. If there's none of the same family, look for a bird of the same order, recognizing such a label by the Latin ending *-iformes.* Generic and specific labels do not have fixed endings, though all must be Latin or Latinized spelling, but in the official binomials the genus is always first, the species second, showing clearly which is which.

You may be surprised to learn how often you'll find

that the very species named in Bible lines is also listed in your North American bird book. Seventy-eight species are found both in Israel and on this continent (see pp. 201–211 for complete listing), appearing either as regular migrants or as year-round residents. Some 40 more Israeli species come as "accidental" visitors, usually seen only along the coasts and often blown here by gale winds. Many of these "accidentals" have worn metal tags that prove they were hatched overseas, ringed as nestlings by one of the many groups that make bird banding a lifework or earnest hobby. So far, no bird has been found with a band that means "born in Israel," but we can't help hoping that some day such a one may come. The place most likely for this arrival is surely Alaska, for many Eurasian species have begun to make Alaskan meadows their summer home.

Most of these far travelers come from India or China, Siberia or some other nearer shore. But other individuals of these very same species also winter in the Holy Land and each year fly toward the Pacific to seek a nesting ground. Someday—driven by storm or famine or drought or wartorn acreage—they may keep flying till they join an Alaska-bound flock and with them find a new land that will be "home" to their nestlings, calling them back across the ocean each following year. The species most likely to make this adventure would seem to be the small grayish songster of the thrush clan known as the wheatear, *Oenanthe oenanthe,* for wheatears that winter in western Africa have already established new migration routes all the way to North America's Atlantic shores, instead of always stopping in northern Europe as their ancestors did. And wheatears that winter east of the Sahara and migrate toward the Indian Ocean and the Pacific have already found Alaska and Canada a summer home. Perhaps —some day—a wheatear flock that made its winter gleaning beside Galilee will reach this far outpost, too, and with a metal leg band to prove the journey. At least we can picture how that coming would be:

When spring gives back Alaska's icebound earth
To greening grass and short-stemmed tundra flowers,
And earlier sun and lingering twilight hush
Give back each day its winter-stolen hours—
Across the northern ocean's ice-fringed foam
A small gray bird wings in to claim a home.

With warbling song it courts a listening mate,
Now perched on twig or rock, now high a-wing,
As if the selfsame ecstasy were power
To bid its wings to soar, its heart to sing.

Where have you been, small wheatear, winter's while?
What Old World homeland marked migration's mile?
Was it in Persian vale? Or Syrian strand?
In Egypt? Or some farther sunny land?

Do I dare hope that other home you know
Is in a field where Christ walked, long ago?

But even if you never see a bird that has actually been
in the Holy Land, you will see many birds just like the ones
you would see if you wakened some morning in Jerusalem.
You will find many more that can serve as "stand-ins" since
they are members of the same genus as their Israeli cousins,
near enough in looks and manner to illustrate the same Bible
line. You will find still more that are in the same family, and
therefore have the same general structure.

Indeed, family likeness is the best way to match Bible
birds with our own, for many of the Bible bird names were
intended only as family labels—hawk, heron, swallow. Since
there are no more than 60 bird families in Israel (see pp. 201–
211 for variant classifications of 55 to 60) and all but 11 of
them are well represented in North America, a search to see
and know the bird families named in the Bible can be almost
as complete here as in the Holy Land itself.

If you follow the King James Version, only one bird
named there—the ostrich—has no American family cousin.

The New English Bible adds three more non-Americans—bustard, hoopoe, and sand-partridge. The New American Bible—like the King James—names only the ostrich, unless you count that mythical bird the phoenix, named also in several other Bible translations, which cannot be assigned to any order, since it is a bird of fable, not fact. It appears in Job 29:18 in a passage that some scholars interpret with "as uncounted as the sands" or "as long-lived as the palm tree." Whether you want to consider it among the Bible birds is up to you—and the translation you follow.

If you are puzzled because translators can't agree on such passages, remember that Hebrew was long a forgotten language, seldom written or spoken after the Jews were scattered by their conquerors and forced to live in alien lands, using alien speech. Some of the bird words—and other words, too—had only local use in the first place, or had changed in meaning over the years, as words are wont to do in any language, especially when there is no continuous preservation of books to keep them in mind. Then, too, the original Hebrew alphabet was made up only of consonants, and the proper vowels to complete each word had to be remembered by the rabbis—and sometimes memories differed. Furthermore, the ancient scrolls were copied by hand, of course, always with an easy chance for error, and even one letter added or omitted or written in the wrong sequence can change a word's meaning completely. Also, some query or comment written in the margin by one scholar might be thought a part of the original text by the next copyist—and then copied again forever after with no clue to prove it in error. When such an addition was found, there was no way to be sure whether it belonged there or not, for no one official text had ever been put aside. About the beginning of the Christian Era certain Hebrew scholars tried to establish such a key text, calling themselves the Masoretes, because they were preserving the *masorah*, the tradition.

This Masoretic text was then followed by the translators who first published the Bible in Latin for European Chris-

tians; but scholars have also followed another version written
in Greek a few centuries earlier, called the Septuagint, and
a Syrian text called the Peshitta, followed by Eastern Orthodox churches. Lately scholars have also looked for guidance
to the Dead Sea Scrolls, which sometimes have wording different from the other earliest manuscripts.

When you combine the conflict of many languages with
all the normal confusion that comes with the centuries, it is
no wonder that Bible translators cannot always agree on one
word to match each bird. Some of the arguments have come
about because the translators are trying to be too precise—
disputing whether one Hebrew word meant swift or swallow,
for example, when surely one name described both birds of
such similar flight in olden days when watchers had neither
guide book nor binoculars to make clear distinction. We have
both—and we'll put them to good use on Bible bird-walk
trail, wherever it may take us.

three

THE TRAIL BEGINS

The best place to begin is at the beginning, so the old saying goes, and if you are of that logical mind you will want to look for each Bible bird in the order in which it first appears in Bible text. To mark your way there is a listing of each birdlore passage given on pp. 185–200.

But it is equally logical to look for these birds by the "family plan"—all hawks together, all herons in one waterfront safari, all owls on night watch, and so on, each with others "of their kind"—for Moses himself used just such phrasing when he recorded the birds and beasts that could or could not be eaten. The Mosaic Laws given in Leviticus, chapter 11, stand as the first attempt at zoological classification ever put on written record, and so the name of "first scientist" could well be given to this great Hebrew leader. Indeed the Mosaic term "four-footed"—*quadrupedes* in Latin—remained the primary division in the Animal Kingdom through all the centuries thereafter until Linnaeus originated the division of mammals in its place, identifying them as creatures that nurse their young on mother's milk, regardless of foot count. The Mosaic definition of birds as "creatures that fly" remained in effect for centuries, too, until the new definition of "creatures with feathers" finally avoided the

long-puzzling confusion between bird and bat or bird and
insect. Further subdivisions of Mosaic "winged ones" were,
of course, suggested by every scientist from Aristotle down
to Linnaeus and the latest publications of the ornithologists.
The current accounting of Bible birds by order, family, and
genus is given on pp. 201–211 for all who want to mark their
Bible bird-walk trail by these signposts.

But birds have a habit of turning up when you least
expect them, rather than in any given sequence—either
biblical or scientific. It seems more useful, therefore, to mark
the trail here with an alphabetical listing of the English bird
names found in the most used translations, so that the bird
of any passage can be found quickly with a few turned pages.
Along with each of these English names you will find its
Hebrew equivalent—or at least the closest we can come when
using our own alphabet instead of the Hebrew characters that
sometimes were voiced with guttural overtones no English
letter truly equals. Not every scholar chooses the same
English letters for this transliteration, so you will sometimes
find other spellings in Bible dictionaries and concordances—
oph instead of *ahf,* for example—but if you test by ear instead of eye you will not be confused.

By chance—since the alphabet sometimes makes strange
bookfellows—the first name on the list isn't a bird at all by
our definition, but the bat. However odd that seems now, the
bat belonged with the birds by Mosaic classification, and
that's where we will place it, too.

The translations from which we have taken our English
names are: King James (Authorized) Version, American
Standard Version, Revised Standard Version, New English
Bible, Douay, New American Bible, The Complete Bible:
An American Translation (also known as the Chicago trans-
lation), Moffatt, Jerusalem Bible, Holy Scriptures of the
Jewish Publication Society of America and the 1962 Torah,
Georg Lamsa edition of the Peshitta, and the Thomson-
Muses Septuagint. By their variant interpretations (and my
own), the English names of Bible birdlore are these:

bat
bee-eater
bird (fowl)
bird conservation
birds of abomination
birds of doom
birds of prey
birds of sacrifice
birds of the Ark
birds of the hills (mountains)
bittern
bustard
buzzard

caged birds
charadrion
chicken, cock, hen
cormorant
crane
crow
cuckoo

darter, dart-snake (bird)
decoys
desert cock
dove and pigeon

eagle
eggs

falcon
fattened fowl
firebird
flamingo
fledglings
fowl, fowler, fowling

gier eagle
glede
griffon (griffin, gryphon)
grype
guinea fowl

gull

hawk
hen
heron
hoopoe (hoop, houp)

ibis

jackdaw

kite

lamia
lapwing
larus
lilith

magpie
mew
migrating birds

neophron
nestlings
nests
night birds, night crow, night-
    hawk, nightjar, night raven
no more birds

osprey
ossifrage
ostrich
owl

parrot
partridge
peacock
pelican
pelican of the wilderness
phoenix
pigeon
plover
porphyrion
poultry

quail

raven
ravenous birds
ravens of the valley
ring dove
ringtail

sand-partridge
sea gull, sea mew
singing of birds, songbirds
sparrow
speckled bird (of prey)
stork
swallow
swan
swift
symbolic birds

thrush
turtle, turtledove

visions of birds and winged
    creatures
vulture
vulture of the wilderness

wagtail
wandering birds
water hen
wings
wren
wryneck

young birds

These are the signposts, then, that mark the trail for our bird walk with the Bible, and we will follow them one by one.

Bat

HEBREW: *atalaf,* night flier. Leviticus 11:19; Deuteronomy
14:18; Isaiah 2:20

APOCRYPHA: Baruch 6:21 (*or* owl)

This "bird that is not a bird" flies last among the winged
ones banned for eating by the Mosaic Laws (*see* Birds of
Abomination: No. 20, atalaf). Ironically, this is one of the
few bird names translated almost without argument. Only a
few scholars suggest that just possibly some real bird might
have been meant here—some other night flier such as the
marsh hawk or hobby falcon, most often seen at dusk rather
than broad daylight. Owls fit the label best, of course, but
they are named by too many other words on the list to suggest
that last-of-all atalaf is an owl also.

If we sort out living things as Moses did—animals that
go on all fours by paw or hoof; those that swim in the waters;
those that creep or creep-and-fly; winged ones of the air—
there is no place to name the bat except among the birds.
Bat it must be, and it is named also in Isaiah 2:20 and Baruch
6:21 with the disagreeable overtone usually given this mysterious flutterer in the dark.

If you don't see bats in your own yard, try going at dusk
to an abandoned farm, waterfront, cave, or old mine tunnel.
Or just look at the pictures of bats in an encyclopedia, if you
must. But don't miss the gargoyle grimace that watchers of
Bible times surely knew well.

Bee-eater

HEBREW: *shalak,* plunger. Leviticus 11:17; Deuteronomy
14:17

The Eurasian bird known in English as the bee-eater—
Latin label *Merops apiaster*—was listed among the birds forbidden as food in the Georg Lamsa translation of the Peshitta,
a Bible manuscript in the Syrian language. This bee-eater's
name in Syriac and Hebrew means "the plunger"—because
of its spectacular aerial acrobatics as it skims and skydives on
its insect hunt.

32

Three more birds are also called "plungers" in Bible lands: the cormorant because of its remarkable underwater diving; the kingfisher because of its high dive from lookout post to water surface; the tawny owl or the barn owl because of the way it plummets from branch to meadow grass on mouse hunt.

Which of these plungers would Moses have banned as unsuitable food? See the discussion of shalak-the-plunger in the entry *Birds of Abomination* (No. 12).

Since no birds of the bee-eater's genus or family come to North America, watch the kingfishers, which are in the same Order of Coraciiformes. Or watch swifts and swallows, which also do some pretty fancy skydiving. Also, see the entry *Swallow* for further word on the bee-eater.

Bird (Fowl)

HEBREW: *ahf*, the flier. Genesis 1:20–22, 26, 28, 30; 2:19–20; 6:7, 19–20; 7:2–3, 8–9, 14, 21–23; 8:17–19, 20; 9:2, 10; 40:17, 19; Leviticus 1:14–17; 7:26; 11:13, 46; 17:13; Deuteronomy 14:11, 20; 28:26; 1 Samuel 17:44–46; 2 Samuel 21:8–10; 1 Kings 4:33; 14:11; 16:4; 21:24; Job 12:7–9; 28:7, 20–21; 35:11; Psalm 79:2; Jeremiah 4:25; 5:27; 7:33; 9:10; 12:4, 9; 15:3; 16:4; 19:7; 34:20; Ezekiel 17:23; 29:5; 31:6, 13; 32:4; 38:19–20; 39:17; 44:31; Daniel 2:38; 7:6; Hosea 2:18; 4:1–3; 7:12; 9:11; 11:11; Zephaniah 1:2–3
baʿal kanaf, possessor of a wing. Proverbs 1:17
banoth-shir, daughters of music. Ecclesiastes 12:4
kanahath, winged ones. Ecclesiastes 10:20
zamir, singing of birds. Song of Songs 2:12
zippor, zipporim, chirper(s). Genesis 7:14; 15:10; Leviticus 14:4–7, 49–53; Deuteronomy 4:17; 22:6–7; Nehemiah 5:18; Job 41:5; Psalms 8:8; 11:1; 104:12, 17; 124:7; 148:10; Proverbs 6:5; 7:23; 26:2; 27:8; Ecclesiastes 9:12; 10:20; 12:4; Isaiah 16:2; 31:5; Lamentations 3:52; Daniel 4:12, 14, 20–21; Hosea 11:11; Amos 3:5.
APOCRYPHA: Tobit 2:10–11; Judith 11:17; Wisdom 5:11;

17:18; 19:11–12; Sirach (Ecclesiasticus) 17:4; 22:20; 27:9; 43:14, 17; Baruch 3:9–17; 6:21–22, 69–70; Song of the Three 1:58 (Daniel 3:80); 2 Maccabees 9:15; 15:33
GREEK: *peteinon,* winged ones. Matthew 6:26; 8:20; 13:3–4, 31–32; Mark 4:4, 31–32; Luke 8:5; 9:58; 13:19; Acts 10:12; Romans 22:23; 1 Corinthians 15:39; James 3:7–8; Revelation 19:17, 21
petomai, wing openers. Acts 11:6
ornea, bird of prey, large bird. Revelation 18:2

To people of Bible times, as to all primitive people everywhere, birds seemed creatures of mysterious power, for they are the only things of earth able to soar up to the realms above the clouds where the one God or the many gods were thought to dwell. In primitive eyes the power of winged flight was the one thing that made a bird a bird, and when the Hebrews of old wanted to express the thought "birds of every kind" what they said was "birds of every wing."

These winged ones, bound by neither road nor path, were a symbol of a freedom no earthbound man or beast could know. Even their name in Latin marks this freedom, for the word *aves* is said to come from *a* plus *via*—without path or roadway. "As unmarked as the path of a bird," the Apocryphal book of Wisdom 5:11 makes awed comparison. And there was wonder, too, at the swiftness of bird flight, for Proverbs 1:17 notes how useless it is to spread a net while watching birds can see you and take to quick wing.

Indeed, anything that moves swiftly was said to go as if on wings, from the Lord himself and all his angels to clouds in the sky and even the latest shred of tattletale gossip. "That which hath wings shall tell of the matter," warns Ecclesiastes 10:20, and while this may be a reference to the effectiveness of news-carrying pigeons, many readers thought only of magical talking birds—and perhaps moved away from the window when there were secrets to share.

The marvel of flight, as well as tender meat, made birds acceptable for sacrifice—an offering even the poorest could afford. The use of birds in altar ritual is set down in Leviticus and Deuteronomy in some detail, naming a choice of doves or pigeons for some occasions and any bird, or any young bird, for others.

Only seven books in the Old Testament have no reference to birds: Joshua, Judges, Ezra, Esther, Joel, Jonah, Haggai. And though there are fewer birdlore passages in the New Testament, birds of some kind are named frequently in the four Gospels and in Revelation. The Apocryphal Books name birds in eight of the 14 sections, especially in the two called Wisdom of Solomon and Wisdom of the Son of Sirach. From Sirach (Ecclesiasticus) come the lines that are surely the origin of our saying "birds of a feather flock together" (Sirach 27:9), though this is not the literal translation, and there are also picturesque comparisons of birds to scudding clouds and snowflakes.

But of all the books that make up the one Book, the Psalms stand first in Bible birdlore, with more such passages than any other can mark. The shadow of rustling wings hovers in line after line, symbol of the protecting shadow of the Lord God. Many a psalm has been set to music, those with birdlore passages among the rest, and one of the loveliest comes from Psalm 11:

> In the Lord put I my trust:
> How say ye to my soul,
> Flee, as a bird, to your mountain?

Bird Conservation
GENESIS 1:26–28; Deuteronomy 22:6–7; Psalm 104:10–12; Isaiah 5:8; Hosea 2:18; Ezekiel 34:18; Romans 14:20

The idea of bird conservation, the need to save the last survivors of vanishing species, seems to belong only to the destructive years of the twentieth century. Yet the oldest law of conservation on record comes from the laws of Moses as given in Deuteronomy:

If a bird's nest chance to be before thee in the way, in any tree or on the ground, whether they be young ones or eggs, and the dam sitting upon the young, or upon the eggs, thou shalt not take the dam with the young:

But thou shalt in any wise let the dam go, and take the young to thee; that it may be well with thee, and that thou mayest prolong thy days.

Today's legislators and game commissioners who have charge of modern hunting regulations might be surprised to learn that twentieth-century conservation laws are based on these words set down around 1290 B.C. when the Children of Israel were escaping from Egypt, yet today's laws also call for sparing the mother bird and taking only young birds or males. We realize now, of course, why the rule works: because a hen that has lost one brood of chicks or a setting of eggs will usually start raising another family at once—and because cocks of several species collect a whole harem of hens in their charge, so that fewer males than females are needed to keep the flocks at survival level.

But oddly some Bible students have refused to believe that the people of Mosaic times had this same practical thought in mind. Instead, they have tried to read some idea of magic into the lines, as if sparing a mother's life would somehow work a charm to protect the hunter and give him added years. What sparing the female of bird and hunted beast did, of course, was to prolong the hunter's years by giving him a steady food supply through preserving the species.

Modern conservationists have also learned that preserving wild habitat is the way to preserve a species, and there is more than a hint of this in Isaiah 5:8:

Woe unto them that join house to house, that lay field to field, till there be no place, that they may be placed alone in the midst of earth!

Still more pointed comment comes from this query in Ezekiel 34:18:

Seemeth it a small thing unto you to have eaten up the good pasture, but ye must tread down with your feet the residue of your pastures? and to have drunk of the deep waters, but ye must foul the residue with your feet?

Water conservation is part of the modern concept of maintaining habitat, too, and this thought lies behind the words of Psalm 104:10–12:

He sendeth the springs into the valleys, which run among the hills. They give drink to every beast of the field: the wild asses quench their thirst. By them shall the fowls of the heaven have their habitation, which sing among the branches.

And the dire prediction of Rachel Carson's monumental book, *Silent Spring,* was foreshadowed centuries before in the words of the prophets. No more birds, no birds, all have gone—that is the warning given by Jeremiah 4:19, 23–25, and 9:10; by Ezekiel 38:19–20; Hosea 4:3; Zephaniah 1:2–3. We read these lines and Rachel Carson's book—and shudder.

Yet we should do something more than view the wreckage of pollution and vanishing wildlife with dismay, for the Bible also makes clear our stewardship. "Into your hands are they committed," is the word from God to man in Genesis. They are ours, not to destroy, but to hold in trust so that there will always be some part of the world where growing things and beasts and birds can live in their own way, replenishing the earth as God directed.

Birds of Abomination

HEBREW: *nesher, peres, ozniyyah, da'ah, ayyah, oreb, bath-ya'annah, tachmas, shahaf, nez, kos, shalak, yanshuf, tinshemeth, ka'ath, rahama, hasidah, anafah, dukifath, atalaf.* Leviticus 11:13–19
ra'ah, dayyah. Deuteronomy 14:11–20

For the first presentation of this list in Leviticus, the time is the year of the escape from Egypt—around 1290 B.C.; the

Birds of Abomination

LEVITICUS 11:13-19

Phonetic Hebrew	King James Version	Douay Bible	Jewish Holy Scriptures (JPS)	Revised Standard Version	New American Bible	Torah (JPS 1962)
1. nesher	eagle	eagle	great vulture or eagle	eagle	eagle	eagle
2. peres	ossifrage	griffon	bearded vulture	ossifrage	vulture	vulture
3. ozniyyah	ospray	osprey	osprey	osprey	osprey	black vulture
4. da²ah	vulture	kite	kite	kite	kite	kite
5. ayyah*	kite	vulture	falcon	falcon	falcons	falcons
6. oreb*	raven	raven	raven	raven	crows	raven
7. yaᶜannah	owl	ostrich	ostrich	ostrich	ostrich	ostrich
8. tachmas	night hawk	night hawk	night hawk	night hawk	nightjar	nighthawk
9. shahaf	cuckow	larus	sea mew	sea gull	gull	sea gull
10. nez*	hawk	hawk	hawk	hawk	hawks	hawks
11. kos	little owl	screech owl	little owl	owl	owl	little owl
12. shalak	cormorant	cormorant	cormorant	cormorant	cormorant	cormorant
13. yanshuf	great owl	ibis	great owl	ibis	screech owl	great owl
14. tinshemeth	swan	swan	horned owl	water hen	barn owl	white owl
15. ka²ath	pelican	bittern	pelican	pelican	desert owl	pelican
16. rahama	gier eagle	porphyrion	carrion vulture	vulture	buzzard	bustard
17. hasidah	stork	heron	stork	stork	stork	stork
18. anafah*	heron	charadrion	heron	heron	herons	herons
19. dukifath	lapwing	houp	hoopoe	hoopoe	hoopoe	hoopoe
20. atalaf	bat	bat	bat	bat	bat	bat

* These names followed by "of all kinds" or "and its kind."

	Jerusalem Bible	New English Bible	American Standard Version	Moffat Version	Chicago Translation
1.	tawny vulture	griffon vulture or eagle	eagle or great vulture	griffon	griffon
2.	griffon	black vulture	gier eagle	vulture	vulture
3.	osprey	bearded vulture	osprey	eagle	eagle
4.	kite	kite	kite	kite	buzzard
5.	several buzzards	all falcons	falcon	buzzard	kites
6.	raven	all crows or ravens	raven	raven	raven
7.	ostrich	desert owl	ostrich	ostrich	ostrich
8.	screech owl	short-eared owl	nighthawk	nightjar	nighthawk
9.	seagull	long-eared owl	seamew	seamew	seamew
10.	several hawks	all hawks	hawks	hawks	hawks
11.	horned owl; night owl	tawny owl	little owl	cormorant	screech owl
12.	cormorant	fisher owl	cormorant	owls	cormorant
13.	barn owl	screech owl	great owl	owls	eagle owl
14.	ibis	little owl	horned owl or swan	water hen	horned owl
15.	pelican	horned owl	pelican	pelican	jackdaw
16.	white vulture	osprey	vulture	carrion vulture	carrion vulture
17.	stork	stork or heron	stork	stork	stork
18.	several herons	all cormorants	heron	heron	heron
19.	hoopoe	hoopoe	hoopoe	bittern	bittern
20.	bat	bat	bat	bat	bat

N.B. In the Thomson Septuagint—differing verse order—the words used are: eagle, osprey, sea eagle, vulture, all kites, ostrich, owl, all gulls, all crows, all hawks, night raven, cormorant, ibis, flamingo, pelican, swan, heron, all plovers, hoopoe, bat.

In the Lamsa translation of the Peshitta (used in Syriac churches)—also a differing verse order—the words used are: eagle, vulture, raven, ostrich, nighthawk, little owl, pelican, great owl, cuckoo, hawks, stork, bee eater, swan, hoopoe, heron, peacock.

Birds of Abomination

DEUTERONOMY 14:11–20

Phonetic Hebrew	King James Version	Douay Bible	Jewish Holy Scriptures (JPS)	Revised Standard Version	New American Bible	Torah (JPS 1962)
1. nesher	eagle	eagle	great vulture or eagle	eagle	eagle	eagle
2. peres	ossifrage	grype	bearded vulture	vulture	vulture	vulture
3. ozniyyah	osprey	osprey	osprey	osprey	osprey	black vulture
4. ra'ah	glede	ringtail	glede	buzzard	various	kite
5. ayyah	kite	vulture	falcon	kites and	kites and	falcon
6. dayyah*	vulture	kite	kite	their kind	falcons	buzzard
7. oreb*	raven	raven	raven	raven	crows	raven
8. ya'annah	owl	ostrich	ostrich	ostrich	ostrich	ostrich
9. tachmas	night hawk	owl	night hawk	night hawk	nightjar	nighthawk
10. shahaf	cuckow	larus	sea mew	sea gull	gull	sea gull
11. nez*	hawk	hawk	hawk	hawk	hawks	hawk
12. kos	little owl	heron	little owl	little owl	owl	little owl
13. yanshuf	great owl	swan	great owl	great owl	screech owl	great owl
14. tinshemeth	swan	stork	horned owl	water hen	ibis	white owl
15. ka'ath	pelican	cormorant	pelican	pelican	desert owl	pelican
16. rahama	gier eagle	porphyrion	carrion vulture	carrion vulture	buzzard	bustard
17. shalak	cormorant	night crow	cormorant	cormorant	cormorant	cormorant
18. hasidah	stork	bittern	stork	stork	stork	stork
19. anafah*	heron	charadrion	heron	heron	herons	heron
20. dukifath	lapwing	hoop	hoopoe	hoopoe	hoopoe	hoopoe
21. atalaf	bat	bat	bat	bat	bat	bat

* These names followed by "of all kinds" or "and its kind."

	Jerusalem Bible	New English Bible	American Standard Version	Moffat Version	Chicago Translation
1.	tawny vulture	griffon vulture or eagle	eagle	griffon	griffon
2.	griffon	black vulture	gier eagle	vulture	vulture
3.	osprey	bearded vulture	osprey	eagle	eagle
4.	kite	kite	glede	glede	buzzard
5.	several buzzards	all falcons	falcon	buzzard	kites
6.			kite	kite	kites
7.	ravens	all crows or ravens	raven	raven	raven
8.	ostrich	desert owl	ostrich	ostrich	ostrich
9.	screech owl	short-eared owl	nighthawk	nightjar	nighthawk
10.	seagull	long-eared owl	seamew	seamew	seamew
11.	several hawks	all hawks	hawks	hawks	hawks
12.	horned owl; night owl	tawny owl	little owl	barn owl	screech owl
13.	barn owl	screech owl	great owl	eagle owl	eagle owl
14.	ibis	little owl	horned owl	water hen	horned owl
15.	pelican	horned owl	pelican	pelican	jackdaw
16.	white vulture	osprey	vulture	carrion vulture	carrion vulture
17.	cormorant	fisher owl	cormorant	cormorant	cormorant
18.	stork	stork or heron	stork	stork	stork
19.	heron	all cormorants	heron	heron	heron
20.	hoopoe	hoopoe	hoopoe	bittern	bittern
21.	bat	bat	bat	bat	bat

N.B. Thomson's Septuagint uses these names: eagle, osprey, sea eagle, vulture, all kites, ostrich, owl, gulls, heron, swan, ibis, cormorant, all hawks, hoopoe, night raven, pelican, all plovers, flamingo, bat.

Lamsa translation: eagle, vulture, raven, ostrich, hawks, owl, pelican, crow, little owl, nighthawk, bee eater, stork, hoopoe, desert cock, peacock.

place is Mount Sinai. Moses and his brother Aaron have been called up on the mountaintop to hear the voice of the Lord giving out the laws which the Israelites must now obey and describing each kind of creature they might or might not use as food.

In naming over the forbidden flesh, the birds never to be eaten, the wording of the King James Version is: "These are they which shall be an abomination among the fowls: they shall not be eaten, they are an abomination. . . ." Other translators have changed this word of banning (*abomination*) to *loathesome* or *detestable* or *vermin*.

Whatever the choice, it seems at first reading to be a term of utter hatred, and you read on, half expecting that the following lines will bring a command to hunt and harry such terrible creatures from the face of the earth. But no. The only command is simply *Do not eat them*. Only as food are they labeled *shekes,* an abominable, detestable, and verminous thing.

Mystic taboo on the eating or touching of certain plants or animals has always been so much a part of ancient magic and ritual that you can't help wondering if there is a hint of witchcraft behind this banning, too. But then you remember that the laws were handed down at a time of hardship, with hunger threatening on every day of the journey through alien lands, and you feel sure that there must have been good reason for the *"do not eat"* ruling. And then glancing at the list, that reason seems suddenly clear, for most of the names are those of well-known predators and scavengers, birds that find their own food in gutter and dungheap, gulping down filth and rotting flesh and the foulest carrion and excrement, or at least feeding on rats and mice and other such creatures that carry disease with them wherever they go. Even the predators that are clean in their killing do not always wait for death before they feast, thus breaking the law of Genesis, so that people who eat such birds would be breaking the law, too, if only at secondhand.

Predator and scavenger alike break the laws for clean

living which Moses now heard on Sinai: do not eat animals that die of their own illness; do not eat flesh that has been torn by beasts; do not eat living flesh and blood. Therefore predator and scavenger were banned as food, not in mystic taboo—magic for magic's sake—nor yet merely as a matter of discipline, but only as sensible, practical reasons of good health.

Bible scholars of earlier times evidently did not understand these reasons behind the rules—or perhaps did not know enough about birds to realize why these species and not others are unfit food. As a result they had no yardstick to measure by when the right translation of a name on the list was doubtful, and they sometimes decided on birds such as the swan, cuckoo, and lapwing—species that are not in either scavenger or predator category, and so eat nothing that makes them unfit for the cookpots. Most modern Bible scholars, however, agree that such birds were not on the original list, and so they have put others in their place. But no two scholars ever seem to agree completely on just which birds really do belong on the list; therefore we will look at the entire roster name by name.

Twenty birds are named for banning in Leviticus. The Book of Deuteronomy, repeating the laws at a later day, names 21, but perhaps the altering is only a copyist's error. The translation called the Jerusalem Bible puts 21 in Leviticus, also. The New English and the New American Bibles make 20 the count in both books, considering the Deuteronomic word *raʾah* a miscopying of Levitican *daʾah* (since the characters for *r* and *d* are almost identical in Hebrew) and the additional word *dayyah* merely another spelling of *daʾah*, perhaps the plural form instead of the singular.

The word *shalak* is on both lists, but moved from twelfth place in Leviticus to seventeenth in Deuteronomy, as if the writer of this later listing thought it belonged with a different group of birds. Scholars do generally agree that the names are arranged in some sort of related groupings, for the whole chapter is one of classification, the putting of like with like under a general label. But the text itself does not explain the distinctive features or habits that define the likeness and we can only guess at the rules.

Perhaps the most natural sequence for this era, when there were no binoculars or microscopes or scientific tests and texts, would be an arrangement by size, with the largest species either first or last. Pliny, the famous Roman naturalist of the first century, used this system, beginning his history of birds with the ostrich. But when we see that the 8-inch little owl is right in the middle, with larger birds on either side, we have to admit that a stair-step pattern was not intended. Instead, there seems to be an arrangement by the pattern and shape of the wings, or by the manner of flight, and this seems well in keeping with the Hebrew expression, "birds of every wing."

If this is the guide rule, then first come three names for birds of widest wings—the soaring eagles and vultures; then three more with the swooping wings of the raiders—kites, falcons, and ravens; and then the bird with useless wings— the ostrich. Next are three of hawklike flight; followed by three (or perhaps four) silent-winged owls; then six (or only five, if there are four owls) for birds alike only in having white wings trimmed in black. Last and least comes the little fur-winged flutterer we call the bat.

Half of these 20 names appear only on this list of "do not eat" taboo and are not mentioned again in any other Bible passage. The other 10—eagles, vultures, kites, owls, falcons, ravens, ostrich, cormorant, pelican, and stork—are all named elsewhere and will be described in alphabetical entries of their own. Here we will consider them all only as the listeners must have done that day on Sinai, seeing for ourselves that they would indeed be abominable food.

Those of Widest Wings

1. Nesher: Depending on which Bible you follow, nesher is either the eagle or the griffon vulture. Actually, the name seems to have been used for both species at different times and places. But here it surely put taboo on all kinds of eagles, especially the golden eagle, for predators of such huge size—and therefore ample meat—would scarcely have been omitted from the list and there is no other name among the 20 to include them.

Eagles do not eat the putrid carrion and offal so normal to the vulture menu, but they do feed on animals that have died in sickness, on the torn prey left by lions and hyenas, on rats and rodents that they catch themselves and tear apart in bloody feasting. You may never see them at such work yourself—except on TV nature film—but you may well see them gleaning on the mangled bodies of woodchucks, opossums, and pheasants left by speeding cars on the highway and so know of your own proving that they do indeed warrant *shekes* banning.

If the bird you see at such feeding is the golden eagle, *Aquila chrysaëtos,* then you are seeing the very same species that roamed over Mount Sinai when Moses set down the laws —and is still seen there occasionally to this day. The golden eagle has been found the world around, in all lands above the equator, and by its size and majesty—and by its golden crown—has been the one eagle named "king of birds."

Five other eagles of very similar feathering and the same genus come to the Holy Land in winter and so share the banning, and two especially—the imperial and the tawny eagles—probably were not recognized as separate species by watchers of Bible times, who had neither binoculars nor bird books to point out the differences. On the seacoast was another bird of unmistakable eagle mien, the white-tailed sea eagle, *Haliaeetus albicilla,* a congener of our American bald eagle, *Haliaeetus leucocephalus,* and so our national bird may be a stand-in on Bible bird walk, even though no birds of this species have ever winged over Israel.

All of these eagles will come up for charting when the alphabet gives "eagle" due turn. Here we stop only to realize that their own diet was warrant enough to take them off the Israelites' dinner plates.

2. *Peres:* This Hebrew word means "the breaker" and therefore surely names the one species known for its skill at taking bones aloft to drop and break open on the rocks below and provide a meal of juicy marrow. The trick gave it the name of ossifrage—from *os,* bone, and *fragor,* breaking—in both Latin and English in the early days. But it is famed and named also for wearing a pirate-like black beard of dangling feathers and so has the species label of *barbatus*—the bearded one. Just what genus it belongs in has been of much dispute, for it has the pointed wings that mark the falcon clan, the well-feathered head of an eagle, but the weaker foot structure of the vultures. In spite of awesome size and pirate boldness, these feet prevent the bearded one from winging away with any large-sized prey, so that it either eats carrion like the vultures or seizes nothing larger than a newborn lamb or fawn. Lamb has been so consistently on its menu that it has been called by names that mean "lamb vulture" (lammergeyer, lamgam, etc.) in several Old World lands, but bearded vulture, *Gypaëtus barbatus,* is its official label. Actually, "vulture-eagle" is the literal translation of its genus, and it is the only member to wear this split-personality label.

Now and again it has a chance at the larger prey that true eagles sometimes feast on, for peres has also learned the trick of swooping down full speed at some goat or ram perched unwarily atop the cliffs, coming with such a rush that the animal is startled into a quick leap that sends it plunging to its death on the rocks below. But when this ruse fails, then the bearded bone-breaker has to follow the ways of all vultures and wait for death to serve its dinner.

Peres has never soared across New World skies, so we will have to look for a stand-in. Since no other bird of its genus exists, we will have to make substitution by size and menu, choosing the largest North American vulture, the California condor. Since this is a rare species, with only some 50 or 60 survivors and found nesting now only in the Los Padres National Forest and on remote cliffs in Baja California near Diablo Peak, we may have to choose instead the smaller

North American birds that also developed the bone-breaker's trick—ravens, crows, and gulls, who often break clam shells instead of bones. Or in peres's place we can also chart the osprey, a small edition of the ossifrage, with the same dark-feathered body and resplendent white crown. The osprey breaks no bones, eats no carrion, but lives almost entirely on fish, so it scarcely merits the full count of *shekes* taboo. However, an all-fish diet certainly gives its meat an unpalatably fishy taste and people of every nation have generally been willing to eliminate it from the menu except in times of great hunger.

Even if we counted osprey meat a delicacy we would have little chance of eating it these days, for the concentration of DDT and other pesticides in the fish it eats daily has made osprey eggs infertile and reduced its numbers, so that we can only hope for a comeback. Sports fishermen, jealous of the osprey's skill, have also killed this species in great numbers, even though examination of stomach contents generally shows that ospreys take the more easy-to-catch trash fish than the wily trout and salmon.

But if the California condor and the osprey are hard to find these days, so is peres. The three have that much in common, at any rate. If we do find an osprey as a stand-in of smaller size, at least we will be seeing the same species that watchers of Bible times knew well, for *Pandion haliaëtus* encircles the globe. We will also be seeing the species named in third place by several Bible translators—perhaps on circumstantial evidence for its resemblance to peres and perhaps because its English name sounds so much like Hebrew *ozniyyah*.

3. *Ozniyyah:* With *nesher* and *peres* banning eagles and vulture-eagles, this third name of taboo surely bans the true vultures. And if *ozniyyah* means "watchers" or "dark watchers" as its root words seem to indicate, the name is a perfect match for the vulture category.

Watching is a vulture's way of life. With blunter beaks than the eagles or peres and with weaker feet, these birds must be scavengers, for they can neither kill nor carry off any large

and healthy animal roving with herd or flock. Instead, they
must wait and watch for a wounded or sickly animal left to
die alone, or for newborn young. And since the newborn are
guarded better than the dead, death most often serves the
vultures their dinner. So, they soar aloft, one over this patch
of grazing land, the next miles away, and when one drops
down to a potential feast, the others see and follow, for their
eyesight is unbelievably keen.

Even when they gather beside a carcass they must often
continue watching and waiting—until death is assured or until some stronger bird or beast tears back the hide. They
watch, too, while birds and beasts higher up in the wildlife
hierarchy take their turn first, for the order of precedence on
jungle and prairie was established long ago.

There were—and still are—several different kinds of
vultures in Bible lands. Only one—the neophron, which
comes later on the list—is white and of only medium size.
The other three are all huge and all dark-feathered of body
and bare-necked. From a distance, one looks much like the
other, and so it is reasonable that "dark watcher" could name
them all. One of them will be the "common" vulture today
in one valley, with either of the others taking the same label
some place else. Even today, many farmers or shepherds do
not know one from the others, calling them all "black vulture."

But "black vulture" is the official name for the smaller
of the two American vultures never seen in the Old World,
and so it seems that "great vultures" ought to be the name
listed here for *shekes* taboo. It would include the griffon vulture, *Gyps fulvus,* which is the most common of these three
watchers in most areas, and also the cinereous vulture, *Aegypius monachus,* most common in the Jordan Valley today,
and *Torgos (Aegypius) tracheliotus,* the eared vulture, also
seen in many wasteland areas.

Since none of these takes up its sky-hook watch in New
World skies, look instead for our *Cathartes aura*—called turkey vulture or turkey buzzard because of its red-as-a-turkey
neck—or the smaller black vulture, *Coragyps atratus.* Neither

matches the ozniyyah in huge size, but both keep skywatch for death with the same effortless soaring glide that caught the eye of Moses and everyone else in Bible times. Both also have the same scavenger menu that should keep all of their kind off our own dinner plates.

Those of Swooping Wings

4. *Daʾah:* Daʾah is still the common name for kites in Israel today and there is little argument that both bird and word belong on this list. The only question seems to be whether daʾah names only one of the two kinds of kites seen there, or both.

The obvious answer is that one word suffices for taboo on both *Milvus milgrans,* the black kite, and its congener *Milvus milvus,* the red kite. In spite of those distinguishing color labels, both birds are actually feathered in mottled brown tones that loom darkly blackish in bright tropical sunlight. In Mediterranean lands, the black kite is by far the more abundant, the common street scavenger of town and city, often lined up in rows across the rooftops, waiting for kitchen boys or scullery maids to toss a bucket of refuse into the gutters or atop the dung heap.

Their customary food includes almost anything you can name—rodents, scraps of fish or flesh from fishmonger or butcher, the foulest carrion or offal, or perfectly good meat from the dog's dish at the doorstep. In Old Testament times, when fresh meat was placed on the outdoor altars for sacrifice, the kites would swoop down to snatch it from under the priest's hand, and these always hungry raiders would also feed on corpses left to dangle in grim warning to other possible enemies or evildoers. Everybody knew the kites in those times and nobody had to be told why they were unfit food.

Neither red nor black kite is found in America, but we do have other members of this same fleet-winged clan to mark on Bible bird trail. As it happens, our kites are more insect eaters than scavengers, so what you'll look for is the graceful flight pattern that gave the Israeli birds their name.

Most graceful of all is our swallow-tailed kite, *Elanoïdes forficatus,* but there is beauty, too, in the flight of the white-tailed kite, *Elanus leucurus,* and the Everglade kite, *Rostrhamus sociabilis,* and the Mississippi kite, *Ictinia misisippiensis.* The Everglade kite feeds only on fresh-water snails, but all the others have a reptile-and-insect diet, with an occasional rodent, and only the white-tail coming close to the scavenger fare of its Old World cousins.

5. *Ayyah:* "The ayyah and its kind" is the listing in fifth place, so there is no doubt that more than one species is taken off the list with one word—each alike in having the screaming cry that *ayyah* echoes in imitative syllables, yet each different in size or coloring. These screamers are none other than the falcons, kin to the hawks but different from them in having pointed wings (not rounded) and longish tails (not fan-shaped). The distinctive falcon silhouette can be told from the hawk outline even without field glasses, and there is little doubt that people of Bible times made the distinction between these two kinds of raiders. Also, falcons are by far the fastest fliers, famous for their flashing dive-bomber attacks, not for patient soaring.

Nine different species of falcons roam the Bible lands now, as they did when Moses made his listing, and so the added phrase "of all kinds" was needed. Two of them are— or were—found all across North America: *Falco peregrinus,* called peregrine falcon or duck hawk; and *Falco columbarius,* the pigeon hawk or merlin. Also, our prairie falcon, *Falco mexicanus,* is much like one of their most common species, the lanner falcon, *Falco biarmicus.*

Listen for their ringing *ai-ee* scream or watch their swift dive on unwary prey, and you will be seeing and hearing the sights and sounds that every shepherd on Judean hills knew well. Carrion is not often on their menu when fresh-caught mouse or rabbit is available, and their blood-stained beaks and talons are reason enough for *shekes* banning here.

6. *Oreb:* "The oreb and all its kind" bans another group similar in voice and habits. Eventually, closer watching gave

each member an added name. The raven—seen everywhere
in Israeli hill country—is oreb shihor, the "black oreb." The
much smaller hooded crow, abundant in farmlands, is named
"dusty oreb" for its dust-colored breast and back. The Eurasian jay—much like North American jays in voice, though
not in looks—is the "complaining oreb." Also included in the
clan are the less-numerous carrion crow, fan-tailed raven, and
black-billed magpie, as well as the migrant rook and jackdaw.

Besides sharing the hoarse voice which *oreb* echoes, the
family traits are boldness, a penchant for picking up bright
objects to store in nest or hideaway—a habit which made
oreb the word for thief—and a fondness for eating meat,
even carrion. The only other inveterate meat-eaters among
the small birds are the shrikes and the blue roller, and
watchers of olden times probably counted them among the
òrebim also. Since it is meat-eating that puts these birds on
taboo, roller, shrikes, crows, magpie, jay, and ravens are all
banned with oreb name, though surely the raven—far and
away the largest—is chief of clan, and "ravens of all kinds"
the right translation.

Corvus corax, the raven of Israel, is seen here also, as
are *Lanius excubitor,* the northern shrike, and *Pica pica,* the
black-billed magpie. Our crows are not the same species as
the Old World crows and we do not have their rook or jackdaw or their jay, but any of the three duplicate species or all
their act-alike cousins will show you why birds of raven-kin-
ship could not be counted fit food and why "eating crow" has
become our synonym for something very distasteful to swallow
(*see* Birds of Doom; Crow; Jackdaw; Magpie; Raven).

Useless—or Slowest—Wings

7. *Bath-ya‘annah:* Ya‘annah is either echoic of a lonely,
loud, and mournful voice or the word for greediness—or
both. And since loneliness goes with desert solitude, there is
also an overtone of meaning that suggests desert or wasteland
habitat. In other passages a full description of this bird proves
beyond doubt that ya‘annah is the ostrich.

But what is *bath*-ya‘annah? The prefix *bath*—literally "daughters"—may mean female ostriches, especially female chicks, but there could be no dietary reason for banning these birds and leaving cocks on the menu. Reconsider, and you realize that *bath*—like its masculine counterpart *beni* for "sons"—may also mean "of the same kind" or even "smaller creatures of the same kind."

And the smaller birds of the same general appearance as the ostrich—to nonscientific eyes—are the bustards. Their very name means "slow flier," and since they live in open country where trees and other cover are seldom handy, they often rely on long-legged running to take them away from their four-footed predators whose speed seldom equals their own. Bustards can fly, while the ostrich cannot, but nevertheless their reluctance to fly, their long legs and necks and plump bodies surely suggest ostrich kinship if looks alone make the only standard for judging.

Xenophon, the Greek historian, mentioned ostrich and bustard together as the two desert birds well worth the chase, adding that the bustard was far the slower of the two. A man on horseback could catch up with one if he started soon enough, "for they fly only a short distance, like the partridge, and soon tire; and their flesh was delicious."

But—delicious or not—bustards are eaters of rodents and reptiles, to make them seem unclean food by the standards Moses followed, so of course they would get a "do not eat" label. Also, one species of bustard found in Africa has such nauseous-tasting flesh that Africans who have once eaten it—and spit it out—never try to cook any similar bird, so travelers report. All three of the bustards in the Holy Land, however, have good-tasting meat and all are plump, so if they were not to be eaten for good health's sake, the Israelites would surely have needed special taboo. The most common of these is the houbara bustard, *Chlamydotis undulata,* a year-round resident. Two others—the great bustard, *Otis tarda,* and the lesser bustard, *Otis tetrax*—come only as winter visitors. All three of them—and the ostrich also—were probably included in bath-ya'annah banning, though all have been eaten in other lands.

Neither ostrich nor bustard is found in North America, so we will have to look for stand-ins, or go to a zoo. For the bustards, at least, we can find family cousins, for modern ornithologists classify these birds among the cranes. One of the smaller subspecies of sandhill crane will show you something of the same silhouette that bustards give against desert skylines and follow much the same menu.

Hawklike Wings

8. *Tachmas:* When it comes to translating this word, scholars agree on only one point—it's one of the most puzzling names on the entire roster. Translators of the first Latin Bible put it down as *noctua,* which means "night bird"— which would seem to mean "owl." But the Night Bird of ancient mythology was one with night's color—black—and usually meant the one called Night Crow or Night Raven or Night Bird—now enrolled as *Nycticorax nycticorax,* black-crowned night heron.

It looks far more like a raven or a hawk than like a typical heron, for both legs and neck are fairly short. In flight it could easily be mistaken for hawk kin and justify its placing here with sea hawks and land hawks in close sequence. Like all herons, it dines on fish, reptiles, amphibians, and rodents, and the rather rank flavor of adult birds is said to be unpleasant. However, young birds are fed mostly on aquatic plants and have always been considered tasty fare. Audubon once wrote that they were as delicious as young pigeon—and that was a compliment. The birds that he saw—and that you can see today—are the same species that still nest in the Holy Land. If tachmas is the night heron, it needs no stand-in on Bible bird walk.

But other translators are sure that Moses was banning the nightjars. The Nubian nightjar, *Caprimulgus nubicus,* is still a year-round resident in Israel, and the European nightjar, *Caprimulgus europaeus,* comes as a passing migrant.

Both dine principally on insects, but both have been seen gulping in small songbirds and nestlings, either by mistake or by hungry intent. Their small beaks immediately take them out of hawk classification by our standards, but they do have long wings and strong, hawklike flight—so hawklike, in fact, that their American cousin is actually called "nighthawk." But our American nighthawk, *Chordeiles minor,* is never seen in the Old World, and using its name on a Bible list gives readers the wrong idea. "Nightjar" would have to be the best choice if a bird of this family is to stand in tachmas's stead.

Nightjars do fly at dusk rather than broad daylight most of the time, to match that *noctua* translation of the Latin Bibles. And since the Hebrew word *tachmas* may mean "torn face," that makes a match, too. For all birds of this family open mouths of such incredibly wide gape that they do look torn apart. Another bird for torn-face naming is the African skimmer, *Rhynchops flavirostris,* much like our own black skimmer, *Rhynchops nigra.* Both have a peculiar hinged bill that opens at a jagged angle as it scoops up its dinner from the water and both are black-feathered to further match the tachmas qualities.

The same root word for "torn face" is also the Hebrew root word for "laughter" and all three of these birds—skimmer, nightjar, and night heron—have the laugh on us because we can't be sure which one wore the tachmas name when Moses set down his laws.

9. Shahaf: This word names a bird of "long and slender" wings, and though King James scholars mistook it for the cuckoo, there should be no argument over which long-winged bird Moses had in mind. *Shahaf* is still the word for gulls in Israel today and since all gulls are much alike in looks and appetite, all must have been included in the banning. Quite possibly it could have included all species of terns, shearwaters, petrels, the skimmer, and the skua, too—for all of these have sometimes gone under the alias of "sea hawk" in folk speech around the world. No roster of dietary taboo would be complete without them, for all are fish-eaters with resultant unpalatable flavor, and the gulls are garbage cans in feathers, eating everything and anything, alive or dead.

Gull watching on Bible bird walk is a delight, for many are the same species as the birds you'd see in the Holy Land itself. Duplicates include the skua, *Stercorarius parasiticus,* and all but three of the 17 Israeli gulls, terns, and kittiwakes. The most abundant wintering gull there—the herring gull, *Larus argentatus*—is also one of the most abundant species all across North America, on inland lakes as well as on the coasts. The mew gull, *Larus canus,* is a common bird in Israel and is often abundant on the North American Pacific coast.

Any gull, for that matter, will show you why Moses took them from the menu, why he placed them here just before he named the hawks.

10. Nez: No one disputes that the phrase "nez and all its kind" bans hawks of all sorts. This is one Bible bird word all translators read alike. The group includes 10 hawks not already banned as kites or falcons: osprey, honey buzzard, two slow fliers of the genus *Buteo,* three harrier hawks of the genus *Circus,* and three bird hawks of the genus *Accipiter.* Perhaps the three smaller eagles were included also—serpent eagle, booted eagle, and Bonelli's eagle.

None of the eagles will be found in this hemisphere, but three of the same hawks roam our skies: the osprey, *Pandion haliaëtus,* often called fish hawk; the goshawk, *Accipiter gentilis,* largest of the bird hawks; and the marsh hawk, *Circus cyaneus.* Our red-tailed and broad-winged hawks are much like the *Buteo* Israelis call "common buzzard" and our rough-legged hawk, *Buteo lagopus,* makes a good stand-in for their long-legged *Buteo ferox.* Our two smaller Accipiters, sharp-shinned and Cooper's hawks, are almost identical with the Accipiters that Israelis call "sparrow hawks," so there is full scope for sighting nez and all its kind.

Silent Wings of Night

11. Kos: Like many bird names in any language, *kos* is the echo of a repeated cry—the best of all ways to name a night bird more often heard than seen. The same half sneeze, half snort produced the German word *kauz,* which is the basic name for several kinds of owls having a similar coughing voice but different terrain or size.

To watchers who know these coughers well, an added word of description gives a fuller name, so that a forest-dweller is distinguished from a canyon-dweller, or large from small. And usually there is one species among them that is best known—"the" kos, when no adjective is added. For the Israelites, as for many Mediterranean peoples—"the" owl was a little round-headed, big-eyed fellow once sacred to the Grecian goddess Athena and now down in scientists' Latin as *Athene noctua.* In everyday language it is usually "little owl," with the adjective a part of the official folk name, not just a size marker.

In Bible times its *kos* name was probably shared by another small owl of similar 8-inch length, *Otus scops,* different only in having ear tufts instead of a round-head silhouette. Neither of these is found in North America. In their stead look for two of the same size and silhouette: the screech owl, *Otus asio,* is our small tufted owl and *Aegolius acadius,* the saw-whet owl, is our round-head. Both of them are able mouse-traps—as are their Israeli counterparts.

Boiled owl has been eaten by starving mountain men in our own pioneer times, and no doubt by hungry wayfarers elsewhere, but no one really objects to taking owl off the daily menu as Moses suggested here, listing three kinds of owls at least and perhaps four.

12. Shalak: Since shalak is named here with the owls in the first recording of Leviticus, it was surely intended to name a bird of this silent-winged family. And since the little *Athene noctua* precedes it, while the largest owl species follows, it is reasonable to assume that shalak is a medium-sized owl.

However, *shalak* means "plunger" and almost the same word is the name today for birds that plunge into water—the cormorants and the kingfisher. But a similar name also marks the midair dives of the bee-eater, and it seems obvious that a "plunge" could be into meadow grass after a scampering mouse. Nevertheless, it was evidently the association of "plunge" with water that led whatever scribe rearranged the taboo list in Deuteronomy to remove it from the owl sequence and place it among water birds.

Some translators try to reconcile the two listings by giving this place to the fisher owl, *Ketupa ceylonensis,* the only species noted for hanging around the waterfront. But *Ketupa* is one of the biggest owls in the family—a good 20 to 24 inches —and doesn't match shalak's middle placement. Also, it has so much the same size and horned silhouette as the more common eagle owl that the two probably went by the same name in common speech. After all, how well can you see in the dark to tell owl from owl, except by size?

Four owl species still seen in the Holy Land have a middle-sized 12-to-15-inch length to fit the sequence. Two have ear tufts and are only passing migrants or winter visitors: the short-eared owl, *Asio flammeus,* and the long-eared owl, *Asio otus.* Two others are round-heads: the tawny owl, *Strix aluco,* and Hume's tawny owl, *Strix butleri,* smaller and paler to match its desert terrain. Of them all, the tawny owl is by far the most abundant and best known, surely the best candidate for the "plunger" name—as all small field mice would surely agree.

Only one other owl disputes the tawny's claim—the barn owl, *Tyto alba. Tyto* has the same tuftless head and much the same size, the same reputation for being a living mouse-trap, and so one name could have served them both. But *Tyto* does have one distinctive trademark that has long given it a name of its own—a monkey-like, heart-shaped face. There are other monkey-faced owls in other lands, but none in Israel—or in North America—has the weird hobgoblin face that *Tyto* shows to trembling farm folk as it peers down from rafter or church steeple. *Tyto* flies in almost every land the world around and so it has picked up a ragbag of nicknames. It comes in a range of buffy tones from pale to dark, but its front and underbelly are almost completely white, and so watchers who see it only from below call it the white owl. Its back is of yellowish mottling and so those who see it flying away call it the yellow owl. Or sometimes the name is "silver" instead of white and "golden" instead of yellow. In Hebrew its name could have been *tinshemeth,* next taboo but one in Leviticus and set apart from the three-size "small, medium, and large" owl sequence because of its monkey-like face. But there are other candidates for tinshemeth identity, too—none of them owls—and so the barn owl could have been included with the two tawny owls, the short-eared and long-eared owls in one-word-for-all-middle-sized listing.

When you look for their 12-to-15-inch shadows, you will find no tawny owls in America. In their stead look for three of the same genus: *Strix varia,* barred owl; *Strix occidentalis,* spotted owl; *Strix nebulosa,* great gray owl. The other three —barn owl, short-eared, long-eared—are world roamers, the same species here in our own woods and fields as in Old Judea. The short-eared owl, which often hunts by daylight and often nests in the far corners of city airports, will probably be the "plunger" you see most often, and you will agree it earns its name.

13. Yanshuf: This name may be an attempt to echo the weirdly hoarse voice of the Old World's largest owl, or it could have been derived from the Hebrew word for horns. "Horned owl" is certainly the most common name for our own very similar owl species, *Bubo virginianus.* Officially, our bird is "great horned owl," for its larger size is a factor in identification that almost automatically has to be part of the label. Europeans have given their *Bubo bubo* the same indication of superior size with the label eagle owl, but whatever words mean "great owl" in any Old World tongue surely point to this abundant species above all others.

The New English Bible lists seven kinds of owls for

taboo—three ahead of the hawks and four following—so that all but two of the nine owls seen in the area are banned. But what species are meant by "desert owl" and "screech owl" is uncertain. The latter is sometimes a European nickname for the barn owl, but the American species officially enrolled as the screech owl is unknown overseas. Moses was talking to simple folk, not expert ornithologists, and surely three owl names—four at the most—would be sufficient. "Do not eat small owls, middle-sized mouse-catching owls, or the big owls with horns" would have been ample banning to include all species. Only monkey-faced, heart-faced *Tyto alba* might have called for additional naming.

14. Tinshemeth: If you want to place this name among the owls, you'll find its match easily on Bible bird walk if you know of an abandoned barn or little-used country church where these birds of night could find a home. In fact, "church owl" is one of Tyto's Old World names. Find them in spring and see the half-grown owlets pop up to defy the searchlight's beam with hissing threat and bobbing hobgoblin war dance, and you'll agree that if this Hebrew word means "hisser" or even "astonishing hisser" it is rightly applied. But don't make up your mind about which bird matches the word best until you take a further look.

White Wings Trimmed with Black

14. Tinshemeth: One thing is certain—tinshemeth is not the swan, as both the King James and the Douay Bibles declared. While swans do hiss, they are clean eaters, feeding on neither flesh nor filth to warrant dietary taboo. Indeed, roast swan was long counted the most delicate meat to be served at royal banquets, jostled out of this honored place only by the discovery of American turkeys.

But barn owls are hissers, too, and we would give over this name to the barn owl without further thought, except for one thing. There has been a strong oral tradition that some water bird was intended for banning, some bird like the swan but with different eating habits. And the bird that fits the bill actually has "swan" as part of one of its common names—the swan-grebe, officially known now as great crested grebe, *Podiceps cristatus.*

The great crested grebe fits tinshemeth requirements in several ways. First of all, *tinshemeth* (or a very similar word) is also used as the name of a kind of lizard. And grebes have the same kind of horny, lobed toes that lizards do. Perhaps it was the hissing voice, not the toes, that led to duplicate naming, but since few birds have lobed toes it is a case in point.

Also, if "astonishing puffer of air" is part of the name's root meaning, the grebe fulfills the role to perfection as a courting male goes into full display, ruffling its feathers and seeming to tiptoe across the water in unbelievable ballet prancing.

Furthermore, grebes do dine on rodents as well as fish, to make inclusion logical. If they were not banned by special naming, their size and plumpness would certainly put them on the menu in hunger times, even if a fishy flavor would keep them from being prime favorites.

No Bible translation has ever named the great crested grebe here as tinshemeth, but it could have been the species intended by the vague label of "water hen," a name applied to several marsh birds. If you want it on your list, look for our western grebe, *Aechmophorus occidentalis,* which it closely resembles in looks and courtship dancing. Any of the smaller grebes will show you those lobed toes, if the westerner isn't in your area, and three of them will be the same species still seen by birders in the Holy Land—*Podiceps grisegena,* the red-necked grebe; *Podiceps caspicus,* the eared grebe; and *Podiceps auritus,* the horned grebe.

Also any of them will show you the grebe custom of suddenly sinking beneath the water without a betraying ripple, leaving only heads and necks to wave in sinuous, snakelike twisting as they keep danger lookout—perhaps another reason for their sharing a reptile's name.

Only the great crested grebe, however, has the white feathers with a darker trim that form the only common bond to unite tinshemeth with the following names for six-of-a-kind. Whether the grebe belongs here or not, white-with-black is the bond-mark for the next five names in Leviticus.

15. Ka'ath: The meaning of this word is "vomiter," but so many birds regurgitate their food to feed their young—or to lighten body-weight for fast take-off or to wage war against an intruder—that the label could apply to almost any bird on any list. But only the pelican wears an enormous throat pouch as visible evidence of supreme ability to disgorge on demand, and so it seems well-entitled to keep the ka'ath name given it in traditional texts.

If the throat pouch is indeed the namesake mark of the ka'ath, then any other birds with this same equipment might share the pelican's Hebrew name. Best known among them would be the cormorant—another fish-eater with unpalatable flavor—which has a smaller but still noticeable gular sac, as do gannets and darters. A bird with an even more prominent pouch is the long-legged desert scavenger, the marabou stork, and this species is a likely candidate for the phrase "ka'ath of the wilderness" that comes in Psalm 102:6 (*see* Desert Cock; Pelican of the Wilderness).

Wait by any waterhole in lion country and you will soon see the marabou coming to feed on whatever carcass the king of beasts has abandoned. Often it asserts its rights to bloody gleaning even before the griffon vulture takes its turn, and there's no doubt that this species would be on taboo list, either here or later with herons of all kinds, since it has heron-like long legs.

Whether pelican, cormorant, and marabou are all three banned by ka'ath name, or whether the pelican stands alone in blame, is difficult to decide. The pelican is named by most translators and the North American white pelican, *Pelecanus erythrorhynchos,* is very close to being an exact duplicate for the white pelican of Israeli lands. Our brown pelican, *Pelecanus occidentalis,* at least matches in pouch size, if not in

color. Neither is as abundant as formerly, but both can still
be seen on many waterways.

If you cannot see a living white pelican in flight, look
for it in TV nature films or in books so that you can see how
the wings make the only trademark for the pelican in flight
—white wings edged in black. Once the bird is airborne, the
recognition by pouch, squat body, or waddling awkwardness
is impossible—all we really see are those wide wings. The Old
World white pelican wingspread has been measured at 10
feet, 4 inches; the marabou at 12 feet, widest span of all living
birds.

16. Rahama: This Hebrew bird name has been translated many ways—gier eagle, carrion vulture, white vulture
—and all of them are aliases for just one species, *Neophron
percnopterus* (usually known in English now as the Egyptian
vulture), probably the best-known scavenger of Mediterranean lands. For one thing, it is a bird of all habitats—city or
country—and of just one habit, namely, the eating of the
filthiest carrion and offal that ever accumulated in gutter and
dung heap. Its white coloring, when other vultures are dark
of feather, and its smaller size—23 or 24 inches to their 39
and 40 or more—and its prevalence in city streets all would
cause it to be named apart. In soaring flight, it shows white
wings bordered with black—sufficient reason for its placement here.

Certainly it would have to be named somewhere on a
list of "do not eat" taboo. Its role as a scavenger was so ap-
preciated by the pharaohs of old Egypt that they absolutely
forbade anyone to harm these street-cleaners, and the rule
led to the nicknames "Pharaoh's pets" and "Pharaoh's chickens" and to the official name, Egyptian vulture.

Yet like many birds that bear a geographical label, they
are seen in many places besides the namesake area, and they
were abundant in Bible lands in the time of Moses. They are
still seen in modern Israel, too, and are generally protected
wherever they are found.

If *rahama* does mean "bird of tender care," as some

scholars suggest, it fits this protected species very well. If it means "white-and-black," as other scholars claim, that meaning fits just as well.

In Neophron's place you can look in the zoo for the only white American vulture, the king vulture, and remember that it was once seen in Florida. Now it is not found north of Mexico. Or you may substitute the black vulture, *Coragyps atratus,* a match in size and with the reverse color scheme— black trimmed with white.

17. Hasidah: Hasidah is another bird known in flight by a pattern of white wings trimmed in black—the white stork. We are so accustomed to thinking of this bird in its legendary role as a bringer of good luck to the homes where it builds its rooftop nests—and bringer of babies—that we overlook its practical role as scavenger, eater of mice and rats and lizards and snakes or any scraps that might be tossed aside from the butcher stalls at the oldtime city market. In the olden days storks were common sights in the market square, stalking about on sanitary patrol, calm in their assurance of ample food and a warm welcome.

Hasidah is said to mean "bird of kindness," with the goodwill a mutual exchange between people and birds, but protecting them as scavengers was a matter of good sense, even without the Hebrew law against unclean food to take them off the menu.

The Old World stork of Bible lines does not come here, but we do have one family cousin, *Mycteria americana,* the wood ibis or wood stork, to give the same long-legged, wide-winged silhouette. Look for the kinship as you drive along the Tamiami Trail in Florida or take a tour through the Everglades or on the Carolina–Georgia sea islands. In autumn you may see them almost anywhere, for they become great wanderers as the southern marshes dry up and they are forced to look elsewhere for food. White wings edged in black are their trademark, too. You can't miss it.

18. Anafah: "Anafah of all kinds" is the phrase of banning, so once again—as with the taboo against all of raven-kind and all hawks and falcons—there must be a large group of similar species, each different enough in small ways to have individual names, yet with a strong family resemblance.

Cormorants, named here by the New English Bible, would surely not need the "of all kinds" label, for the three wintering species seen in Israel are so much alike that a bird book and binoculars are needed to tell them apart for positive identification. Besides, *anafah* is still the word for herons of all kinds in Israel today, and through the centuries nearly all translators have reaffirmed this identity.

If you were asked to name the trademarks of heron family resemblance, you'd probably say "long beaks" or "long legs," and it seems that the Hebrews of old had the same idea. At least *anafah* could mean "big and noselike beak." To them, as to ornithologists today, it included herons, ibises, spoonbills, bitterns, egrets, and the flamingo. Their purple heron, *Ardea purpurea,* much like our great blue heron, *Ardea herodias,* is the most abundant of the larger species and therefore would seem to be "the" anafah. But if you are looking for the bird with the most noselike beak, you would have to choose the flamingo. The flamingo is actually named in one American version of the Greek Septuagint Bible. Also, its wide white wings edged with black fit the sequence bondmark better than do heron wings, for most Old World flamingo wings have only a touch of pink to tinge their whiteness, not the full deep rose coloring of American and some African flamingos. See them flying in bright tropic sunlight —as you often do on travel films—and white-with-black seems the only color pattern. They could be "the" anafah beyond all doubt.

Besides the flamingo, other members of the anafah clan still seen in the Holy Land and in North America as well are these three: *Bubulcus ibis,* the cattle egret; *Plegadis falcinellus,* the glossy ibis; and *Nycticorax nycticorax,* the black-crowned night heron. All our other herons, bitterns, spoonbills, and ibises make good stand-ins and all will show you the menu of field mice, rats, snakes, toads, and shrews—as

well as fish—that would have made this family liable to
Mosaic dietary taboo. Whether heron or flamingo was named
head of the clan makes small difference on Bible birdwatch,
for both would have been included by the "anafah of all
kinds" banning.

19. Dŭkifath: The word *dukifath* names a bird with
lofty crest and lusty voice, and early English translators immediately thought of the crested lapwing, a bird whose wail-
ing complaints echo into legend over all moors and meadows
of the British Isles. This very species, *Vanellus vanellus,* sometimes wanders to North American shores, and if you want to
follow the birds of the King James Version, you may be able
to add it to your list. If you can't find this original, look for
a stand-in from the plover tribe to which it belongs—our kill-
deer, *Charadrius vociferus,* which does not have the crest but
does have an equally persistent and repeated cry.

But almost all translators agree that the bird still known
by dukifath name in Israel is the species intended: the hoopoe, *Upupa epops.* It does have a crest, and it does have a
lusty cry—which the name *hoopoe* tries to imitate—and it
does have a diet of unsanitary stench, poking into dungheaps
for grubs and worms and such. An insect diet is generally
counted "clean," since insects do not have the red blood forbidden by Judean law, but any creature feeding among garbage cannot get away wholly clean. Besides, the hoopoe
mother raises her young in one of the filthiest nests ever to
offend a birdwatcher's nose. Part of this malodorous aroma
is due to a dark and oily spray discharged from her preen
glands whenever her babies are threatened by an intruder,
and the "keep away" melody lingers on long after the intruder has discreetly gone elsewhere for its dinner. Also, the
droppings from both mother and babies are left in the nest
to add further filth. Most parent birds remove the feces from
their nests—and the babies themselves soon follow instinctive
command to back up to the edge of the nest and let their
droppings fall outside where sun and rain will supposedly
lessen their unpleasant odor and the danger of passing on any

germs. But the hoopoe mother and her young let the droppings stay in the nest, since the female herself does not leave
it during the entire four weeks of incubation. The male
hoopoe feeds and protects her meanwhile in an exemplary
display of devotion—but that does not make the nest smell
any sweeter.

In northern Europe, where hoopoes appear only on late
summer wanderings, as a rule, and do not nest, they were
counted good food in earlier days when songbirds of all kinds
were on the menu. But anyone who had had his own nose
tweaked with that nesting stench would have agreed with
Moses on the "do not eat" warning.

Since no hoopoes come to North America, nor any members of the Family Upupidae, we will have to look for a member of the same order, the Coraciiformes. The only candidate
is the belted kingfisher, *Megaceryle alcyon,* which has both
crest and voice as well as kinship to mark the claim. The
kingfisher, however, does not have the wide white-with-black
wings that have been the common marking of this sequence.
Actually, the hoopoe itself falls far short of the wide span
shown by grebe, pelican, neophron, stork, flamingo, and
heron. Even the smallest of these—the neophron—measures
from 23 to 26 inches, while the hoopoe is but 12 or so from
tail to beak.

But the hoopoe does have a striking zebra pattern of
black and white on its wings, and again that color combination makes the identifying clue as a fawn-toned bird flies
away. The fawn-brown of its body, by the way, leads in transi-
tion to the last flier on the list, also small and brown.

20. Atalaf: The name means "night wings" or "night
flier" and almost all translators agree that it is the bat (*see*
Bat). Scientists today may argue that bats are clean creatures,
not at all earning their evil name of ancient legends. Only
the New World vampire bats suck blood to warrant taboo,
by Mosaic standards. But even bats that dine on insects and
fruit juices live in caves amid incredible filth of heaped
droppings that sometimes accumulate for centuries, and some

investigators have been made ill merely by inhaling bat-cave air. Also, bats seem to be frequent carriers of rabies and perhaps other diseases, and while modern science removes the bat from the bird category, few want it on the menu.

The only true birds suggested as possible wearers of the atalaf name are these: the marsh hawk, *Circus cyaneus,* which often begins its hunting in midafternoon or dusk; the nightjars—probably already banned as tachmas—and the hobby and red-footed falcons, which also hunt at dusk more often than in broad daylight; the night heron, another contender for the tachmas label; and the stone curlew, also called "thick-knees"—an eerie-voiced flier tangled in many an Old World superstition because of its night-time flying.

But the bat still seems to have first claim, and so the forbidden names most probably should read: *Do not eat* eagles, the bearded vulture, the great vultures, the kites, or any kind of falcon, or the raven and all its kindred, the ostrich and bustards, the nightjars, the gulls, hawks of any kind, the little owls, the rodent-eating owls or the great horned owls, the great crested grebe, the pouch-wearers (pelican and marabou and cormorant), the neophron vulture, the stork, the flamingo and heron and all their kind, the hoopoe, or the bat.

The dietary laws set down by Moses also forbade the eating of certain animal flesh, and during the early Christian centuries there was much discussion about whether Jewish converts to Christ's teachings should continue to observe these Mosaic taboos.

A revelation to the apostle Peter (Acts 10:9–16; 11:4–10) gave him a message from God saying that the old bans were no longer part of the law and that men should henceforth decide for themselves which foods were to be eaten and which put aside. None at all needed to be put aside merely as an act of required sacrifice, but only if the abstinence came from inner soul need.

This discussion shows clearly that the Mosaic taboos had come to be considered as a matter of ritual, not as a matter of good health, however the forbidden foods had been chosen in the beginning.

The challenge here is not for us to decide why and wherefore, but to look for whatever species may best represent these names on the Bible's longest bird list—look for them, learn to know their ways, learn all they can tell us of the wonders of God's world.

Birds of Doom
HEBREW: *ka'ath, kippod, yanshof, oreb, ya'annah, lilith, kippoz, dayyoth,* Isaiah 34:11–16
ka'ath, kippod, kol, oreb, Zephaniah 2:14

Twice in Bible passages, the prophets rely on a naming of birds of eerie cry or lonely wasteland wandering to help their listeners picture a scene of utter desolation. Beasts may be named, too—wolves, jackals, dragons—but the birds alone could set listeners shivering in remembered awe as they pictured the sort of lonely place where they themselves had heard owl hoot and bittern croak, seen vultures gathering beside sun-bleached bare bones.

The ka'ath, named first in both warnings, would surely be that stalking scavenger the marabou, rather than the pelican (*see* Birds of Abomination, No. 15). The cormorant, which may well have shared the name, might be a bird of doom, also, because of its black feathers. A flock of them will gather along a waterway, sitting with wings widespread to dry and looking like funeral drapery, as you may see for yourself some day if you go where cormorants make their home on seacoasts or inland waterways.

Kippod, twice named also, means "the bristler," and several early translators mistook it for the porcupine or hedgehog. But birds bristle, too, though they do not have spiny quills, and when they are angry enough—or frightened enough—their feathers stand on end in fearsome array. And the bittern bristles not only in threat or fear, but every time he brings out that deep-toned croak that echoes across the

Birds of Doom

ISAIAH 34:11–16

Phonetic Hebrew	King James Version	Douay Bible	Jewish Holy Scriptures	Revised Standard Version	New American Bible	New English Bible
ka'ath	cormorant	bittern	pelican	hawk	desert owl	horned owl
kippod	bittern	ericius	bittern	porcupine	hoot owl	bustard
yanshof	owl	ibis	owl	owl	screech owl	screech owl
oreb	raven	raven	raven	raven	raven	raven
bath ya'annah	owls	ostriches	ostriches	ostriches	ostriches	desert owls
lilith	screech owl	lamia	night monster	night hag	lilith	nightjar
kippoz	great owl	ericius	arrow-snake	owl	hoot owl	sand-partridge
dayyoth	vultures	kites	kites	kites	kites	kites

ZEPHANIAH 2:14

Phonetic Hebrew	King James Version	Douay Bible	Jewish Holy Scriptures	Revised Standard Version	New American Bible	New English Bible
ka'ath	cormorant	bittern	pelican	vulture	screech owl	horned owl
kippod	bittern	urchin	bittern	hedgehog	desert owl	ruffed bustard
kol	voice	voice	voice	owl	call	tawny owl
oreb (harab)	raven	desolation	desolation	raven	raven	bustard

silent marsh like sudden voodoo drumbeat. So of all birds he is surely "the" bristler, and his solitary ways second his impact as omen of doom and desolation. The American bittern, *Botaurus lentiginosus,* has much the same coloring and customs as the Old World *Botaurus stellaris,* and the generic name they share gives each the title of "bull-voiced."

When you take up bittern watch in some lonely marsh you may think you're hearing a suction pump instead of a wild bull. First there is an ominous sucking in of breath to make you imagine a giant pulling his boots out of the ooze, and then the booming drumbeat—a *woomph* against the silence, a *ploongh* . . . a *choongh*—certainly no sound you can duplicate by ordinary words. Sometimes that boom can be heard a mile away, but somehow it always seems right at hand in threatening nearness—and if you can hear your first bittern while you are standing alone in a lonely place, and not want to turn and run, then you must have a clear conscience indeed.

To top it off, the bittern's mottled feathering and long neck enable it to pose in veritable duplication of waving marsh grass, so that you can look right at it and not see it is there. Then suddenly it moves, seeming to materialize out of thin air like any ghost—one more reason why the prophets of old thought their listeners might tremble at a world turned into a haunt for the bristler. Also, the bittern's splay feet enable it to walk in safety across slime and ooze where hunters following in pursuit will sink in up to their knees, as if trapped by the bird's magic powers. And if it is cornered, it suddenly gives up its hunch-necked pose for a lightning jab with its dagger beak, piercing a hunter's arm clear to the bone at a distance no one could believe—unless he knew how long that hunched-in neck could really stretch. No wonder "haunt of bitterns" was a warning of doom!

Whether the next name Isaiah spoke in warning was yanshuf, the horned owl, or yanshof, a different bird, the scholars cannot quite decide. Certainly the largest owl in the land—or an owl of any size—could be a bird of doom, as owls have been in all places and all times. But if *yanshof* is the word, the bird to match might be the glossy ibis, the stone curlew, or the night heron—all birds of eerie cry often heard at night and in lonely places. Evidently the name was intended to echo the cry, and you can listen yourself to both the ibis and the heron, for these are birds you can find on Bible bird walk in many parts of North America.

Oreb and ya‘annah, the next two birds of doom in Isaiah's warning, are already named among the Birds of Abomination as raven and ostrich. Lilith—which is also the folk name for a certain witch or hag—might be the ghostly barn owl or the pale Hume's tawny owl that lives in the desert. The last name on the list—dayyoth—is surely the plural of da'ah, the kite, another scavenger already named among Birds of Abomination. But next to last is a name that gives translators considerable trouble, for kippoz is listed among the birds but seems to mean "snake" or "darter."

If you have followed bird trails through the Florida Everglades or other southern swamps and marsh country, you will immediately picture the dark feathers and sinewy neck of *Anhinga anhinga,* actually known as both snakebird and darter, even though *anhinga*—a Tupi Indian word from Brazil—is the recommended usage. The snakebird of the Old World tropics is very similar, *Anhinga rufa,* but since it is not seen in northern Europe, Bible translators of olden days probably were not aware of its existence.

The anhinga does look like a snake, for often only the head and neck come thrusting out from dangling vines or show above the waves. And "darter" is certainly the one word to describe the sudden thrusting of slim dagger beak as the anhinga spears an unwary fish for its dinner.

Like the bittern, the anhinga is a bird of lonely places and eerie ways that seem like magic to watchers who do not understand bird life. It can soar on wide wings like an eagle or a hawk, hang there riding the air currents like a vulture, dive underwater like a cormorant—and spread its wings to dry, cormorant-style, too—and paddle like a duck or deflate to instant submersion like the grebes. As it climbs out on a tangle of tree roots overhanging the bank it seems to hang onto them like a cat, for it has both claws and webs on those remarkable feet. Up, up, it goes, from roots to bole to twisted upper branches in writhing, snakelike progress. The special structure of its neck muscles and the central kink in the neck vertebrae enable the anhinga to make its typical darting jab at food or foe, and the spearlike beak has both the hooked tip of the predator birds and serrated edges to ensure that even the slipperiest fish or frog will be held firmly.

In tropic lands all around the world, the anhinga has been counted a bird of special omen, its feathers prized for fans and robes and chieftains' headdresses and even as a sign of royalty. Surely it is a more fitting denizen for Isaiah's land of desolation than the owls—already named by other words —or the friendly and gentle sand-partridge of the New English Bible. Surely you will want to look for the darter on some coming southern marshland bird walk, whether you count it a Bible bird or no.

Zephaniah, in repeating the same forecast of doom, named ka'ath, kippod, and oreb—marabou, bittern, and raven —and added another name, the kol, the voice. Of course this could be any ghostly sound, even the wind, but it also could be the blue roller, *Coracias garrulus,* known by almost this same word in Israel today. The roller's voice issues forth from its beautiful blue throat in an unbeautiful crowlike croak— in fact, "blue crow" or "blue rook" are some of its nicknames —and like any corvine croak it seems to carry an ominous overtone. Also, the roller is a bird that keeps to itself in lonely places, not visiting city gardens or backyards where its croak could become familiar, as well known as the similar harsh voice of our jays.

Any of the American jays will be a good match for the roller on Bible bird walk, and so will the kingfisher—actually a roller relative in the Order Coraciiformes. And you may also want to look for a sandhill crane as a stand-in for the bustards in this passage, for some Bible scholars feel that the bird on the abandoned doorstep was not the oreb but the harab or houbara bustard (see Birds of Abomination: No. 7 *Bath-ya'annah*). Other scholars think it was neither bird, but *horeb,* meaning "desolation."

Birds of Prey

HEBREW: *ayit,* screamer(s) or flesh-tearer(s). Genesis 15:11; Job 28:7; Psalm 50:11; Isaiah 18:6; 46:9–11; Jeremiah 12:9; Ezekiel 39:4

GREEK: *ornea,* large bird. Revelation 18:2

See also Birds of Abomination; Ravenous Birds; Vulture

Bird watchers of Bible times were far from having the precise steps of classification that rule ornithology today, but they did use group labels. First, birds were clean or unclean —that is, edible or not edible by Mosaic Law—and beyond that there were songbirds (see Singing of Birds, Songbirds) and birds of prey. For the predators the Hebrew word was *ayit,* which may be an echo of the screaming cries of kites, hawks, and falcons, or stem from root words that mean "tearers of flesh." This latter meaning would allow the label to include vultures—which only grunt and hiss—for they do tear flesh with their hooked beaks, if not with their talons.

The ayit are first named in Genesis when Abraham comes to spread sacrificial meat upon the outdoor altar, only to find that some hook-beaked, hungry birds are on watch, ready to swoop down and snatch his offering from the stones. We do not sacrifice meat today, so we cannot act out this very scene. But we do picnic in the out-of-doors—and spread our food upon a picnic cloth or table. If a crow or a jay pounces on a bun the moment our backs are turned, we can at least understand how it was that day when the ayit came swooping down and Abraham drove them away.

Birds of Sacrifice

HEBREW: *ahf,* any bird. Genesis 8:20; Leviticus 1:14–17; 7:26; 17:13; 20:25

tor, gozal, turtledove or young bird. Genesis 15:9–10

tor, beni-yonah, turtledove or young dove (pigeon). Leviticus 1:14–17; 5:7–13; 12:6–8; 14:4–7, 22–30; 15:14, 29; Numbers 6:10

zipporim, any small bird. Leviticus 14:49–57

GREEK: *trugon, neossos,* turtledove or young bird. Luke 2:24

No one word names the birds that may be used for Old Testament sacrifice, but the requirements are given in some detail in Leviticus, along with other ritual actions. Turtledoves, young pigeons, and young birds or nestlings are usually named in particular, although sometimes any bird seems suitable (*see* Dove and Pigeon; Young Birds).

Birds of the Ark (*see* Dove and Pigeon; Raven)

Birds of the Hills (Mountains)
HEBREW: *ayit-harim.* Psalm 50:11; Isaiah 18:6

Since mountain country is usually sparsely settled or not settled at all, while low country has farms and towns, it seems possible that "birds of the mountains" simply means the wilder species seldom seen around dwellings, especially the predators of solitary habits, such as eagles and the bearded vulture.

Bittern
HEBREW: *kippod,* bristler. Isaiah 14:22–23; 34:11–16; Zephaniah 2:14

A nickname like "the bristler" could be applied to many birds (*see* Birds of Doom), but it is an apt label for the bittern, traditional translation for these passages. The American bittern, *Botaurus lentiginosis,* is much like the Old World bittern, *Botaurus stellaris.*

Bustard
HEBREW: *bath-ya'annah* (*see* Birds of Abomination: No. 7, ya'annah)

kippod (*see* Birds of Doom; Bittern)
harab. Isaiah 34:11–16 (*see* Birds of Doom)

Harab is the Semitic name for *Chlamydotis undulata,* a year-round resident in Israel known in English as the houbara or houbara bustard. If *harab,* rather than *oreb,* is the word in Isaiah, then undoubtedly the bustard belongs among Bible birds. Very possibly it was also named as a kind of ostrich (bath-ya'annah) not to be eaten because it feeds on small animals and rodents, and some scholars believe it was kippod, the bristler. The great bustard, *Otis tarda,* is the species most deserving of this name, for it does have bristling feathers around its throat that stand out like quills in courtship display. However, the great bustard comes to Israel now only as a winter visitor, when courtship is out of season, and if this were true in Bible times also, the bristling display would not be seen often enough to make it a common byword.

The great bustard seems to have more the contour of a turkey than any other American bird as it struts across the plain, but in flight it stretches out its long neck crane-fashion (bustards belong to the Order Gruiformes, as do cranes) and then looks much like a goose. In fact, when European explorers in North America first saw our Canada goose, *Branta canadensis,* they mistook it for a bustard. If you are reading pioneer journals and come to a passage about bustards, you are reminded once again that even outdoorsmen of the seventeenth and eighteenth centuries did not describe birds accurately—and how much less could be expected of watchers in Bible times.

Buzzard (*see* Vulture)
To Europeans, a buzzard is a hawk of the genus Buteo or any slow-flying bird of hawklike manner. The osprey, for example, was once called the moor buzzard or the bald buzzard. Another hawk that eats bees and bee larvae is called the honey buzzard. In the United States, however, buzzard is used only as another name for vultures.

Caged Birds

HEBREW: *zippor,* any small bird. Job 41:5; Ecclesiastes 10:20;
    Jeremiah 5:27

yonim, doves. Isaiah 60:8

APOCRYPHA: Sirach (Ecclesiasticus) 11:30

GREEK: *peristera,* dove. Matthew 21:12; Mark 11:15; John
    2:14–16

ornea, large bird of prey. Revelation 18:2

See also Dove and Pigeon; Fowl, Fowler, Fowling; Peacock

"Will you play with him as with a bird?" is the question
in Job 41:5, proving that birds were caged as pets in Bible
times as well as for food (*see* Fowl, Fowler, Fowling) and for
sacrifice (*see* Dove and Pigeon), and for display (*see* Peacock).
Indeed, the taming of birds as playmates goes so far back in
man's history that the very word *pet* may have come from
Greek *peteinon,* the word for small birds or birds in general.

Goldfinches, nightingales, magpies, blackbirds, and
starlings were all favorite cage birds before the Christian Era,
with jackdaws, crows, and hoopoes also popular. Parrots were
brought to Greece from Persia and India by the time of
Alexander the Great—about 323 B.C. Probably the rock
doves, *Columba livia,* ancestors of our own park pigeons,
were among the first—or at least the most common—caged
pet birds in Bible lands, since they were bred both by private
families and by dealers to use in altar ritual.

"Like doves at the lattice window," Isaiah wrote (60:8)
when he saw the white sails of ships in the harbor.

And perhaps the writer of Ecclesiastes 10:22 had messenger pigeons in mind when he warned gossipers that birds
might tell others what they were saying. Swallows and other
small birds that nest on windowsills carried messages, too,
at a very early date. Their tiny legs could not bear the weight
of a capsule, as pigeons may do, but a twist of blue or red silk
thread—for instance—could be tied to the leg of a nesting
mother swallow. When the bird was taken to a chariot race
and released just as the race was over, the color told watchers

at home which horse had won long before any courier on horseback could come with the news, for the mother bird would lose no time in winging home to her eggs or babies.

If you are thinking of having a caged bird for a pet, remember that both federal and state laws prohibit the taking of wild birds for pets. Only canaries, parakeets, parrots, and certain other foreign birds imported under permit may be kept in confinement in homes.

Charadrion (*see* Birds of Abomination: No. 18, anafah)

Chicken, Cock, Hen
HEBREW: *tuhoth, sekvi,* meaning uncertain. Job 38:36
   tamara, to lift oneself up (by extension, to act the male, i.e., strut like a cock). Job 39:18
   zarzir mothnayim, one with well-built (well-girt) loins or legs: cock, greyhound, warhorse. Proverbs 30:31
APOCRYPHA: 2 Esdras 1:30 (sometimes omitted); Tobit 8:11 (or 8:18, or omitted, or translated as "dawn," "morning")
GREEK: *alektor,* cock. Matthew 26:34, 74–75; Mark 13:35; 14:30, 68–72; Luke 22:34, 60–61; John 13:38; 18:27
   ornis, hen. Matthew 23:37; Luke 13:34
   nossion, chickens. Matthew 23:37, Luke 13:34

There is no reference to cocks, hens, or chickens in the King James translation of the Old Testament, and it has long been thought that domesticated barnyard fowl had not been brought from India—where they originated—at this early date. But nevertheless there were words in those times for male and female birds and young—several words—and just like English "cock," "hen," "chickens" they eventually slipped into use to mean barnyard birds, not wild fowl. When a translator comes upon one of these words in an old manuscript, he has to decide whether the "cock" of the passage was just any male bird—like Cock Robin and Cock Sparrow in the nursery rhymes—or a bird like the old red rooster in many a barnyard.

The red jungle fowl of India, *Gallus gallus,* were domesticated in their own homeland around the year 2500 B.C., and by 1400 B.C. they were known in China. Two centuries later Phoenician ships were making long voyages and returning with all sorts of foreign wonders, and perhaps domesticated jungle fowl were among the cargoes. Even earlier—1435 B.C.—Egyptian pharaohs had a hen (that is, a female bird of some sort) that laid an egg every day, and the account said it had been brought from Babylon. Very likely there were chickens, as we use the word, among the "fattened fowl" served King Solomon nearly a thousand years before the Christian Era.

And certainly there were crowing, strutting barnyard chanticleers in Bible lands before Jerusalem fell to Babylon in 587 B.C. in the reign of Nebuchadnezzar, for 2 Kings 25:23 tells of a man named Jaazaniah who lived then, and we know he used the picture of a rooster as his seal. The seal itself, made of onyx, has been found at Mizpah, just north of Jerusalem, and it is now in the keeping of the Pacific Institute at Berkeley, California.

So it does seem possible that the men who wrote the Book of Job might have made comparison to the "wisdom" of the barnyard cock, and those who wrote the Proverbs might have described its strutting step. At least several modern Bible versions give the cock its place in one or two passages from these books, and some translators add a third in Job 39:18 (*see* Ostrich).

Oddly, there are two words that might be translated as "cock" in Job 38:36—*tuhoth* and *sekvi.* The King James line reads: "Who hath put wisdom in the inward parts (*tuhoth*)? Or who hath given the heart (*sekvi*) its understanding?" Now *tuhoth* does sound as if it comes from the same roots as *tohoroth,* the word for food that is ritually clean and not prohibited by Mosaic Law. And since chickens were unknown in the time of Moses they were indeed among the fowl to earn this label. Also, there seems to be a double play on words with the phrase "inward parts," for the entrails of a common barnyard cock or hen were often used by Roman

soothsayers to foretell the future or at least to predict whether
the time was auspicious for good fortune. "Auspicious" actually derives from the Latin word for "birds"—*aves*—plus
the Latin for "look." And our slang phrase "to chicken out"
comes from all the ancient Romans who looked at the spread
entrails of a cock and then decided not to wage war or carry
out some business project after all, just because the signs of
those "inward parts" were not favorable.

Sekvi seems to get into the picture because it was one
of the poetic names for the constellation of Orion the Hunter
and Sirius the Dog Star seen during the early morning hours
when cocks begin to crow and signal the farmer to start his
day's work, the soldier to change guard. The Hebrews themselves—and other ancient peoples, also—very early learned
to use the rising of these well-known star patterns as a clock,
and perhaps they thought that roosters set their own crowing
time by the stars.

But besides these fanciful—but very possible—explana-
tions of *tuhoth* and *sekvi* meaning, there is also good founda-
tion for believing that "inward parts" and "heart" are exactly
what the writer meant to name. We still say that we get fore-
warning of danger by a certain feeling in our bones or in our
bowels or the pit of the stomach. We say "heart" when we
mean "courage," and "guts" when we mean "daring."

The most common Hebrew word for "heart," by the
way, is not *sekvi* but *leb,* and this is written with characters
very much like the Egyptian word for the sacred white ibis.
Consequently, the translation might be, "Who has given the
ibis its understanding?"

What the ibis understands is when to migrate. What
the cock understands is when to crow. What the human heart
knows is more complicated, but whatever doubts there may
be about the wording of the question, the expected answer is
certain: God is the giver of understanding to cock or ibis or
man.

Turn to Proverbs 30:29–31 for the third name that may
give the rooster a place in Old Testament lines and you find

zarzir mothnayim, which possibly means "he of the well-girt loins" and certainly names a creature with pride to match its stride.

There be three things which go well, yea, four are comely in going: A lion which is strongest among beasts, and turneth not away for any; a *zarzir mothnayim:* and an he goat also; and a king against whom there is no rising up.

Four absolute rulers walking in pride make the picture: a king of men before loyal subjects; a billy goat, boss of barnyard and meadow flocks; a lion, king of the jungle; and zarzir mothnayim. Since human kings, jungle kings, and flock kings have already been named, this other high stepper almost has to be a bird. "Strutting cock" is so familiar a phrase now that it almost immediately leaps to mind, yet there is that nagging question of doubt as to whether barnyard roosters really were well known in Israel when the lines were written.

King James translators thought this proud stepper was a greyhound. American Standard authors chose the war horse, certainly "well-girt" when caparisoned for battle. But Jewish scholars who wrote the Talmud—a compilation of traditional wisdom—suggested the raven, which indeed does walk proudly. Other scholars point out that *zarzira* and *zurzur* are local names for the starling.

But bossy as starlings may be when backed up by a huge flock, the male is not set off from the females by brighter plumage—as the name suggests—nor does one male starling strut before a flock to match the picture. So, if roosters weren't yet common enough to make instant comparison—or even if they were—this kingly walker among birds could well have been the peacock, surely as proud-looking a strutter in bespangled dress as the bird world knows. Peacock, he-goat, lion, and a king of men—now there is a strutting foursome beyond all doubt.

Or, if the phrase simply means well-made limbs, rather than brightly colored, this stately walker could be the mara-

bou, lordly carrion bird of lion country. Hide behind a bush
—or watch a television travel film—and you can see how
this vulture-on-stilts comes stalking up to the feast of an
abandoned carcass, taking kingly precedence over the
hunched figures of the craven vultures who give way before
him. And in ancient eastern legends you can find the marabou
named as *zahir mora,* one who carries a magic stone em-
bedded in his skull, a magic stone that would cure you of any
poison dosage, if only you could get hold of it with proper
ritual. And *zahir mora* sounds enough like *zarzir mothnayim*
to suggest that the writer may have been thinking of the
marabou all along (*see* Desert Cock).

Most recent translators, however, give this line to the
barnyard rooster and you have only to watch for a moment
to see how well he illustrates the passage, whether he was
meant to have it or no.

By New Testament times, of course, barnyard fowl were
well established in the Holy Land and "cock crow" was the
phrase used by soldiers to mark one of the four periods of
sentry duty. The day began with Cock-crow Watch, then
Early Watch followed next, then Late Watch, and Midnight
Watch. So it was a definite time-span that Jesus had in mind,
not random rooster crowing, when he said:

Watch ye therefore: for ye know not when the master of the
house cometh; at even, or at midnight, or at cock-crowing, or in
the morning (Mark 13:35).

"Cock crow" may also have been the original phrase in
the Apocryphal Books 2 Esdras 1:30 and Tobit 8:11, although
the translation is usually just "morning." According to Hebrew belief, the words a crowing rooster was trying to pro-
claim in this clarion voice meant "Remember thy Creator!"
To medieval Christians, however, the crowing voice seemed
to be saying, "Christ is born!" And of course the story was
told that a rooster in the stable at Bethlehem had been first
to announce the Child's birth, and the custom of making

weather vanes in the form of a crowing cock was supposed
to remind all passersby of this great message.

But of all crowing cocks in Bible lore or elsewhere,
surely the best known is the one that fulfilled the prophecy
of Peter's denial of his Lord. The story is told in all four
Gospels—Matthew 26:34, 74–75; Mark 14:30, 68–72; Luke
22:34, 60–61; John 13:38, 18:27.

The Gospels, too, show how well known was a hen's
tender care for her flock, how she gathered the little chicks
under outspread wings, and Jesus likened his own yearning
for giving protective love to hers (Matthew 23:37; Luke
13:34). Barnyard cock, hen, and chickens are indeed Bible
birds.

Cormorant

HEBREW: *shalak,* the plunger. Leviticus 11:17; Deuteronomy
14:17

ka'ath, the vomiter. Isaiah 34:11; Zephaniah 2:14

See also Birds of Abomination: No. 12, shalak, and No. 15,
ka'ath; Birds of Doom

Three species of cormorants winter in Israel today, all
much like each other and all much like the kinds of cormorants seen in North America. The European cormorant (*or*
great cormorant), *Phalacrocorax carbo,* is seen on our Atlantic
coast as well as in Israel, and is the only actual duplicate for
Bible bird walk; but any cormorant shows you typical black
feathering, typical plunging dive.

Crane

HEBREW: *agar* (traveler, gatherer). Isaiah 38:14; Jeremiah 8:7

Two birds—crane and swallow—are named together in
the traditional translations of both passages, though sometimes there has been a confusion as to which word—*agar* or
sis—stands for which bird. Both words seem to define a
species that flies in large flocks with continual calling voices.

Since the ringing and raucous boom of a crane could scarcely be represented by a word that sounds like *sis, agar* must be the crane, if the choice is between these two.

Translators of the New English and New American Bibles believe that the crane was not mentioned by Isaiah at all, and instead find a sound word to describe the swallow's repeated calls. Both these texts also see other birds than the crane in the passage from Jeremiah, and for this discussion see the entry, Migrating Birds.

The King James Version makes Isaiah's comparison to the "chatter" of cranes, and if you have ever heard the resonant calls of the sandhill cranes, *Grus canadensis,* you will agree that "clamor" of the Revised Standard Version better matches the voice—at least as we understand these two sound words today. If you can't hear cranes in the wild, listen to any of the recordings of bird songs now available and picture a tall bird in gray plumage with a mark of bright scarlet on the forehead—much the same coloring that marks *Grus grus,* the Old World crane that still flies over Israel, though no longer in the great numbers that once made it a common bird of passage. The smaller demoiselle crane—more the sandhill's size—is also a migrant there, but shyer and seldom seen. The crane voice can also be heard for comparison in recordings of one of North America's rarest birds, the whooping crane, *Grus americana.*

There is good reason for its ringing call, for crane voices come winding up out of a long and curiously convoluted windpipe with all the resonance of a lusty blow on a brass hunting horn. The "horn" lengthens its coils with each year of the bird's growth, even penetrating the wall of the breastbone in older birds, so that a wise old leader of the flock blows out with a trumpeting that can carry more than a mile.

If Isaiah wanted his listeners to picture an enraged monarch roaring out with angry blast of words one minute only to fall away to sibilant mumbles and mutterings, then crane and swallow would have carried his message to those who knew both bird voices well.

Crow

HEBREW: *oreb,* echoic (*see* Raven, since "crow" is substituted
     for "raven" by some translators)
APOCRYPHA: crow, Baruch 6:54; scarecrow, Baruch 6:69–70
GREEK: *korax,* echoic. Luke 12:24

There is no doubt that crows and ravens belong to the
same family and are so much alike that each may be mistaken
for the other by beginning watchers who do not know how
to estimate the raven's larger size or other trademarks. To
recognize a raven, look for the shaggy jabot of throat feathers
—the crow is smooth-throated unless it is bristling all over
in threat display. Also look at the tail—a raven tail is wedge-
shaped; the crow is fan-tailed. In flight a raven flies with
wings outspread at even level with its body in between-beat
soaring; the crow seems to halt its beat with wings in up-
turned slant. Also, listen for the voice—the raven has a deep
and ominous croak; the crow a rasping caw.

Hebrew watchers had additional clues, for their most
common crow species, the hooded crow, *Corvus cornix* (or
Corvus corone cornix, to authors who count it only a subspecies), is not of all-over blackness, but has a dusty-gray
breast and back—in fact "dusty oreb" is its Hebrew name.
The less-often-seen carrion crow, *Corvus corone,* is all-black
like our own common crow, *Corvus brachyrhynchos,* however.
In most Bible passages, raven, rather than crow, seems the
right translation of oreb, though scholars differ—perhaps because the crow is more abundant and familiar. But there is a
scarecrow in Baruch 6:69–70, as well as oreb of all kinds in
the Birds of Abomination, to give crows their place on Bible
bird walk.

Cuckoo

HEBREW: *shahaf,* slender wings. Leviticus 11:16; Deuteron-
     omy 14:15 (King James Version)
     barburim, fattened fowl. 1 Kings 4:23 (Jerusalem Bible)

Most Bible scholars agree that the cuckoo—or cuckow, as it was written in the older versions—was not intended for naming in any Bible line. Oddly, it has been translated once as the name of a bird never to be eaten, and then listed in another passage—by other translators—as a bird especially suited for table fare.

The Eurasian cuckoo, *Cuculus canorus,* and the more abundant cousin of the Holy Land, *Clamator glandarius,* the spotted cuckoo, are both bigger and far fatter than North American cuckoos and would obviously make much meatier fare. In the days when robins and larks and every other songbird were counted good game, the cuckoos were probably eaten as often as any other species.

The King James scholars who named them among the birds of abomination were following a footnote suggestion in the still earlier Geneva Bible. Probably both groups were giving the cuckoo a name of shame because it lays its eggs in the nests of other species, always letting a foster parent rear its young. Such an act seemed abominable enough to warrant *shekes* taboo (*see* Birds of Abomination) regardless of whether the birds themselves were clean-eating. Now in this more scientific age most of us understand that the cuckoo is obeying an instinct it cannot control, and while we may wonder how it lost—or never developed—the nesting instinct, we do not blame cuckoos as we would human parents who go off and abandon their babies on an alien doorstep.

Since the two Israeli cuckoos are unknown in North America, we can look for the yellow-billed cuckoo, *Coccyzus americanus,* or the black-billed cuckoo, *Coccyzus erythropthalmus,* to assure ourselves that long and slender wings are a family trait. However, these two American cuckoos usually build their own nests and rear their own young, and so to observe the cuckoo custom of demanding unpaid baby-sitters, we will have to look for the American brown-headed cowbird, *Molothrus ater,* that somehow acquired this same custom.

Both cuckoos and cowbirds usually lay their eggs in nests of smaller birds, so that the foster child will have the biggest beak and therefore be oftenest fed. Adult cuckoos—and cowbirds, too, sometimes—will actually remove an egg of the nesting bird. The young cuckoo or cowbird often ejects a foster-brother, too—not viciously, but simply in the process of getting more room for itself. This is just one of the many facets of bird behavior we do not understand, yet watch with interest. A song sparrow mother standing on tiptoe to feed a cowbird baby nearly twice her size is really something to see (*see* Partridge).

Darter, Dart-Snake (bird)
HEBREW: *kippoz,* coiler. Isaiah 34:15

This word has troubled every translator, and it has been rendered as great owl, dart-snake, arrow-snake—even ericius by those who mistook it for *kippod*—and hoot owl, a folk term that lets the reader make his own choice of owl species. Unaccountably, the New English Bible gives the line to the sand-partridge. Whether they mean the desert partridge or the sandgrouse by this mix-match label is uncertain, but neither species is a bird of doom and gloom that the lines seem to require. The African darter, still seen in Israel, seems to fit the context far better (*see* Birds of Doom; Sand-partridge).

Decoys
HEBREW: *yonah,* dove. Hosea 7:11–12
APOCRYPHA: *kore,* caller, partridge. Sirach (Ecclesiasticus) 11:30

The men of Bible times who set out decoy birds or lures or traps of any kind were hunting for food, not mere pastime pleasure. God had given them the right to eat meat, and that carried with it the right to hunt for food. Yet there is always something pathetic—something wrong and cruel—in the use of living decoys, birds set out without choice of their own to lure their kindred to destruction. It is especially cruel when the bird is blinded—each eye stabbed with a red-hot needle—before it is tied to a stake in an open place where others of its kind will be passing overhead. Sightless, the bird crouches in fear freeze, without heart to struggle until it hears the calling of the migrant flocks and then flutters and cries in answer, beating its wings in an attempt to join them. There is no overtone of warning in its cries—only thankful recognition—and so the flocks overhead come down to see what food or resting place offers welcome. Some have already touched the ground, others are still hovering in air, when suddenly the net comes whistling out from the fowler's hiding-place and catches them all in its meshes.

Hosea 7:11–12 shows just such a scene, though the wording of the translators is not so clear to us as it must have been to Hosea's listeners, who no doubt had set many decoys of their own:

Ephraim also is like a silly dove without heart: they call to Egypt, they go to Assyria. When they shall go, I will spread my net upon them; I will bring them down as the fowls of heaven. . . .

Doves—the common rock dove, *Columba livia,* now better known as the common pigeon—were the birds most frequently used as decoys. Our own slang phrase "stool pigeon" proves that people of Mediterranean lands were not the only ones to use this trick, for "stool" was the English name for the little open cage that kept the decoy in place. But other species that followed the custom of going in flocks and calling to their mates were also used, especially quail and partridge. In Sirach (Ecclesiasticus) 11:30–31 a mind that twists good into evil is likened to a decoy partridge in its cage.

None of us is likely to want to hear a blinded decoy's calling, or even see wooden or canvas decoy ducks on a pond beside a hunter's blind. Instead, we can get a better understanding of how the decoys were used as we read the moving autobiography of Dr. Axel Munthe, *The Story of San Michele,* which tells how he tried to stop the slaughter of migrant birds on the island of Capri in the years before World War I. The islanders refused to give up their traditional springtime assault, explaining what a good price larks and quail and thrushes would bring in mainland city markets, and the doctor had to buy up large tracts at a fantastic fee so that the weary birds could have their midway resting place on the long flight.

Sanctuaries have been set aside in many places now—but not in every place. The Bible lines written so long ago still carry a meaningful message.

Desert Cock

This is probably the marabou, named among the birds of abomination in Georg Lamsa's translation of the Peshitta, the Syrian text of the Bible used by Middle East Christians.

Dove and Pigeon

HEBREW: *yonah, yonim,* mourner(s) (doves or pigeons). Genesis 8:8–12; Psalms 55:6; 68:13; Song of Songs 1:15; 2:14; 4:1; 5:2, 12; 6:9; Isaiah 38:14; 59:11; 60:8; Jeremiah 48:28; Hosea 7:11; 11:11; Nahum 2:7

beni-yonah, sons or kindred or young of the yonah. Leviticus 1:14; 5:7, 11; 12:6–8; 14:22, 30; 15:14, 29; Numbers 6:10

hari-yonim, dove's dung. 2 Kings 6:25

yonim-gai, doves of the rocky gorge (valley). Ezekiel 7:16

tor, echoic (turtledove). Genesis 15:9; Leviticus 1:14; 5:7, 11; 12:6–8; 14:22, 30; 15:14, 29; Numbers 6:10; Psalm 74:19; Song of Songs 2:12; Jeremiah 8:7

GREEK: *peristera,* plump-bodied or mourner (dove or pigeon). Matthew 3:16; 10:16; 21:12; Mark 1:10; 11:15; Luke 3:22; John 1:32

trugon, echoic (turtledove). Luke 2:24

The difference between a dove and a pigeon is difficult to define now and probably always has been, for birds known by these names are so much alike that their kinship is obvious. Even scientists cannot find any structural differences—internal or external—to separate doves from pigeons. Usage has made a thin line of distinction: usually the smaller birds of blond or brownish tones are called doves. The bigger and darker-hued species—usually bluish—are called pigeons.

The reason for this change of name seems to lead back to the kitchen and to the Norman-French conquest of Anglo-Saxon England. "Dove" has Saxon roots—with similar words in other northern languages all meaning deaf, dumb, blind, or confused, and all pointing to the ease with which these birds were captured, with or without decoys. "Pigeon" was a French word, coined to imitate the piping cries of squabs in the barn loft, where they were kept handy for use in pigeon pies. After the Norman Conquest, French became the language for courtly conversing, and "pigeon"—along with French-coined "mutton," "veal," "pork," and "beef"—became polite table talk, while Anglo-Saxon terms were relegated to the barnyard, woods, and farm fields. And since the bigger doves were the ones that were most often served at table as pigeon pie, these larger species were the ones to acquire the new French name and keep it most consistently over years of use.

Meanwhile, certain doves had such a persistent and repeated cry, different from the others, a haunting *tur-tur-tur* or *tor-tor* so easily echoed that it became the bird's special name, much the same in various languages. To the ancient Romans it was *tur-tur*—with the "u" long to rhyme with "poor." To the Anglo-Saxons it was the *turtla* or *turtil*—still with the same long "u" sound. To the Hebrews it was *tor*—another echo. And when the first English Bible translators came upon this word, they wrote it down as "turtle"—of course—for that was their word for it. Using this same word as the name for a hard-shelled amphibian didn't come about till later—apparently from sea captains and traders mispronouncing the French word *tortue,* the creature that provided the shell for tortoise-shell combs, suddenly the new fashion fad. So then the bird had to become turtledove, for clarity's sake—only the King James translators didn't always get it down that way and left a confusing "voice of the turtle" as one of the sure signs of a returning spring (Song of Songs 2:11–12).

"Singing turtles!" you can imagine some startled reader exclaiming in olden days, shaking his head in doubt and wonder. Other readers, of course, would frown or sneer or complain—thinking that the translators or the printers had made a mistake, not understanding how much the meaning of the simplest words can change in daily use.

In the Holy Land today there are four species of doves in the genus *Streptopelia,* all with something of the same *tor-tor-tor* call that gave the turtledove its name. "The" turtledove is *Streptopelia turtur,* always the best known and most abundant, the one that gladdens everyone's winter-weary heart as the migrant flocks return each spring. The others are year-round residents but until recently were seldom seen: *S. senegalensis,* the palm dove; *S. decaocto,* the collared dove; *S. risoria,* the ringed dove. The latter two are sometimes named together as Barbary doves and perhaps were fixed in their markings by artificial inbreeding as caged birds, later escaping to the wilds. All have their feathering sparkled with typical dove-family iridescence, all have a basic coffee-with-cream coloring, or cream-with-coffee, rather, for only the palm dove has the darker fawn tones.

No bird of tor's genus is native to North America, but two have become naturalized residents, brought here as pioneer flocks and making good their freehold claim. *Streptopelia risoria,* down on the A.O.U. *Check-list* as ringed turtle dove, was released in both Los Angeles, California, and Miami, Florida, and has spread northward from both sites, especially on the west coast, and others may be gaining a foothold around New York City. The other, *S. chinensis,* the spotted dove, was brought from China to Hawaii and also to Los Angeles, and it, also, is moving out to adjacent terrain.

If neither of these turtledoves comes near your listening

post, you may listen instead for the call of the mourning dove, *Zenaidura macroura,* seen in all of the North American continent except the snowbound Arctic, even in Alaska. In many places it lives the year around; in others it comes as springtime migrant, like the tor; but in all places its repeated calling is part of the springtime symphony, a gentle *Ah-h, coo-oo, coo-oo, coo-oo!*

"That's the turtledove," my grandmother used to say when she heard it, for most birders of the last century still used European names for similar American species. And then she would repeat in loving cadence the Bible lines she knew by heart—the flowers . . . the singing of birds . . . the voice of the turtledove. . . .

I learned those lines, too, along with the proper name of mourning dove that the bird books insisted was correct, and though this was not the same voice heard in Bible lands, it seemed to carry the same message.

"Mourning dove" might also serve as a translation for the Hebrew word *yonah,* the name for all doves and pigeons in general and the rock dove in particular, for the name is meant to echo the mournful sound of their cooing cry. To the birds themselves it is not at all sad, but a love-note, a word of reassurance from a devoted mate. But since all doves and pigeons sound mournful to human ears, the name of *yonim gai,* "mourners of the rocky gorge," gave the rock dove a special name when there was need to set it apart from others, for only this species nested on cliffs rather than in trees, and when farmers began making similar little niches or "pigeon holes" in their barns, the yonah nested in them and felt right at home. They were at home in the Ark, too, and after the raven failed to bring Noah the proof of a reborn earth, he sent one of his doves on this same errand, thus creating the first messenger pigeon in history.

This rock dove that we call "common pigeon" was the only year-round resident among the three larger dove species in the Holy Land. Two others—the wood pigeon and the stock pigeon (*or* stock dove)—come only in winter. Both

were beni-yonah, but not "the" yonah. Neither of these two
species comes to North America, but in our western states
look for the band-tailed pigeon, *Columba fasciata,* if you
want to see how birds of this sort and size behave as free
wildlings, not park-pigeon panhandlers.

The family name of Columbidae has nothing to do with
Christopher Columbus. *Columba* is simply the Latin word
for dove, and all official labels have to be in Latin—or at
least have a Latin ending. But Columbus, nevertheless, has
a part in their story, for when he returned to the Caribbean
in the fall of 1493 with 1,500 eager Spanish colonists, he
brought caged rock doves along with other farmyard birds
and beasts—the first birds of this Old World genus ever to
coo and nest on New World shores. He also mentioned seeing
fantastic numbers of doves unlike those of Europe—some that
flew in flocks so vast they darkened the sun, probably the
now extinct passenger pigeon; and some with a white crown,
the now rare white-crowned pigeon of Florida and the Caribbean. But in spite of this promise of plenty of birds for pigeon
pie, most of the later colonists from every European country
also brought more captive rock doves when they came a-pio-
neering, and when these birds escaped from the dove cotes
and went pioneering themselves, they established themselves
as one of the most abundant bird species in the land, making
themselves at home on office windowsills, bridges, and other
manmade shelves when the natural rocky ledges of their
homeland were not available.

Jesus himself used the comparison "as harmless as doves"
(Matthew 10:16), and these birds have become everyone's
symbol for gentleness, love, and peace. But the record of the
rock dove shows that "adaptable as a dove" makes an apt
phrase, too.

"Mournful as a dove" is another comparison, heard in
Isaiah 38:14; 59:11; Ezekiel 7:16; Nahum 2:7.

The lovely gold and silvery iridescence that glints on
dove feathering was recalled by David in Psalm 68:13, and
the beauty of dove wings and eyes are chanted over and over

in the Song of Songs. Songs 6:9 likens an only child to a young dove, and it is true that dove parents often raise only one chick, although usually two eggs are laid.

Since doves nest in large colonies, and on the same rocky ledges year after year, the white splattering of their droppings was a familiar sight in Bible lands, and when a little springtime flower made a similar white pattern over the meadows, it was often called "doves' dung" or "doves' milk." Doves and pigeons do not actually feed their young on milk, but both male and female let the food in their crops soften to a milky texture, and when the hungry young birds dive in for dinner—or the parents try to make delivery—the resultant splatterings make another pattern of dotted whiteness to suggest the whiteness of the meadow flowers. In 2 Kings 6:25, we are told that doves' dung was sold for a high price in wartime siege and eaten as starvation's last resort, but whether this food was actual dung or the bulbs of the meadow flowers, scholars do not agree. Nowadays these meadow flowers keep the old name with the Latin label of *Ornithogallum*—literally, bird milk—but they are also known as Star of Bethlehem.

Bethlehem has an even closer link with doves, for these were the birds that Mary took to the temple for altar sacrifice to rejoice in the birth of a Son. The ritual requiring such an offering was described in the ancient laws of the Hebrews, called the Torah, and set down in Leviticus 12:6–8; a mother who cannot afford the cost of a lamb, may offer two turtledoves or two beni-yonah—two pigeons. And legend—though no Bible verse—tells that there were doves in the stable at Bethlehem on the night that Jesus was born, cooing him a first lullaby.

And when Jesus became a man and was baptized in the River Jordan, the spirit of God came to hover over him in the form of a dove, and although the Bible itself does not say that these hovering wings were white, a white dove has always been portrayed by the artists who have sought to picture this scene in paintings or wood carvings, chiseled stone or woven embroideries. In the portrayal of other scenes, too, a white dove has come to be the accepted symbol for the presence of God.

We will find no flocks of all-white doves in the wild, in North America or in Bible lands, for the pure white doves often seen in pet shops and stage shows have been developed in the past from cage birds with an inherited tendency to albino feathering, a lack of pigmentation, or to more white than black or gray in mottled plumage. Even among park pigeons today an all-white or nearly white bird may be hatched among darker nestlings, giving passersby a sudden startling reminder of the white dove in folklore and Bible verse. The turtledoves, too, often seem pure white in bright sunshine, their jet-black collar hidden by lifted wings.

But doves of all colors bring reminder of many Bible lines.

Eagle

HEBREW: *nesher,* golden-chaplet wearer, consecrated one. Exodus 19:4; Leviticus 11:13; Deuteronomy 14:12; 28:49; 32:11–12; 2 Samuel 1:23; Job 9:26; 39:27–30; Psalm 103:5; Proverbs 23:5; 30:18–19; Isaiah 8:8; 22:17; 40:31; Jeremiah 4:13; 48:40; 49:16, 22; Lamentations 4:19; Ezekiel 1:10; 10:14; 17:3–7; Daniel 4:33; 7:4; Hosea 8:1; Obadaiah 1:4; Micah 1:16; Habakkuk 1:8 *beni-nesher,* sons, kindred, young nesher. Proverbs 30:17
GREEK: *aetos,* echoic, or radiant ones. Matthew 24:28; Luke 17:37; Revelation 4:7; 8:13; 12:14

The voice of God in Exodus makes the wings of eagles the symbol of his power. The *nesher* name itself bears witness, for the *nezer* was the golden chaplet of consecration to mark Israel's holy priests as the anointed of God, and *nezer* sounds enough like *nesher* to suggest that both words came from the same roots.

Of course *nesher* could be—as some scholars suggest— a phonetic word to imitate the sound of rushing air through eagle wings as the great bird plunges in a power dive. But the golden feathers on the eagle's head seem to make stronger claim. The priests of earth have golden chaplets, the kings of earth wear golden crowns, and a golden sheen on the head of one of the largest and most powerful birds of the air would surely have seemed to be a sign of honor and consecration, too.

The glint of this shining crown is reflected in both the common name and the Latin label of the bird we call golden eagle, *Aquila chrysaëtos*, for *chrysos* is the Greek word for "gold." It has been counted the king of birds and the bird of kings all around the northern half of the globe, for it flies, or used to fly, in every land above the equator. It is becoming rare now over most of its range, not often seen now in Israel, not seen at all in many parts of North America where it was once abundant, coast to coast. But you can see it if you look for it in the lonely hills that have become its last retreat, perched atop a crag or a power pole—whatever may be the highest lookout point around—and as the majestic head turns slowly in wary watching, a sudden gleam of crowning radiance tells you why this bird of all-over brown feathering has been called golden eagle and king of birds.

In North America no other eagle wears a golden crown. But in Israel five other eagles of the genus *Aquila* come as passing migrants or winter visitors, and the two largest and most abundant species also are marked with nape feathering that is paler than the body plumage and with a yellowish sheen. Surely these two—*Aquila heliaca*, the imperial eagle, and *Aquila rapax*, the tawny eagle—were both thought of as birds that shared the nesher name. Even today, with binoculars and bird book in hand, it takes a sharp eye to name birds of these three species apart—especially young birds only two or three years old—for the eagles of all species seldom get their full adult plumage until they have passed the four-year mark. All three are much the same size—at least 30 inches, beak to tail—with the golden eagle often the largest by two to five inches more.

The other three eagles of this same genus are noticeably smaller—around 26 inches or so—and not so likely to be confused with the golden king. Spotted eagle, lesser spotted eagle, and Verreaux's eagle are the names to look for in a guide book of Eurasian birds. However, they do have the same silhouette, the same regal pose, and perhaps they also shared nesher names in olden times. Even the sea eagle, white-tailed *Haliaeetus albicilla,* may have been known by this name as well as others, for while it has no glint of golden crown, it does have paler feathering around the head than elsewhere and in size it equals or surpasses the golden eagle.

Because all these eagles are scarce today and the griffon vulture still common and well known by the Arabic name of *nisr,* some scholars have thought that the *nisr* of the Arabs had to be the *nesher* of the Hebrews. The two languages are much alike and have the same Semitic roots, but that does not mean that usage is identical. Just think of all the words that have different meanings in England and the United States—little ordinary words like "suspenders" and "garters" that you wouldn't think could get twisted—and you will understand at once why Arab and Hebrew usage can be identical for some words and widely different for others. *Nisr* and *nesher* may both stem from words that indicate consecration, but that doesn't mean they mark the same bird. The griffon vulture was indeed a sacred bird to the Egyptians. Its likeness is painted on pharaoh tombs and molded in gold and jewels for royal crown and scepter. Its ability to survive in the desert heat that gave the Egyptians themselves such ordeal must have seemed a symbol of its supernatural powers, and its wide wings spread aloft to ride the air is an awe-inspiring sight. But when the griffon comes to earth, humping in hunchback waddle to carrion feast, cringing aside to let the stalking marabou feed first, waiting its turn with low-hung head—how then could it be a king to watching Hebrews or counted the wings of the Lord?

Only the gold-touched eagles of the genus *Aquila* fully match this role, and surely the eagle name should be placed in all the Bible lines where the word *nesher* stands in Hebrew script. Even the line that speaks of enlarging baldness like the nesher (Micah 1:16) calls up the familiar eagle likeness, for the golden sheen does get bigger and brighter as the birds get older. With the imperial eagle particularly, the golden snood becomes lighter and lighter each year and in old birds is almost pure white. Remember that the word "bald" once meant "white" rather than "hairless," and that our own national bird has a full head of white feathers as an adult, in spite of being called a bald eagle, and the words used by Micah are clearer still.

When the collector of the Book of Proverbs named the four things most impossible to understand (30:18–19) "the way of an eagle in the air" came first. When the voice of God hurled at Job his challenge of power, one question was: Does the eagle mount up at your command? Isaiah 40:31 promises the strength of eagles to those who serve the Lord. Renewed youth like the eagle's is the pledge of Psalm 103, for people of olden times saw magic in the way an eagle's beak stays scimitar sharp and strong, even in old age—never guessing that it was daily stropping and cleaning that kept youthful strength renewed.

Eagle swiftness is praised in nearly a dozen passages, and both golden and bald eagles have been clocked in power-dive spurts at around 120 miles per hour. Their usual cruising speed is much slower, however, and even their fastest dive to defend nest and mate can be bettered by gyrfalcons and peregrines, timed at 190 miles per hour. Eagles were often preferred as trained hunting birds, however, simply because they have the size and strength to capture larger game.

These kingly birds have tenderness to match their power, usually mating for life and guarding their young with patient care. Deuteronomy 32:11–12 gives one eagle watcher's report of their home life, describing how the female arranges and rearranges the nesting material—as you may see both golden and bald eagles do today—how the mother spreads fluttering wings over the downy young, shielding them from rain or hot sun or biting wind; how she coaxes the full-feathered young to follow her in gliding flight, letting them find their wing power in triumph—or buoying them with updraft current from her own wings.

Many ornithologists have thought that the Bible picture of an eagle carrying her young was merely figurative, but in recent years certain reliable observers have actually seen a parent bird let its young rest for a moment on the feathered back—especially when there was no other roosting place in sight. When an eagle nests on the ledge of a sheer-walled canyon, many feet above the earth, with no jutting tree root or protruding rock to break the fall, the quick movement of a mother bird to offer her own back to a frightened fledgling may be the only way to let it live to try its wings again. Just so did the power of God reach out to Jacob, the Bible lines add, and the translation of the Jewish Torah makes it a chant of triumph:

> Like an eagle who arouses his nestlings,
> Gliding down to his young,
> So spread He His wings and took him,
> Bore him along on His pinions;
> The Lord alone did guide him,
> No alien god at His side.*

Watch an eagle in flight yourself, the lines seem to suggest, and know how great the strength of the Lord must be.

Eggs

HEBREW: *betsaw,* eggs. Deuteronomy 22:6; Job 39:14–15; Isaiah 10:14; Jeremiah 17:11

challamuth, slime of the yolk, white of an egg (or slime or juice of mallows). Job 6:6

APOCRYPHA: Tobit 11:13

GREEK: *oon,* eggs. Luke 11:12

* Reprinted from THE TORAH: A New Translation, with permission of the publisher, The Jewish Publication Society of America.

The good nourishing value of eggs as food must have been well known in Bible times, for Jesus compares bread and a stone, eggs and a scorpion as symbols of best and worst. Long before then the prophet Isaiah had compared the treasure store of worldly wealth to eggs in a wild bird's nest, with the boastful king of Assyria bragging that he had plundered people of their wealth with the same quiet ease of the fowler gathering eggs from partridge, duck, or quail. Wild bird eggs were staple food in all lands, long before the barnyard fowl with day-after-day supply were known, and they would continue to be a food source for seafarer and wayfarer, hunter and countryman down to our own times.

Falcon

HEBREW: *ayyah,* echoic, a screamer. Leviticus 11:14; Deuteronomy 14:13; Job 28:7

Falcons, swiftest of the hawks, marked by pointed wings and shrill cries, are included in the picture whenever the ayit—birds of prey—are named in Bible lines. The nine kinds of falcons seen in the Holy Land are also banned as food in the Mosaic Law (*see* Birds of Abomination: No. 5, ayyah), under their own name of ayyah.

But aside from being known for swift wings and sharp talons, the falcons are also honored for keen eyesight. Job 28:7–10 reminds us of this well-earned reputation, describing a hidden path that no bird of prey has found, not even the falcon. This keen vision is aided, so ornithologists now believe, by the swatch of black beneath the eyes. Supposedly this dark encircling prevents sun-blindness, and certainly a bird that darts from sheltered perch on ledge or branch directly into the sun's rays in pursuit of foe or food needs such protection, some means of instant adjustment.

We know also that the eyes of falcons—all birds of prey —can adjust far more quickly than our own to the swift change from seeing some scampering rabbit at a distance to one right beneath its talons. So far we have not been able to add this trick to our own repertoire with much success, but we have borrowed the falcon's sun-guard of the black eye-swatch. Football players started the custom, and fishermen and other sportsmen who face the sun have copied it, too.

In some Bible translations, this keen-eyed bird of Job is named as the vulture, rather than the falcon. The problem here is not whether vulture or falcon has the sharper vision —both have eyes incomparably keener than our own—but whether the original Hebrew word was *dayyah,* for kite or scavenger, or *ayyah,* the falcon.

Fattened Fowl
HEBREW: *barburim abusim,* edible fowl (cocks). 1 Kings 4:23

This descriptive term for the birds served at the tables of King Solomon has been interpreted by many readers as proof that this famous monarch had barnyard fowl like our own, domesticated offspring of the wild red jungle fowl of India (*see* Chicken, Cock, Hen). Others see it only as evidence that he had domesticated birds of some sort or at least fattened wild birds in coops. Since *barburim* implies only cocks, these fat ones may be capons, castrated to make them grow up plump and tender.

Solomon died around 932 B.C. Archaeologists have found evidence that pigeons were domesticated in the Middle East around 4500 B.C., but the yarding of tame chickens, ducks, geese, and guinea fowl came much later—perhaps in Solomon's reign and certainly soon afterward. Also kept for fattening but never fully domesticated were partridge, quail, and pheasants, an Oriental species native as far west as the Black Sea, where Greek legend says they were first found by the hero Jason, who named them for the River Phasis nearby. All of these birds and peacocks, too (*see* Peacock), may have been among the barburim on Solomon's table, and swans may well have been included also (*see* Swan).

Swans, geese, and ducks were among the earliest birds tamed to barnyard residence because the adult birds lose their flight feathers all at once in molting and are unable to fly and escape capture. If the wings are clipped to keep them flightless, the birds eventually adjust to being grounded and hatch out broods of young that are kept flightless also. Swans do not submit as easily as ducks and geese and seem to need a lake or river to keep them contented enough for breeding. Also, they have smaller broods than ducks or geese and so were never as popular for barnyard flocks as descendants of wild mallard ducks or the wild graylag goose.

Guinea fowl, another early barnyard bird, was domesticated in the Middle East as early as 450 B.C. and perhaps before then. At least one Bible scholar (Moffatt) lists them here as the one bird intended by the *barburim abusim* label. The Jerusalem Bible lists fattened cuckoos. Other scholars feel that *barbur* (singular of *barburim*) meant the male of any fowl for table use—swan, goose, duck, guinea fowl, or even songbird—eaten instead of the hen birds because of Mosaic Law (*see* Bird Conservation).

One thing is certain, the birds served to Solomon were fattened to tender plumpness in some sort of semidomestication, at least. No king so wise and wealthy would have made do with scrawny birds straight from the hunter's game bag.

Firebird
HEBREW: *beni-reshef,* sons of burning coals. Job 5:6–7
reshef. Habakkuk 3:5

So many bird names are figurative, rather than factual description, and so many are prefixed with *beni*—sons—to show a kindred group, that the name *beni-reshef,* "sons of the burning coals," stands a very reasonable chance of belonging to some bird of fiery color or nature or flight.

The King James Bible translates it very literally as "sparks" in Job and "burning coals" in Habakkuk. The likeness of the word *reshef* to words for thunder and lightning led the Jerusalem Bible to give this name to the birds that soar up to the heights where thunder and lightning are born

—the eagles. Others simply say "birds" or "wild birds" and some suggest that the firebirds in Habakkuk were vultures, always the companions of pestilence and death. This bird of fire could also be the phoenix, the mythical bird said to arise from its own ashes, and the comparison of Job could then be:

Yet man is born to trouble, as surely as the phoenix rises anew.

If you believe in the phoenix, that's a very certain outcome, indeed.

Flamingo
HEBREW: *anafah,* big noselike beak

The flamingo is listed among the birds of abomination in a translation of the Greek Septuagint Bible made by Charles Thomson, secretary to the American Continental Congress, at the end of the eighteenth century. It was revised and republished by C. A. Muses in 1954. The Greek word *porphyrion* named among the birds of abomination in the Douay Bible may also list the flamingo, since this was one of its names in ancient times.

The Septuagint Bible was prepared by Hebrew scholars living in Alexandria, Egypt, around 250 B.C. It was in Greek, the language spoken in more places and by more Hebrew exiles than any other tongue at the time, and was said to have been given its name—which means "70"—because 72 translators worked for 72 days to get it ready, and perhaps because it could be read in 70 or more different lands, all conquered by Alexander the Great, who forced his own language upon his conquered subjects. Only the Old Testament was included, of course, and the sequence of names in the birds of abomination is not the same as in the Masoretic Bible, compiled by other Hebrew scholars two or three hundred years later. The first Latin Bibles followed the Masoretic Text, the first Greek Bibles followed the Septuagint, and modern scholars who try to use them both have to make a choice (*see* Birds of Abomination: No. 18, anafah).

Fledglings (*see* Young Birds)

Fowl, Fowler, Fowling
HEBREW: *yakosh,* partridge-catcher, fowler. Psalms 91:3; 124:7;
     Proverbs 6:5; Hosea 9:8
See also references to fowling: 1 Samuel 26:20; Proverbs 1:17;
     7:23; Ecclesiastes 9:12; Isaiah 10:14; Jeremiah 5:26–27;
     Lamentations 3:52; Hosea 7:11–12; 11:11; Amos 3:5
See also references to nets, traps, gins, snares: Psalms 9:15–16;
     11:6; 18:5; 25:15; 31:4; 35:7–8; 40:1–3; 64:5; Proverbs
     29:5–6, 8, 25; Ezekiel 12:13 (no reference to birds)
APOCRYPHA: Baruch 3:17
GREEK: *struthion,* sparrows, small birds (sold at market). Mat-
     thew 10:29; Luke 12:6
     peristera, doves (sold in the temple). Matthew 21:12;
     Mark 11:15; John 2:14–16
See also reference to snare: Luke 21:35

"Surely He shall deliver thee from the snare of the
fowler," is the promise in Psalm 91:3. And Psalm 124:7 fulfills the pledge with "Our soul is escaped as a bird out of the
snare of the fowlers."

These two passages—and all the other texts that tell of
trap and snare and net and fowler's wiles—prove beyond all
doubt that people of Bible times made many meals on fresh-
caught partridge, quail, duck, goose, and wild dove, and on
many a smaller bird, even if it made only one mouthful when
skewered on a spit and roasted over the brazier coals.

And since the very word for "fowler" is "catcher of the
black partridge" there seems little doubt which kind of bird
was preferred or most often captured. Oddly, *yakeb,* the word
for the black partridge itself—*Francolinus francolinus* by
Latin label—is not used in any Bible line. All three kinds of
partridges seen in Israel are mentioned only by the name
kore (*see* Partridge). *Yakeb*—or *yakibu*—means "spurred
heel" and points to the armor that all chicken-like birds pos-
sess. It is also the root word for the name Jacob, and reminds

us that Jacob, son of Isaac, was so named because at the moment of his birth he was grasping the heel of his twin brother Esau in one outstretched hand, as told in Genesis 25:25–26.

But even the experts—as others named Jacob could have been—did not always catch the birds they sought. "Surely in vain the net is spread in the sight of any bird," is the reminder in Proverbs 1:17. And Proverbs 6:5 adds, "Deliver thyself . . . as a bird from the hand of the fowler." Lamentations 3:52 adds, "chased me sore, like a bird. . . ."

Gier Eagle (*see* Birds of Abomination: No. 16, rahama)
The Egyptian vulture was evidently mistaken for a kind of eagle in olden times—especially by English scholars who didn't know the bird—because it has a well-feathered head, not bare or down-covered like other vultures.

Glede (*see* Birds of Abomination: No. 4, da'ah)
"Glede" was an old English name for kites and soaring hawks.

Griffon (*see* Birds of Abomination: No. 3, ozniyyah)
Griffon, griffin, and *gryphon* are variant spellings of the name for one of the commonest vultures.

Grype (*see* Birds of Abomination: No. 1, nesher; No. 2, peres; No. 3 ozniyyah)
"Grype" means "hooked beak" and is an old group term for eagles, hawks, and vultures.

Guinea Fowl (*see* Fattened Fowl)

Gull (*see* Birds of Abomination: No. 9, shahaf)

Hawk
HEBREW: *nez*, flashing. Leviticus 11:16; Deuteronomy 14:15; Job 39:26

The hawks make their first appearance in Bible lines among the birds forbidden as food under Mosaic Law (*see* Birds of Abomination: No, 10, nez). They are also named in Job 39:26 as one of the birds that wing southward in winter, directed by the wisdom of God (*see* Migrating Birds).

Hen (*see* Chicken, Cock, Hen)

Heron (all kinds) (*see* Birds of Abomination: No. 18, anafah)

Hoopoe (Hoop, Houp) (*see* Birds of Abomination: No. 19, dukifath)

Ibis
HEBREW: *sekvi,* curved in heart shape. Job 38:36 (*see* Chicken, Cock, Hen)
yanshof, echoic. Isaiah 34:11 (*see* Birds of Doom)
yanshuf, echoic, or horned one. Leviticus 11:17 (*see* Birds of Abomination: No. 13, yanshuf)

The glossy ibis is named among the forbidden food birds by a few translators, including the Latin Vulgate Bible of the fourth century and the Greek Septuagint. See the entry Chicken, Cock, Hen for its translation of *sekvi* and the entry Birds of Doom for its appearance in Isaiah.

Jackdaw
HEBREW: *ka'ath, ka'ath midbar,* vomiter, of the wilderness

The translation of the Old Testament by J. M. Powis Smith for the University of Chicago gives the jackdaw its only appearance in Bible lines. This smaller edition of the crow was, of course, included in the ban on eating orebim of all kinds (*see* Birds of Abomination, No. 6, oreb). It is only a passing migrant in the Holy Land today, except for a few nesters, and probably had the same minor role in ancient times, so it seems unlikely that it would have been singled out for mention by special name in any passage.

Smith not only names it in place of the pelican in Leviticus and Deuteronomy, but also among the Birds of Doom in Isaiah 34:11 and Zephaniah 2:14. Apparently he interpreted the name as echoic of the jackdaw's cawing voice. Jackdaws join raven and crow and all black-feathered birds in being counted birds of evil omen in many folk tales, but were probably not common enough in Israel to have had a major role.

Kite

HEBREW: *da'ah,* the swooper. Leviticus 11:14
    ra'ah, possible copying error for *da'ah.* Deuteronomy 14:13
    dayyah, possible plural or alternate spelling of *da'ah.* Deuteronomy 14:13
    dayyoth, probably plural of *da'ah.* Isaiah 34:15
See Birds of Abomination: No. 4, da'ah

The similarity between these Hebrew names for the black kite and the Arabic word *dey* for the cinereous vulture, often called black vulture, gives translators a problem (*see* Birds of Abomination: No. 4, da'ah). And read any travel diary of the Middle East to hear how bold and daring are the black kites, the common street scavengers of many towns. In Elizabethan England the red kite was the same sort of raider and so fond of pilfering any strand of ribbon or lace hung out to dry that Shakespeare (*Winter's Tale,* IV, iii, 23) warned the laundry maids to "look to their linens" when the kites came in sight.

No bird in North America today really comes up to kite reputation as thief, scavenger, raider. But the gray jay of the north woods, *Perisoreus canadensis*—often called "Camp Robber"—comes close in boldness, though not in numbers or in the kite habits of raiding as a gang rather than an individual, and frequenting city streets and rooftops as well as lonely countryside.

For gang-type raiding, you might see how pesky gulls

can be at a waterfront resort where picnickers and tourists encourage their begging. Or go to an open city dump where both gulls and black vultures scavenge, and if you can imagine a flock as noisy and numerous as the gulls and as black as the vultures, you've conjured up a likeness of the kites.

Lamia (*see* Birds of Doom: lilith)

Lapwing
HEBREW: *dukifath* (*see* Birds of Abomination: No. 19, dukifath)

Larus (*see* Birds of Abomination: No. 9, *shahaf*)

Lilith (*see* Birds of Doom)
Lilith is a Hebrew word left untranslated in Isaiah 34:14 in some texts.

Magpie
HEBREW: *orebim anahal,* ravens of the valley. Proverbs 30:17 (*see* Ravens of the Valley)

The bold and clever magpie has found a place in so many Old World legends that it almost has to be included among Bible birds. There is only one species in the Holy Land, the common or black-billed magpie, *Pica pica,* but it has enough personality to make up for a whole tribe of shyer birds, and farmfolk have always given it grudging affection—along with plenty of cursing for its thievery and gluttonous meat eating.

The first European settlers on the eastern shores of North America did not find any American magpies and really seemed to miss these clever ones. Then when Lewis and Clark took the trail west to Oregon in 1804–6, they found plenty of magpies, lively and sassy as ever, and tamed four young ones to ship back to President Jefferson.

A few decades later a yellow-billed magpie was discovered in southern California and was enrolled for science as

Pica nuttalli, in honor of the pioneer ornithologist Thomas Nuttall. This yellow-bill seldom leaves its home state, but my husband and I are among the lucky few to see it here in Oregon, so when you are looking for magpies be sure to check the color of the tell-tale beak.

Mew
HEBREW: *shahaf,* mew gull or all gulls (*see* Birds of Abomination: No. 9, *shahaf*)

Migrating Birds
HEBREW: *selav,* quail. Exodus 16:13; Numbers 11:31–32; Psalm 105:40
   ahf, fowl (quail). Psalm 78:26–29
   nez, hawk. Job 39:26
   zippor, wandering bird. Proverbs 27:8; Isaiah 16:2
   hasidah, tor, sis, agar, stork, turtledove, swallow, crane (and variant translations). Jeremiah 8:7
   zippor, yonah, bird and dove. Hosea 11:11
   zippor, deror, bird (sparrow) and swallow. Proverbs 26:2
   kanaf, wings. Isaiah 18:1
APOCRYPHA: Wisdom 5:11; 16:2

The earliest written record of bird migration that we can still read is in Exodus 16:13, when the hungry Israelites under Moses are fed by a vast flock of quail that come fluttering down from the skies to drop at their feet. As the story is told here, their coming is a miracle, a gift from the hand of God, not the once-each-springtime event that we know migration of the quail to be in these lands. Therefore the quail are often passed over in presenting the Bible story of migration, and the wandering birds of Proverbs and Isaiah and the hawks of Job stretching their wings to the south are forgotten, too.

Instead, the much quoted lines from Jeremiah 8:7 are cited again and again as the oldest known observation on bird migration ever put down in writing. We have read it so many times and in so many other places besides the Bible itself, that the wording of the King James Version seems the only right wording possible:

Yea, the stork in the heaven knoweth her appointed times; and the turtledove and the crane and the swallow observe the time of their coming.

To back up our feeling that stork, turtledove, crane, and swallow are the right birds, we have only to look at the records in the bird books. These four species of birds are among the most regular in timing their migration journeys. Jeremiah could not have chosen four birds that set a better example of the mysterious way in which birds know when and where and how to make their journey to another clime.

When we turn to the old Douay Bible and read the names of "kite," "turtle," "swallow," and "stork" in their place, or to the New American Bible with "stork," "turtledove," "swallow," and "thrush," the New English Bible with "stork," "dove," "swift," and "wryneck," we are curious about the reasons for the changes and even a little disappointed. The old names we know seem so right.

Actually the King James scholars made one mistake in sequence—the Hebrew text reads *sis* and *agar* for the last two names, so the wording should be "swallow and crane," rather than "crane and swallow." The Revised Standard Version and several other translations make this correction but no other change from the reading we know best.

Authors who insist that Jeremiah was talking about swifts instead of swallows are being too particular. The precise distinction in the usage of these two terms is very recent. Even Audubon wrote about "chimney swallows" in describing the birds we now call "chimney swifts." In Bible times, with no binoculars or bird guides to point out distinctions, one name surely served both birds (*see* Swallow).

The change in the Douay Bible from "stork" to "kite" was probably due to an error in writing or reading a manuscript line—quite understandable when you think of all the trials that beset those scholars of nearly four hundred years ago. Their change of the last word from "crane" to "stork" is similarly explained.

This last word is the real trouble spot. First, scholars do not agree that *agar* means "crane"; and second, they are not sure that *agar* was the actual word in the original text. Put both these problems about words aside and consider only the birds: cranes do migrate with remarkable regularity of repeated date and they also migrate in large flocks—like storks, turtledoves, and swallows—so that people are easily aware of their coming at the same time, year after year. The cranes are huge, too—watchers could scarcely help noticing them. But the thrush, suggested by the New American Bible, is a solitary bird, slipping into the garden quietly for midway rest on migration journey, not calling any attention to itself. There are at least 26 different members of the large and varied Thrush Family seen in Israel with some as year-round residents or summer nesters, others as winter visitors only or as passing migrants both spring and fall, and naming any one species or the whole family as a symbol of migration doesn't quite make the picture of a regular and recurring event that Jeremiah's lines suggest.

The wryneck, now named in the crane's place by the New English Bible, also fails to fulfill the description of a bird that observes a regular time of coming. Wrynecks "come" to the Holy Land only as passing migrants bound elsewhere for winter or summer home. In England and northern Europe, where they nest, they are indeed a sign of spring's return, coming early in March or April—almost as early as the cuckoo, the bird that English poets since Cynewulf have hailed as the bird that announces spring's arrival. In fact, "cuckoo's companion" is one of the wryneck's most used names. But they have camouflage feathering of mottled leaf and bark tones, and are much more easily heard than seen; so it does not seem likely that the wrynecks passing over the Holy Land would have been one of the four most remembered species that Jeremiah would have named to mark the migration miracle.

Migration does seem miraculous, unbelievable—no matter what birds you choose as symbols of a flight across pathless skies, the returning year after year at the same place and time. Even today, when scientific research has told us more of the how's and why's of bird behavior than even wise Solomon could have known, we still have our wonderings only half-answered.

Why do birds migrate? To find a place where they will have more food is one obvious answer. But how do they know that such a place exists and just where to find it? Hunger itself is not the prompter that starts them on the autumn journey, for they leave while insects are still flying and fruit and grain still ripening on spear and vine. Memory of landmarks will help to show them the way, if they survive to travel a second year, but many young birds fly alone, or with other yearlings, and have no experienced fliers to show them the way.

Those storks that Jeremiah named, for instance, seem to be hatched with the knowledge of their migration route already mapped in their wobbly heads. When eggs from storks that always migrated over the Strait of Gibraltar after nesting in western Europe were taken from the nest and kept warm until they could be hatched out by storks in eastern Europe, the hatchlings grew to full storkhood with every sign of being contented and happy with their foster parents, not at all aware of the transplantation. Yet when migration time came and the foster parents headed for the Dardanelles Straits—as all storks from eastern Europe do and have always done—the young birds turned west to cross at Gibraltar as instinct bade them.

Young racing pigeons, however, will come home to the loft where they were hatched and raised and took their first flights—not to the place where the eggs were laid. Whatever innate pattern of response guides them, it is not the same as for the stork.

Wild birds hatched in incubators, never seeing their parents or any other birds, will nonetheless show signs of restlessness when the migration time comes. If they are set free, they will wing off in the same direction that others of their kind normally follow. If they are kept caged, they will turn in that same direction, fluttering futilely against the bars. If they are put in a planetarium, where a false sky overhead can be set with stars to match any hour of any night or season, birds will follow the stars they see—not instinct—and turn south in an attempt at migration when the constellations of autumn are there to trigger some inborn mechanism that bids them go.

Other tests have proved that birds are guided by the sun in daytime flights to some degree and are reluctant to fly in heavy overcast when they cannot see it. Whatever sensory organ guides them, therefore, must be keyed to vision in some way, but even when we know this much, we still have to wonder how a bird knows that the sun rises in the eastern sky each morning and sets to westward each afternoon.

We ask, too, why some birds migrate in nonstop flights over thousands of miles, gorging themselves with food before each journey like pilots taking on an extra tank of gasoline, while other birds stop to eat each day. How do they recognize an approaching storm front and wait it out, instead of taking off into the teeth of a gale? How did those storks know that the warmed air currents rising upward from the land will give their wings more support and make easier flying than the cool updrafts over water? How did they learn that Gibraltar and the Dardanelles gave them the least water to cross in all the broad expanse between European summer home and African winter quarters?

How do the swallows—and turtledoves and other birds— time their journeys to so fixed a pattern that we can almost mark the calendar by their coming, at least to the same springtime week, if not to the very day? Even when we know that they are guided in part by the sun and stars and the longer or shorter hours of daylight that all have their own fixed patterns, we still cannot quite explain how the birds have learned to match their own goings and comings to the mystery of the changing seasons. Inside each bird there must be a complicated assortment of timers and triggers more amazing than the workings of the most remarkable computer that man has yet invented. Most of us do not understand the workings of a computer any better than we do the inner drives that govern bird behavior. We can say that both are "programmed" by a master hand, and for the birds it is surely the hand of God.

What birds you choose to mark by way of observation on the "appointed times" in migration calendar does not really matter. If you have been keeping a daily, weekly, or monthly calendar of the birds you see in your own backyard or nearby park or woods, you already know which species are first to return after a winter sojourn elsewhere. If you are only beginning such a record, you will have to wait for another year or two to collect a representative sampling. For an answer right now, check in with the nearest Audubon Society or find a fellow birder who has a list already underway. If you live in northeastern states, you may find that the redwinged blackbird is earlier than either robin or bluebird. If you live in southern California you have no doubts that spring comes with the swallows that return to the chapel at Capistrano. If you live in Hinckley, Ohio, you know beyond all argument that the migrant wings to watch for are those of the turkey vulture. The town has officially declared the "buzzard"—as they call it—the bird that announces spring's return.

As a matter of aerodynamics, they're about right. The wide-winged turkey vultures—like the stork and the crane—depend on the rising currents of warmed air from the ground below to keep them buoyed aloft. In northern winters, the ground isn't warm enough itself to send much heated air skyward, and so the turkey vultures drift north with the sun—and the rising temperatures. They can flip-flap their way across cold gray skies when they need to, but soaring takes warmed air currents and that means they come with the spring—and leave when winter threatens.

Winter sends the soaring hawks southward, too, as Job observed long ago. If you want to go on an autumn hawk watch to match his lines, one of the best places is in Hawk Mountain Sanctuary in Pennsylvania. The updrafts from the north-south ridges of the Allegheny Mountains give the hawks the same sort of aid that Old World storks found in crossing a narrow strait instead of the wide Mediterranean, and on a sunny October day, with a good wind blowing down from the north or northwest to add further assistance, watchers who stare in awed wonder will swear that all the hawks of eastern North America are winging past. Another place for an autumn hawk watch is along the lake shore near Duluth, as birds follow the curve of the shore in order to avoid battling turbulent over-water winds.

Birds with smaller wingspread are not so troubled by wind turbulence, and Point Pelee on the Ontario side of Lake Erie has been set aside as a sanctuary where watchers can come and see hundreds of migrants any spring day.

If you want to know the bird that makes the farthest migration flight in the world, look for the Arctic tern, *Sterna paradisaea,* that spends summers near the North Pole and winters near the South Pole, getting the world's longest day at either season. Each one-way journey charts 10,000 to 11,000 miles.

The next 15 to 20 places in the long-distance records also go to shore and sea birds—in this hemisphere. Baird's sandpiper and the white-rumped and pectoral sandpipers all fly from the Arctic to Argentina, while sanderlings, the sooty shearwater, gray albatross, skua, Wilson's petrel, greater yellow-legs, Eskimo curlew, the golden and black-bellied plovers, ruddy turnstone, knot, whimbrel, Hudsonian godwit, and the phalaropes all do between 7,000 and 10,000 miles each way. Among small land birds in North America, the farthest flier may be the wheatear, whose ultimate migration route has not yet been measured, but goes from southern Africa up through western Europe to Greenland and across to Labrador, then inland for at least half the continent's width—for some individuals—and down coast as far as North Carolina for a few others. Still other individuals take the trans-Pacific route to Alaska and have come downcoast as far as British Columbia, with further journeying expected now any springtime. Other small fliers with champion-length mileage are the barn swallow and the cliff swallow—Alaska to the Argentine; and the blackpoll warbler, Alaska to Brazil and Ecuador, often via the Atlantic coast; and the common nighthawk, Yukon to Patagonia. At least a dozen other small songsters clock 4,000 to 7,000 miles each way.

Perhaps most remarkable among them is the tiny rufous hummingbird that measures under 4 inches, yet flies over 4,000 miles—Alaska to Mexico. Not to be left out on this marvels-per-inch mileage is the 5-inch chimney swift that goes from Canada to Brazil and Peru—over 4,500 miles.

In the Old World, long-distance mileage is usually ceded to the stork, which often flies from South Africa to the Scandinavian countries, and to the common swallow—the same species called barn swallow in North America. The wheatear should be added, along with the common cuckoo, since both fly from southern Africa to northern Europe, and the common crane goes from mid-Africa to far-north summer haunts, as does the wryneck.

So it would seem that all of the birds named for Jeremiah's famous passage by all the translators have some claim to being far-flying migrants as well as remarkably regular. The turtledove does not fly so far as the others, but it makes up in friendliness whatever it lacks in distance and is always watched for and welcomed. Even the wryneck may add a new long-distance record, for a few individuals have been turning up in Alaska—probably wanderers from nests in Siberia or China. Standing in for the thrushes would be the wheatear, for it is counted a member of the Thrush Family.

People of Bible times did not, of course, know how far

a journey the migrating birds had made. They did note directions—the hawk stretched its wings to the south, Job recorded, and Isaiah 18:1 speaks of the land shadowing with wings which is beyond the rivers of Ethiopia. And they marveled most of all at the unmarked skyways that birds could follow so easily. They pass overhead in hordes, leaving no trace or trail, as the author of Wisdom 5:11 exclaimed a century before the birth of Christ. And many centuries later the poet Robert Browning would look at birds with the same wonder and find a message for all of us:

> I see my way as birds their trackless way,
> I shall arrive! What time, what circuit first,
> I ask not: but unless God send His hail
> Or blinding fireballs, sleet or stifling snow,
> In some time, His good time, I shall arrive:
> He guides me and the bird. In His good time.

Neophron (*see* Birds of Abomination: No. 16, rahama)
Neophron is the generic name used by scientists for the Egyptian vulture. It is often used as a common name also, since this vulture ranges far beyond Egyptian territory.

Nestlings (*see* Young Birds)

Nests
HEBREW: *ken, kenim,* nest(s), room, cote, niche. Genesis 6:14; Deuteronomy 22:6–7; Job 39:13–16; 27:30; Psalms 84:3; 104:16–17; Song of Songs 2:14; Isaiah 10:14; Jeremiah 17:11; 22:23; 49:16; Ezekiel 17:22–23; 31:6; Daniel 4:12, 14, 21; Obadiah 1:4; Habakkuk 2:9
aruba, window, lattice (i.e., dovecote). Isaiah 60:8
APOCRYPHA: Sirach (Ecclesiasticus) 14:26; 27:9
GREEK: *kataskenosis,* roosting place, nest. Matthew 8:20; 13:32; Mark 4:31–32; Luke 9:58; 13:19

"Every bird has its nest," Jesus told the disciples in a moment of wistfulness for his own homeless wandering. And other passages tell of the different kinds of nesting places that can be seen on Bible bird walk. Little seed-eating birds in the herb garden among the yellow flowers of the mustard, song-birds of all kinds among the sheltering arms of the cedars, swallows and sparrows on eaves and sills, and the stork that makes her home in a tall fir—before there were plenty of tall chimneys and rooftops—all remind us that if we want to have birds nesting around our own homes we must provide them with shrubs and hedges and trees—especially evergreens. Scholars disagree on the specific kinds of trees and shrubs the Bible lines name, just as they mull over the variant transla-tions of bird names, but you can't go wrong if you provide evergreens of some kind and thorny shrubs and trees—like firethorn, hawthorn, cat briar—that will give birds a place of refuge against hawks, cats, and BB guns or slingshots, snakes and predator birds and beasts.

Birds look after the safety of their own nests, and even the rock doves learn to choose a nesting site "in the sides of the hole's mouth" as the King James Version puts it. Other translations describe the mouth of a gorge, the opening above an abyss, the edge of a chasm—all equally out of reach of all but the most daring climbers.

And the eagles will nest still higher. The golden eagle, among others, nests on a rocky ledge. The bald eagle nests in a tree, by preference. Both choose the tallest tree or the loftiest ledge within the wide range of an eagle's keen vision. Like the kings of old, this king of air seems to demand that no one be placed above him, and observers of Bible times must have noted this trait, for it is marked in Job 39:28 and repeated by others, by prophets speaking with the voice of the Lord—Obadiah, Jeremiah, Habakkuk.

But the lines about nesting places that we most often remember are from Psalm 84:3-4:

Yea, the sparrow hath found an house, and the swallow a nest for herself, where she may lay her young, even thine altars, O Lord of hosts, my King and my God. Blessed are they that dwell in thy house: they will be still praising thee.

Night Birds, Night Crow, Nighthawk, Nightjar, Night Raven (*see* Birds of Abomination: No. 8, tachmas; Birds of Doom: lilith.)

The bird called night crow and night raven in olden times is the same bird now called night heron, *Nycticorax nycticorax*. The nighthawk was probably a nightjar, any *Caprimulgus* species, not an actual hawk. The stone curlew was another late flier often called night bird by superstitious people who always fear what they cannot clearly see. Sailors often gave the name of night bird to petrels and shearwaters and to the skimmer, most often seen feeding at dawn and dusk. Far more birds fly and feed at night than most people realize.

Owls are night birds, too, of course, but they are so different from other birds in shape and voice that they usually had a name—or several names—of their own.

No More Birds
HEBREW: Jeremiah 4:23–25; 9:10; 12:4; Ezekiel 38:19–20;
Hosea 4:3; Zephaniah 1:2–3

The prophets of the Old Testament had a grim warning to give of a land laid waste by God's wrath in punishment for sinful ways. More than once they preached of a land laid bare, fit only for birds used to a desolate terrain: the owl and the ostrich, the marabou, bittern, and raven.

But grimmer still was the prophecy that one day there would be places with no birds at all! No birds, no beasts—only stillness and death. "I cannot hold my peace!" Jeremiah cried out in horror at a vision of a world without form or sunlight, twisted by earthquakes and neither man nor beast nor bird left alive (4:19, 23–25).

"No birds, no beasts—all are gone!" he repeated the dire omen twice again (9:10; 12:4).

Ezekiel, too, foretold a time of trembling before destruction (chapters 29–39) and Hosea called in vain (4:1–3) for repentance, seeing a land in mourning for the wild things it would never see again. And Zephaniah repeated the death-warning for birds, beasts, fish in the sea, and all mankind.

It is a warning we must give ourselves in this age of pollution, overcrowding, and vanishing species—but who can say how many will be ready to listen? Even here in the New World there is already a death count. The last great auk died in 1844; the last spectacled cormorant, in 1852. The year 1875 was the last time anyone saw a live Labrador duck. There have been neither passenger pigeons nor Carolina parakeets since 1914. There are possibly no more than one or two Eskimo curlews left; probably less than a dozen ivory-billed woodpeckers. The 1971 count for California condors stood at only some sixty individuals, and the tally for the whooping crane in the September 1971 issue of *Audubon* was 87—including 56 adults in the wild, 21 in captivity, and a summer hatch of 10 chicks, with no guarantee that there will be more another year or that sometime soon the count will not be none at all.

Which species will be next to vanish? Bald eagle and golden eagle both are threatened, and with them on the danger list are the peregrine falcon, the osprey, the caracara, the trumpeter swan, brown and white pelicans, the Hudsonian godwit, the Everglade kite, a rare sparrow, and two seldom-seen warblers—and perhaps others not yet called to our attention.

It is a time for action, not just for the setting aside of vast acreage for wildlife sanctuaries by government decree and the banning of biocide poisons, but for individuals to take their own stand on home ground, making sure that their own backyards, the nearby parks and fields, offer food and water and homesite to at least a few birds, and shelter in green-growing tree and hedgerow to every winged wanderer that comes by.

Osprey (*see* Birds of Abomination: No. 2, peres; No. 10, nez)

Ossifrage (*see* Birds of Abomination: No. 2, peres)

Ostrich

HEBREW: *ya'annah, ye'enim,* ostrich (es), echoic, or the greedy
    one, or the loud-voiced one; also *bath-ya'annah,* daughter
    of greediness, or daughter of the loud voice, or young
    or kindred of the ostrich. Leviticus 11:16; Deuteronomy
    14:15; Job 30:29; Isaiah 13:21; 34:13; 43:20; Jeremiah
    50:39; Micah 1:8 (all of these passages may also read
    yanshuf, owl)
    ye'enim (no confusion with owls). Lamentations 4:3
    renanim, quill rattlers (or error for *ye'enim*). Job 39:13
    haserah, the lacking one. Job 39:13

As you compare Bible translations, you often find that
the ostrich in one familiar passage becomes an owl in a different version. The two birds aren't being confused—how
could anybody mistake an ostrich for an owl? But *ya'annah*
in written script looks so much like *yanshuf,* one word for
owls—especially in the old script with the vowels omitted—
that misunderstanding is easy. In a passage where this blurred
y-n-? suddenly races off at top speed on long and sturdy legs,
you know—of course—that it's an ostrich. When some la-
menting sinner moans that he looks like a *y-n-?* or feels like
one, you can't be sure. Even the voice doesn't settle the question beyond doubt, for both owl and ostrich give out a defiant
hiss, and the hoot of an owl across the desert silence has much
the same eerie echo as the booming call of the ostrich.

The likeness of the two voices may explain the similarity
of the names, for many birds are known by an echo of their
call. However, *yanshuf* could mean "horned one" and *ya'annah* could mean "greedy one," and since ostriches do not
have an owl's hornlike tufts of feathers, this distinction could
set them apart. As for being greedy—the ostrich has a well-
earned reputation for gobbling down almost everything and
anything that catches its eye, especially if it sparkles. Bottle
caps, nails, bits of broken glass, whole oranges, nickels, dimes,
and silver dollars have all gone down long ostrich throats with

only a momentary bulge to mark their passage. In the bird's gizzard they are slowly ground down to digestible powder— by the action of the gizzard muscles maneuvering the pebbles which the ostrich has also swallowed at the direction of an instinct the bird does not understand but luckily obeys. Barnyard chickens—almost all ground birds—have this same instinctive urge to ingest grit material. But barnyard grit is so small to our eyes that we scarcely notice what the pecking beak picks up, while the size of the pebbles a huge ostrich must gulp down to get the same results sets us blinking in amazement—and started a rumor that ostriches could digest anything. Unfortunately for ostriches, zoo visitors are always eager to test the rumor and toss all sorts of undigestible things into the pen, and sharp edges that can't be blunted even by ostrich gizzard action often lead to the bird's death. The visitor doesn't stay long enough to realize this, of course, and goes on his way repeating the libelous label of "Old Greedy."

Another libel pinned on the ostrich, though not in Bible lines, is that it stupidly hides its head in the sand whenever danger threatens, thinking that it cannot be seen because it cannot see. The grain of truth in this story is that young ostriches, feathered in camouflage coloring of desert sand, will flop down in motionless freeze when an enemy approaches, closing their eyes to gain the protective coloring of the lids rather than betraying brightness and movement of a watching eye. If a desert breeze shifts the sands to half cover them, it is none of their doing, and their ruse is no more than the instinctive quick-freeze of all precocial chicks— quail, partridge, pheasant—that also have the protective coloring of their surroundings. It is movement, not color pattern, that betrays them to predator bird or beast, at least from a distance, and so long as they can remain motionless they will probably not be seen. So the ostrich is not stupid, but wise with instinctive cunning, when it flattens out in the sand— no matter what snickering people believe.

In nine different passages the word for ostrich is *bath*

ya'annah or *ya'annah* or the plural *ye'enim,* meaning "the
boomer" or "the greedy one." But in a tenth passage—the
one that tells most about ostrich ways—one or perhaps two
other names are used and both these words and others with
them are listed as uncertain of meaning, obscure or unintel-
ligible, so that scholars have translated the lines in a confusing variety of ways. The King James text for this puzzle in
Job 39:13–18 reads:

13. Gavest thou goodly wings unto the peacocks? or wings and
feathers unto the ostrich? 14. Which leaveth her eggs in the earth,
and warmeth them in the dust, 15. And forgetteth that the foot
may crush them, or that the wild beast may break them, 16. She
is hardened against her young ones, as though they were not
hers: her labour is in vain without fear; 17. Because God hath
deprived her of wisdom, neither hath he imparted to her understanding. 18. What time she lifteth herself up on high, she
scorneth the horse and his rider.

The middle verses, all pointing out how God has made
the ostrich stupid and cruel, seem so at variance with the
theme of the surrounding chapters—which point out how
wonderfully God has formed the earth and its creatures—that
some scholars believe they were not in the original text at all,
but were added as a marginal note by some later copyist who
was trying to clarify the meaning of verse 13.

This seems very possible, for the phrase for "wings and
feathers of the ostrich" is "of the *haserah,*" which means "the
lacking one" or one that is unequipped, deficient, faulty. Of
course what the ostrich lacks is the ability to fly as almost all
other birds do, but some scribe could well have thought that
other faults were more serious and ought to be set down for
remembering. The ostrich abandons her eggs and even her
chicks and is therefore cruel and stupid, he wrote down with
careful pen, and his words were copied by the next scribe—
or could have been—and became part of the sanctioned text.

This scribe—if he existed—must have been city-bred, for
any desert dweller would have known that the sun on hot

sand does as good a job of incubating eggs as the hen bird herself. Indeed, on a very hot day the heat of her own body added to the sun's rays might have produced too much heat and spoiled the eggs completely. So instinct tells her to cover the eggs and walk away, taking her own sizable bulk out of sight so that any passing predator beast or egg-hunting humans will not have her presence as a clue that a nest is nearby. At night, however, or on cloudy days the ostrich hen sits on the eggs as faithfully as any other bird, and the cock usually incubates during the night.

Later when the chicks are hatched, both cock and hen will keep them in a well-guarded family flock, but the moment some enemy appears on the desert horizon, the parent birds wander off in the opposite direction from the crouching chicks, acting as if they couldn't care less about their offspring. Actually they are giving the babies the best protection possible, offering themselves as easily seen targets to hunter or hyena or hawk in the hope that the motionless young will not be discovered. Scientists remind us that we cannot call this action either bravery or love, since it is only unthinking obedience to instinct, and if that note-adding scribe—and other people of Bible times—had held that same objective view, they would never have called the ostrich cruel and stupid.

At least the scribe put his finger on the source of the bird's faulty behavior, explaining that God had not given her enough understanding, that she was only as God had made her. Scientists today would correct that statement to "as *instinct* made her" and then they could well hear the same Voice that hurled his challenge at Job out of the whirlwind, now re-wording his own question to match the times:

Who gave the birds their instincts?

There has to be an answer, even for the most objective scientists, and some of them reply with the same words that Job cried out in answer to his Lord:

I know that Thou canst do everything.

To do a little more unraveling of the verse 13 puzzle, we find that the peacock of the King James text does not appear at all in other versions. The word translated as peacock —*renanim*—is thought now to be a miscopying for *ye'enim,* plural of *ya'annah,* the traditional name for ostriches. This, too, is quite possible. We can only wonder that there were not more errors in scrolls copied and recopied over so many centuries by so many different hands.

And so now if we put the complaining accusations of the middle verses aside, omitting 14 and 15 and half of 16 and then rewording 13 with the closing lines, we have a very reasonable sequence for this chapter of challenge to open our eyes to the wonders of bird and beast and growing things, and the lines might read like this:

Did you give beautiful wings to the ostriches, yet make each pinion and feather flightless? . . . Or see that even though this bird cannot take wing, it still need not fear its enemies? For what God takes away on one hand, he balances with the other. And when an ostrich stretches out in full run, it escapes even hunters on horseback.

Of course these same verses could be written in dozens of other ways. When the phrases are picturesque rather than plain-spoken and sometimes the very letters of the words in doubt, the variations have to be endless. The word *haserah,* for instance, is written in some texts as *hasidah,* the word for loving kindness and for the stork and sometimes for the heron. The word *notsah,* for feathers, is thought by some to be *nez,* the hawk or falcon.

So the Douay Bible wrote: "The wing of the ostrich is like the wings of the heron and hawk." And the Jerusalem Bible wrote: "Can you compare the wings of the ostrich with those of the stork and falcon?" And the Revised Standard and American Standard Bibles chose: "The wings of the ostrich wave proudly. But are they the pinions and plumage of love?" And with most of these and every other translation there is usually an added note that the exact wording is not clear, not indisputable.

Most of the other verses are translated with little variation, with the last line always making it quite clear that an ostrich can run faster than any horse and rider. And verse 16 always carries at least a hint that the big bird with the little wings keeps flapping them as it runs, as if continually fooling itself into thinking it will really fly if it just flaps hard enough.

Maybe an ostrich does look foolish as it goes dashing off across the sands with flip-flap effort that seems completely wasted. But the experts on speed and motion have now decided almost beyond question that the flapping actually does increase running speed. Sharp-eyed watchers of long ago came to the same conclusion, for the book *Anabasis,* telling the exploits of the Greek historian-warrior Xenophon, in 399 B.C. reports:

. . . no ostrich was captured by anyone, and any horseman who chased one would most speedily yield; for it would out-distance him at once in its flight, not merely plying its feet, but hoisting its wings and using them like a sail . . . (Book I, Section V).

Here was one man, at least, who did not think that God had short-changed the ostrich in its store of good sense. What we call wisdom in wild creatures must begin—as the poets say that beauty begins—in the eye of the beholder, and the better we look, the more "wisdom" we see.

Ostrich running speed, with wing flapping or without, has been clocked at 30, 40, and 50 miles an hour, so ostrich owners claim, and sometimes the boasts go even higher. Horses have set records of 40 miles per hour for a half-mile course and 43 or 44 for the quarter mile. Some record-keepers assert that the fastest race ever run by an ostrich was 37 m.p.h. but surely this must be only a scant measure of the burst of speed the bird could call forth when racing for its life, spurred by fear and the thunder of horses' hoofs and a hunter's wild halloo.

If you have ever seen an ostrich on the run, you know that they do seem to stretch themselves out to taller, thinner, longer silhouette—and an ostrich cock can stand a good 8 feet tall to begin with, so the King James translation of the Hebrew word *tamara* as "lifteth up herself on high" is right to the point. The Georg Lamsa translation of the Peshitta makes it "raises herself high like a palm tree" and that seems quite reasonable since the palm tree is usually the highest outline on the desert horizon. But the New English Bible turns *tamara* into "while like a cock she struts over the uplands"—justifying their interpretation with comparison to a similar Arabic word that gives "to lift oneself up" the added meaning of "to take the part of a male." Now a proud male of any kind may hold its head very high indeed, but no strutting rooster ever ran fast enough to beat an Arab stallion!

The ostrich has never been native to North America even in prehistoric times, and since it is the only bird in the world with only two toes, it is placed alone in an order of its own, the *Struthioniformes,* with its only family the *Struthionidae,* its only generic division the genus *Struthio,* its only species, *Struthio camelus.* The species is divided, however, into six geographical races, recognized by some slight differences in size or in the skin coloring of the unfeathered thighs, head, or long neck. Its closest cousin in the western hemisphere is the South American rhea that once roamed as far north as Mexico, also in an Order and Family all its own.

This label of *struthio* originated with the Greeks and at first meant any sturdy-legged ground bird that walked or hopped as it searched for food—in contrast to birds like swallows and flycatchers that find their food in midair, or to woodpeckers and other insect-eaters that glean on tree trunk and branch. In time, it became applied only to the ostrich, most sturdy-legged of all, but for some reason the Jewish scholars who prepared the Greek text of the Septuagint used *struthion* in the old sense, and the American Colonial scholar Charles Thomson was tricked thereby into filling his Septuagint version with ostriches that winged off to the mountains or perched among the cedars. Anyone who knows birds would have realized immediately that something was wrong, for a two-toed ostrich with a foot more like a hoof than a claw cannot perch on a cedar branch—even a branch strong enough to hold its 200- to 300-pound weight—and it cannot fly anywhere. So once again the puzzle lies in the *word,* not the *bird.*

This category of "sturdy-legged walker" could well have been used by the ancient Hebrews as well as by the ancient Greeks, and the Hebrew label might have been *zarzir mothnayim*—"he of the well-girt loins"—found in Proverbs 30:31. If so, it would have included the ostrich as well as the marabou and the bustard—and the barnyard roosters, too, when they became known in later times—and sparrows, thrushes, wagtails, just as *struthion* did in its original Greek usage (*see* Chicken, Cock, Hen).

But while other birds walk as sturdily as the ostrich, none has feathers quite like the curly ostrich plumes, and these feathers have been gathered for adornment since earliest times. The birds shed their plumes in annual molt and promptly grow new ones, and they feel no more than a twinge when a feather is plucked out quickly before it can fall on the ground and become tangled and soiled. An Assyrian artist of the eighth century B.C. told the story of such a plucking in a carving on a gray marble cylinder now owned by the Pierpont Morgan Library, as other artists must have done many times on wood or stone or plaster wall over the years.

Ostrich eggs have been valued highly, too, for one equals 18 or 20 hen's eggs when stirred into an omelet. Furthermore, they have an exceedingly tough shell—about $\frac{1}{4}$ inch thick —that enables them to be used as drinking cups or serving bowls or (most important of all to desert dwellers) as canteens for water. A small hole in one end will allow the yolk and white to be drained out, and a plug of grass will keep the water safe and cool within, once the emptied shell is rinsed and filled, and the new canteen then fits easily into whatever twist of cloth serves the desert traveler as tote bag or knapsack. Ostrich-egg cups have been found in Assyrian tombs of 3000 B.C., and the rinsed shells once hung in Coptic churches as symbols of the Lord's loving care.

On Bible bird walk you may have difficulty finding an ostrich egg to taste or a shell to measure, and even ostrich plumes aren't always on sale these days. Fifty or sixty years ago they were high fashion, bringing as much as $500 a pound for the best imported plumes, and ranchers in our southern states soon decided to import living birds instead and get rich in the feather trade themselves. California, Florida, Arizona, Oklahoma, Arkansas, and Texas all had good-sized ostrich farms for several years and a few remain today. Now, however, the profit is smaller and likely to be from ostrich leather rather than the ostrich feather—unless those plumes once more become the fashion craze.

In the town of Indio in California, one ostrich owner decided to cash in on the curiosity most people have for finding out how fast an ostrich can run. For some years now an annual ostrich race has been a part of Indio's annual date festival held each February. These long-legged runners can be ridden by a jockey, though not always willingly, and the feature race is for birds hitched to two-wheeled carts driven by boys garbed in the typical flowing robes and twisted head-cloths of desert tribesmen. Off they whirl in a cloud of dust, and if you want to know how fast they run, just have your own stopwatch in hand when you make your match of Job 39:18.

Another place to see ostriches on the run is in the preserves where visitors stay in cars while animals roam free. Even if you go to Israel you would have to see ostriches in captivity, perhaps in the famous zoo that exhibits all birds and beasts named in Bible lines, for wild ostriches vanished long ago from this land. Wild flocks still roam in Africa, but even there they are seldom seen except in remote wilderness or in protected wildlife sanctuaries.

Owl

HEBREW: *bath-ya'annah,* daughter of the loud voice (in some versions the translation is ostrich). Leviticus 11:16; Deuteronomy 14:15; Job 30:29; Isaiah 13:21; 34:13; 43:20; Jeremiah 50:39; Micah 1:8 (*see* Ostrich)

kippoz, darter, great owl. Isaiah 34:13

kos, echoic, little owl. Leviticus 11:17; Deuteronomy 14:16

kos aharboth, kos of the desert. Psalm 102:6

lilith, wavery flier or echoic. Isaiah 34:14

oahim, echoic, doleful creatures. Isaiah 13:21

shalak, plunger. Leviticus 11:16; Deuteronomy 14:15

tachmas, night hawk, torn-face. Leviticus 11:16; Deuteronomy 14:15

tinshemeth, astonishing hisser. Leviticus 11:18; Deuteronomy 14:16

yanshof, echoic. Isaiah 34:11

yanshuf, echoic or horned one. Leviticus 11:17; Deuteronomy 14:16

APOCRYPHA: Baruch 6:21 (*or* bat)

See Birds of Abomination; Birds of Doom

The owl names listed in Leviticus and repeated in Deuteronomy were intended, of course, to forbid the eating of any owl. *Kos, shalak,* and *yanshuf* seem to take care of them all—small, middle-sized, and big. Tinshemeth may or may not make special banning of the barn owl, the only one with heart-shaped, monkey-like face.

But owls in general or certain owls in particular could not help but have other names used in various places at various times, and several of these appear in Isaiah 34 among the birds of doom, and in Zephaniah 2:14. Besides these, there are two more, each used only in a single passage.

Kos aharboth, the "owl of the desert" in the mournful

lines of affliction in Psalm 102:6, is "owl of the ruins" in other translations, or—more simply—"desert owl." Since the little owl, *Athene noctua,* is well known by similar names in various European lands and by its fondness for hiding in lonely places among hills and rocks, the identity of this solitary and hoarse-voiced mourner is scarcely in question. However, watchers in Bible times were not always precise in separating owls by specific labels, and the eerie, long-drawn, mournful cry of any owl coming out from a shadowy outline of tree or rocky crag across the night stillness should tell you just how the speaker felt.

Oahim, the owls of Isaiah 13:21, had a name to echo their cry, too. The name for one owl, one eerie echo, is *oah.* And this is so like the echoic name of the eagle owl that Germans hear as *uhu* and the Dutch as *oehoe* and French as *hibou,* that we cannot help but think that this is the very same species. In the King James Version *oahim* is translated as "doleful creatures," and certainly birds that cry *oah, oah* are as doleful and dolorous and full of doubt and gloom as any bird can be. Listen to the *boo-ah, boo, hoo-hoo-ah* of our great horned owl, *Bubo virginianus,* or the moans of the great gray owl, *Strix nebulosa,* or the cat-voiced yowl of the long-eared owl, *Asio otus,* for your own echo of oahim cry. The French name for the long-eared owl is "midway" *hibou* —with the eagle owl the great hibou and the little scops the petit hibou—and since this long-eared one is known both in Israel and all across America, it is surely one of the first to look for on any owl prowl.

The short-eared owl, *Asio flammeus,* also often seen in both Israel and North America, offers the extra advantage of hunting by daylight as well as dusk and dark and could very likely be found mouse hunting at your nearest airport. Its sneezy barking *kuh-aow* call might also qualify it for the *kos aharboth* role as an owl of lonely wastelands.

And of course do not forget the barn owl, *Tyto alba,* the owl with the long list of nicknames in languages all around the world. As for English nicknames, people who don't know much about birds are likely to call all small owls "screech owls" and all big owls "hoot owls." "Screech owl," of course, is the official name for one North American species, *Otus asio,* which is never seen in Bible lands and does not belong on any Bible bird list, even though it is a common folk name for the barn owl in England. "Hoot owl" has no official standing and belongs only in folk tales and ghost stories, not in Isaiah 14:23 with words of prophecy from God.

Parrot
HEBREW: *anafah,* noselike beak (*see* Birds of Abomination: No. 18, anafah)

The parrot is not named among Bible birds by modern translators, but in the past it was suggested as the bird with noselike beak banned as food under Mosaic Law. Since parrots are not native wild birds in Israel this seems unlikely.

Parrots were introduced in ancient times as cage birds, however, in all Mediterranean lands, with the African gray parrot and the ring-necked parakeet being especially popular. Many of these birds were taught to talk and so they have been cited as the birds in Ecclesiastes 10:20 that sat on windowsills and repeated any overheard gossip. The line in 1 Kings 4:33 telling how Solomon talked about so many things, including birds and beasts, was sometimes translated as talked *to* birds, and perhaps a pet parrot which he had taught to talk in give-and-take chatter that sounded like true conversation may have helped start the legend that he could talk to any bird or beast in its own language simply by touching a certain magic ring that he had on his finger.

Ravens, crows, magpies, and starlings were trained as talkers, too, and since these birds are instantly attracted to anything that glitters, perhaps wise Solomon did twist the ring on his finger to get their attention. For a modern look at this "talking to birds" legend, read one of the most interesting books on bird and animal behavior ever written, *King Solomon's Ring* by Konrad Lorenz.

Partridge

HEBREW: *kore,* the caller. 1 Samuel 26:20; Jeremiah 17:11
En-hakkore, Spring (well) of the Partridge (*or* Spring of the Caller). Judges 15:19
Beth-Hoglah, Place of the (Hen) Partridge. Joshua 15:6; 18:19, 21
kippoz, sand-partridge (?). Isaiah 34:15

APOCRYPHA: Sirach (Ecclesiasticus) 11:30

See Fowl, Fowler, Fowling. *Yakosh,* the word for fowler, is literally "partridge-catcher," derived from *yakeb* (meaning "one with spurred heel"), the current name for the black partridge. Several masculine names are also derived from *yakosh*—Yokshan, Joktan, Jacob—but the *yakeb* is not named in the Bible. The old name for a hen partridge, *hoglah,* meaning "sand-dweller" or perhaps "sand-colored" is used in the Bible only as the name of a place, Beth-Hoglah, or as a girl's name (Numbers 26:33, 27:1; 36:11; Joshua 17:3).

See also Decoys; Caged Birds; Sand-partridge

Three kinds of partridges skitter over Israeli hills: the rock partridge or chukar, *Alectoris graeca;* the desert partridge or sand-partridge, *Ammoperdix heyi;* and the black partridge or francolin, *Francolinus francolinus.* The use of the francolin's present name as the root word for "fowler" suggests that *yakeb*—meaning "spurred"—once named all the chicken-like birds that have this sharp heel claw, and the spur was the sign of the best-tasting birds for table use before the introduction of the red jungle fowl from India. As the francolin decreased in abundance, perhaps through constant hunting, and with the growing use of decoy birds to "call in" the hunted birds, the group name in most frequent usage became *kore,* a word which means "caller" and was probably an imitation of a captive's plaintive cry. Kore is the only partridge in Bible lines.

The likeness of the Hebrew word *kore* to Hindi *cakor* and Sanskrit *cakora*—the root words for English *chukar*—

suggests that these names originally belonged to the same species. But today the book *Birds of Israel* by Paula Arnold, a long-time resident of Jerusalem, assigns the name *kore* to the desert partridge and *hoglah* to the chukar, although *hoglah* seems to be derived from the Hebrew word for "sand-dweller." Getting into a tangled argument over which kind of kore was meant in any particular Bible passage seems a waste of time. Whether partridges live in rocky hills or sandy deserts, they are all "callers" and all have spurs, so that both kore and yakeb are group names. On our bird walk, the matter is easily solved, for none of the three Israeli species is native to North America and only the chukar has become established as an introduced species. The Hungarian or gray partridge, *Perdix perdix,* has also been established in western states, but it is not known in Bible lands. The chukar is our only partridge with both American and Judean nests.

To find a chukar, look in dry and rocky hill country from British Columbia southward, and in Hawaii. Settle yourself down in a sort of hunter's blind beside a water hole—behind a bush or rock or in a little green tent with a peep-hole for your own eye and the camera's lens—and wait, for chukars come to drink at a water hole twice a day, as a rule. You may hear them before you see them, calling to each other with sharp, cackling chuckles, and if you follow the sound you'll see the red legs and chubby bodies and a white, heart-shaped face boldly outlined in a band of jet black. There is a dot-dash patch of streakings along each side of the pale flanks, too, and the rest of the plumage is a blending grayish-brownish tone that makes a crouching chukar sud-denly turn into a rock with an instant-magic camouflage your blinking eyes will scarcely believe.

As long as you remain quiet, with no sound or move-ment, they'll probably not know you're there—but just make a threatening gesture, and they're off and away, those red legs covering the ground with amazing speed. Anyone who has ever challenged a chukar to a race will tell you that this is one of the most elusive ground birds ever to match their

camouflage covering with wily escape strategy. Instinct tells
them they are safer on the ground than in the air, and they
can scuttle in and out of blending bunch grass and rock at
such a fast pace that a hunter and his dogs are often left far
behind. If need be, they can pull the quick-freeze trick, too,
waiting to move till the hunter turns his eyes elsewhere, and
that must have been the very strategy that David used that
day when he hid and ran, ran and hid from a pursuing King
Saul on the hill of Hachilah and called out: "The king of
Israel is come out to seek a flea, as when one doth hunt a
partridge in the mountains" (1 Samuel 26:20).

The birds were as skillful at hiding their eggs as they
were in secreting themselves from the hunter's search. But
nevertheless the keen eyes of the desert and mountain people
found them out and confidently took those that were first
laid, knowing the hen bird would soon return and begin
another set. In watching for the newest nests and the fresh-
est eggs, people of Bible times discovered that sometimes a
second hen laid eggs in the same nest. Then the first partridge
hen would return, lay another egg, and when the full number required by instinct was completed, she would begin
incubation and finally walk off with a new-hatched family,
some of which were clearly not her own.

To the watchers, that seemed outright kidnaping and
thoroughly reprehensible, for they made the mistake of trying to judge birds by human laws and customs instead of by
the demands of natural instincts. The way they saw the matter, that partridge had no right to those chicks and surely
she would be punished in the end. Europeans of the Middle
Ages felt the same way and started the legend that when the
half-grown partridge chicks left the mother and began for-
aging on their own, they had done so because they realized
she had kidnaped them and they no longer wanted to be
near such a wicked creature. The legend may have been
begun by people who actually saw partridges raising chicks
not their own, but chances are that Bible reading, rather than
birdwatching, started the rumor, for Jeremiah 17:11 carries

a similar accusation in wording that has been translated several ways. In the King James text it reads:

As the partridge sitteth on eggs *and hatcheth them not,* so he that getteth riches and not by right shall leave them in the midst of his days, and at his end shall be a fool.

The italicized words are the ones that vary most in translation. In the American Standard Bible they were changed to "which she hath not laid." The New American Bible says: "mothers a brood not her own." The New English Bible has: "Like a partridge which *gathers* into its nest eggs which it has not laid . . ." and seems to suggest that the bird actually steals the eggs from another nest with willful intent, though perhaps that was not the translator's interpretation.

What Jeremiah probably meant to imply was that a hen partridge trying to hatch out an unusually large clutch of eggs—all the ones she laid herself and those laid by one or more other hens who tried to claim the same nest—would probably not be able to brood them all with sufficient warmth for successful hatching, and so in the end would have to go off with her little brood and leave unhatched eggs behind, spoiled and of no use to anyone. A rich man who gets his wealth by depriving others of just wages also gets more worldly goods than he can use in his lifetime, and dies with much that might have been put to good use still unspent.

Perhaps the conclusion should be that at the end both man and bird have been well fooled by fate, the victims of what scholars call "poetic justice." But for the bird there is no cause for moral judgment or name-calling. A good many kinds of birds do lay their eggs in nests that other birds have built, and the partridge is especially likely to do so. Jeremiah was right about that part of his parable, even if he did have to stretch a point to fix the moral lesson. Many observers have seen two birds of different species sharing the same nest, taking turns with brooding chores, neither one willing to give up and build another nest elsewhere. Far more often, one of the hens will yield and go off to make her own nest in another place, raise her own brood, for a good many birds seem to have an almost unlimited capacity for egg laying.

Actually, it seems possible that this instinctive compulsion to lay an egg in whatever nest has been started may be a factor in preserving the species. Two hens can lay the customary number of eggs faster than just one hen could do, since one a day—or one every other day—is the usual limit, so brooding and hatching can get under way that much sooner. And while brooding is going on in Nest Number One, more eggs are being laid in Nest Two, and each will hatch at different times and so avoid whatever hazards of cold or heat or roving predators might destroy the other, or at least have a better chance at so doing. All in all, you would have to say that the label of "fool" applied by Jeremiah fitted the man better than the bird.

But "fool hen" was the very name given to North American grouse in pioneer days, partly because they were mistaken for partridges. No true partridges are native to this continent, but both quail and grouse were often called "partridge" in early days before bird clubs and bird books began making people more aware of proper naming. The ruffed grouse, largest of the group, has been miscalled a pheasant as well as a partridge, and anyone reading oldtime pioneer journals would be quite convinced that partridges and pheasants once abounded in American woods. Our birds earned the "fool hen" sobriquet in earnest, for they continued to rely on camouflage coloring for protection and held their quick-freeze crouch even when the hunter walked up and clubbed them on the head. That crouch had made them invisible to hawk and eagle flying high overhead and to lynx or cougar keeping watch from a distant rock, but it did not keep them from the sharp eyes of hunters two or three feet away.

So the hunters clubbed away, making fool-hen stew a steady diet until they suddenly realized that the birds were getting scarce, in some places no longer seen at all. Looking back, thinking how a little closer observance of good conservation rules would have spared all our vanishing species, you cannot help thinking that "fool *men*" was the tag to use.

In other Bible lines the words for partridge are proper names. Hoglah is a girl in Joshua and Numbers and Beth-Hoglah—meaning "place of the partridge"—is a town in Joshua 15:6 and 18:19–21. In Judges 15:19 we find En-hak-kore—Spring of the Partridge—as the place where Samson slew 10,000 men with the jawbone of an ass and then called aloud to the Lord, bemoaning his great thirst. Instantly God commanded a spring of water to gush forth from the rocks, and so the name by which this place was known forever after was really Spring of Samson, the Caller-on-the-Lord, not of kore the partridge. But partridges no doubt began using it at once and were so often seen there that the name seemed to make it their own.

For anyone on Bible bird walk, the reminder that goes with Samson's story is plain: when you look for a partridge, look for a water hole.

Peacock

HEBREW: *tukkiyim,* echoic. 1 Kings 10:22; 2 Chronicles 9:21
    renanim, quill rattlers. Job 39:13 (*see* Ostrich)

Peacocks do rattle their quills on jet take-off flight, especially when they want to startle a crouching fox or a stalking hunter into missing his mark, so the name of *renanim* —"the quill rattlers"—from Job 39:13 is a word to match the bird. If you want to hear this same sound, but can't find a peacock, listen to a cock pheasant using the same tactics when some prowling house cat comes too near. The ring-necked pheasant is a close cousin of the peacocks and it is also of Oriental origin, first breeding successfully in North America in the 1880s from stock sent to Oregon by Judge Owen Denny, then American consul in Shanghai. Partridges and quail also make a rattling take-off—or at least a buzzing noise —to startle the hunter, and all of them would be equally open to the name *renanim,* "noisy rattlers." However, modern scholars feel that this was a miscopying of the original word, now on the books as *ye^cenim,* ostriches (*see* Ostrich).

The peacock was given an earlier chance for enrollment among Bible birds in the Books of Kings and Chronicles and the story of what fancy foreign goods were brought back to Jerusalem by the far-ranging ships of the Phoenicians under King Hiram, sailing in company with the fleets of King Solomon. The word for them here is *tukkiyim,* and the first English Bibles interpreted it as a phonetic duplication of the bird's *tuk-tuk*—or *turk-turk*—muttering as it stalked about the palace grounds. Scholars have explained that a very similar word—*tokei*—is the name for peacocks in one of the oldest languages in India and Ceylon, the Tamil tongue, and it seems very possible that the sailing ships brought the word along with the bird. Hebrew tongues turned *tokei* into *tukki* and eventually—about the year 1187—English tongues dropped in an "r" and coined the word *turkey*—using it for peacocks and for any big, fan-tailed birds such as the capercaillie grouse that had a proud peacock strut. Guinea fowl were evidently called turkeys, too, for a few years, but in 1523 or 1524 some English adventurers in the Caribbean with Sebastian Cabot sent, or brought, a fabulous American fan-tailed bird back to England and very shortly it was the only bird known by turkey name. Spaniards, who were the first Europeans to discover this new fowl, had called it a peacock—and Englishmen thought they were doing much the same thing, just using the Bible word for peacock and pronouncing it in their own way.

Meanwhile, the Hebrew scholars who translated the Septuagint Bible from Hebrew to Greek did not recognize that word *tukki*—perhaps did not know the Tamil word *tokei*—and they thought it meant carved stones. Other scholars thought it must be the Jewish version of an old Egyptian word for baboons or monkeys. A few have thought it named the parrots and parakeets that were becoming popular cage birds (*see* Parrot). A well-known clergyman of the twentieth century, the Reverend Reinhold Niebuhr, suggested that the word was miscopied and had originally been *sukkiyim,* a word for slaves.

The right answer to the riddle may never be solved, but if any bird matches Solomon's splendid court, with its marble halls and carved panels, its gold and silver trays and dishes, that bird is surely the peacock. If it was not in aviaries in his time, it must have been soon afterward, and it is pictured in many of the mosaics that date from the first Christian centuries. One may date even earlier and was found on the red rocks of Petra, the city that lay on the caravan route between the Gulf of Aqaba and Jerusalem. Once Petra had been a Roman city, but before that it had been Sela, the home for Edomites; and relics of that earlier occupancy have been found near the hill called Umm-il-Biyara, where the carving of the peacock has also been revealed by the patient digging of modern archaeologists (*see* Philip C. Hammond, "Rose-Red City of Petra," *Natural History,* February 1964, p. 24).

Was this peacock carved by an artisan who had learned his trade in some Roman workshop, merely repeating the designs taught by his master? Or was it sketched by a dazzled watcher who had just seen his first peacock being carried by in a caravan of treasures and gifts for King Solomon—and just had to draw it with his own hand to believe that a bird with such a splendid tail really did exist? We do not know, but at least this carved likeness serves witness that the peacock was a bird of Bible lands and times, if not of the book itself. On Bible bird walk, you will find it in a zoo or an aviary—as Solomon himself would have had to do—unless you just happen to know of an estate where half-tamed peacocks roam free or where once captive birds have now gone wild and established themselves much as the pheasants have done.

One place to find these feral peacocks is on Palos Verde Peninsula in California, where the flocks have now increased to such numbers that birdwatchers count them on a bird-

population census along with the house sparrows and starlings
—also introduced species, not natives. The original patri-
archs of this flock, so the story goes, were peacocks imported
by miners who had struck it rich in the gold fields and built
the most elegant mansions they could dream up. When the
ore ran out, the miners left and the mansions moldered away
into rubble, but the peacocks left to fend for themselves
proved that they had something more than just beauty of
feathers to win acclaim.

Pelican

HEBREW: *ka'ath,* the vomiter. Leviticus 11:18; Deuteronomy
     14:17; Isaiah 34:11; Zephaniah 2:14
     ka'ath midbar, ka'ath of the wilderness (*see* Pelican of
     the Wilderness)
See Birds of Abomination: No. 15, ka'ath; Birds of Doom;
     Pelican of the Wilderness

The pelican has long had a special role in the story of
Christianity, quite apart from its place in Bible lines. From
the earliest Christian centuries—the fourth century, at least,
if not before then—it was presented as the "bird of piety" in
those books of moral fables called bestiaries which had been
written by various early churchmen under the alias of Physiologus, meaning one who philosophizes on nature.

There was more philosophizing than naturalizing in
most of the stories, but usually there was at least a shred of
fact, something people could see with their own eyes and
therefore take the whole tale as equally true. For belief in
the piousness of pelicans, the shred of fact is that the throat
and breast of nesting pelicans become suffused with a reddish
tint as they feed their young—a reddish tint that looks like
blood but is simply an excretion from an oil sac that becomes
active only during courtship and nesting. The more the
parent birds preen these breast feathers, the rosier they
glow, and some Physiologus who saw the spreading stain

thought that the devoted birds were feeding their babes with blood from their own breasts.

The moral to add to the tale was obvious—look at the pious pelican and remember that Christ shed his blood for you upon the Cross—and so this bird became the symbol of piety in British heraldry. In 1516 Bishop Richard Fox included it in the heraldic banner for the College of Corpus Christi at Oxford and had a carved stone pelican set up on a pillar in the quadrangle, a reminder for every passing student, teacher, and visitor. The artist who designed the title page for the edition of the Bible authorized by King James of England in 1611 added a medallion below the date line to picture the scene of a pelican feeding its young. The only other birds sharing the honor of being placed here are the dove, symbol of God's presence, and the eagle, placed beside John the Gospel writer, who had been granted a vision of these "wings of the Lord" beside God's throne.

Pelican of the Wilderness
HEBREW: *ka'ath midbar,* vomiter of the wasteland. Psalm 102:6
See Birds of Abomination: No. 15, ka'ath; Birds of Doom

The "pelican" of the wilderness is probably the marabou, a scavenger bird with a throat pouch to give it the pelican name. Its Arabic name was *murabit*—which means "hermit" and well supports its claim to being a bird of the wild wasteland. Just how *murabit* turned into *marabou* when Englishmen took over the Arabic name is one more of the many puzzles that birds and bird names place in the path of those who follow Bible bird walk.

Phoenix
HEBREW: *hol,* phoenix, palm tree, sand (spelling uncertain). Job 29:18 (*See* Firebird)

The verse in the King James Version reads:

Then I said, I shall die in my nest, and I shall multiply my days as the sand.

In other texts, "sand" is replaced by "palm tree" for another symbol of longevity, and in others the symbol is the *phoenix,* that legendary bird that was supposed to burn itself in its own nest and then rise from its ashes completely restored to youth and life. Usually you can help unravel such riddles by consulting the same passage in another language, but the words for "palm tree" and "phoenix" are as much alike in Egyptian as they are in Greek.

The New English Bible solves the problem by putting "sand" in the text and adding "or phoenix" in a footnote. Since the phoenix myth is thought to have been started by watchers who saw drab brown young birds suddenly appear in spring in the brilliant plumage of fully adult males, you can mark this passage on Bible bird walk by looking for young birds of any kind that perform this feat of phoenix-like magic. And since the fabled phoenix was supposed to be fairly long-legged and to wear a crest, what better stand-in could you find than the young cockerel of a ring-necked pheasant just coming into full array? And since the word "phoenix" always carries with it a hint of red—from the red dye developed by the Phoenicians—the enlarged red wattles on the handsome head of a courting cock pheasant will fulfill this part of the description, too. Also, the Phoenicians may have brought the first pheasants to the Holy Land, finding them as Jason and the Argonauts were said to have done in Greek legend, on the shores of the river Phasis near the Black Sea.

Pigeon
HEBREW: *yonah, beni-yonah* (*see* Dove and Pigeon)

Plover
HEBREW: *anafah* (*see* Birds of Abomination: No. 18, anafah)
       dukifath (*see* Birds of Abomination: No. 19, dukifath)

The lapwing, named in the King James Bible for *duki-*

fath, is a member of the plover family. In some of the older texts "plover" was also suggested as a possible translation of *anafah,* the heron-like birds. Among several Israeli plovers also seen in North America are the Mongolian plover, the snowy (or Kentish) plover, the black-bellied plover, and the ruddy turnstone. The lapwing, too, is sometimes seen on our Atlantic coast from Baffin Island on down to North Carolina, South Carolina, and the Bahamas—but more as an accidental visitor, not a regular one.

Porphyrion

This is a Greek word borrowed by the translators of the early Catholic Bibles as a translation of the word *anafah* (*see* Birds of Abomination: No. 18, anafah). Because the meaning of this color word changed from reddish to reddish purple over the years, the bird it named changed, too. At one time it named the flamingo of reddish tinge, but in later years was a name for the purple gallinule.

Poultry (*see* Chicken, Cock, Hen; Fattened Fowl)

Quail

HEBREW: *selav,* echoic, or plump. Exodus 16:13; Numbers
     11:31–32; Psalm 105:40
     ahf, fowl. Psalm 78:26–29
APOCRYPHA: 2 Esdras 1:15; Wisdom 16:2; 19:11–12

The quail flutters into Bible passages because of its custom of migrating in large flocks over long distances—a trait rare among the Order of Chicken-like Birds, the Galliformes, to which quail, partridge, pheasants, peacocks, and barnyard fowl belong, aligned together in the Family Phasianidae, while turkeys, guinea fowl and grouse are each in a different family within this same order. All of these others change terrain only by wandering afoot, coming down from the hills to the warmer valleys each autumn, moving in eat-as-they-go journeys from windswept uplands to sheltered thickets along the streams. But the *Coturnix* quail launches out from its winter home in Africa on whirring wings, and when at last it crosses a river, or a marsh, or a desert where it dare not stop, using the last ounce of stored energy, it flutters down in utter exhaustion, making just such an easy-come-by meal as the wandering Israelites found in answer to their prayers to God.

The vast numbers of quail described in this scene sound almost unbelievable, yet only fifty or sixty years ago the fowlers of Egypt were netting over two million quail each year and exporting them to gourmet markets in Europe. In the 1920s they still came in great numbers, but by the end of the 1930s there were only small bands or none at all. They are not yet extinct, like our passenger pigeons which also once came in vast hordes that darkened the sky, but it is not likely that anyone ever again will see flocks of the size that fed Moses and the Israelites.

These *Coturnix* quail have been domesticated in Japan and seem such a valuable game bird that there have been several attempts to get them established here as breeding wild birds, like the pheasants. Hundreds of birds were released in southern states and seemed to nest successfully, but when autumn came they migrated in the same southerly route that instinct told them to follow—and never reached land. The restless, sky-to-sky waves of the Atlantic Ocean offered no safe resting place.

In their stead we can look for the bobwhite quail in eastern states and even in some western ones. They turn up almost anywhere along country lanes, scurrying ahead of your car like so many little old ladies in brown shawls and peaked bonnets of Queen Victoria's day. By contrast, the California quail and the mountain quail seem Spanish knights in armor, little helmeted Don Quixotes off to tilt at windmills.

Besides these three most abundant species, there are three more little stand-ins for selav the plump one: the scaled quail, the Gambel's quail, and the harlequin quail—all birds of the southwest. And just in case that the name *selav* is both the word for chubby plumpness and also an echo of the quail's liquid whistle, you'll want to listen as well as look. If what you're listening for is the echo of *see-lav, see-lav* rather than *bobwhite,* well, *see-lav* is probably what you'll hear. In the old days, farmers used to say that the bobwhite whistle was a weather forecast, announcing rain in a two-syllable call of "More wet! More wet!" and clearing weather in a three-note "No more wet! No more wet!" Whether that's the role for quail in your bailiwick is something you'll have to find out for yourself.

Raven (and all raven kin)

HEBREW: *oreb, orebim,* echoic, the croaker(s). Genesis 8:7; Leviticus 11:15; Deuteronomy 14:14; 1 Kings 17:4–6; Job 38:41; Song of Songs 5:11; Isaiah 34:11; Zephaniah 2:14

beni-oreb, sons, young or kindred of oreb. Psalm 147:7–9

orebim anahal, orebim of the valley. Proverbs 30:17

GREEK: *korax,* echoic. Luke 12:24

See Birds of Abomination: No. 6, oreb; Crow; Jackdaw; Magpie; Young Birds

The raven is the first bird to be mentioned by a specific name in the Bible, and its early appearance in the story of Noah's Ark (Genesis 8:7) makes it one of the first birds on written records. The raven holds claim to unwritten birdlore, too, for it is known all around the northern half of the globe, and has many a role in Nordic sagas, the legends of North American Indian tribes, and the folk tales told around desert campfires and Eskimo snow lodges.

Here in Genesis it is offered the role of messenger when Noah seeks to learn whether the glimpse of distant mountaintops means that there is enough dry land for his family to begin rebuilding homes, find food and growing things again. Only a bird would be able to bring back such word, yea or nay, and Noah must have thought that the raven—strong of wing and adventurous of spirit—would be the best choice. Then, too, its black wings would be easily followed by watch-

ers at the Ark windows, even against gray skies, while those
of a smaller or paler bird would be lost.

So Noah brought it to the window, his fingers cupped
over the folded wings, then opened his hands to let the bird
launch skyward with alternate flap and soaring glide—the
typical raven flight pattern—and then disappear from sight.
Presently those at the window could see it again, and it would
continue to appear and disappear all through the day, but it
did not return to the Ark, at least not while watchers at the
Ark windows could see any shadow of wings against twilight
sky. Then Noah must have remembered that raven is an eater
of carrion and would have found plenty of such fare exposed
by the falling waters . . . that it is a bird of the hill, not used
to nesting in cotes along a garden wall, which the Ark resem-
bled, and would not have had any need or instinct for returning to such quarters, as doves would do. The fault had been
Noah's for making the wrong choice, but down through the
ages the raven has had to bear the blame, becoming the symbol of ill omen and even death, the companion of witches and
wizards and the embodiment of lost souls.

The raven's black feathers and ominous croak added to
this superstitious aura, especially for ravens that learned to
talk, and it permeated the beliefs of other religions besides
the Judeo-Christian lore. But whatever evil clung to the raven's feathers from pagan tales was enhanced by its failure as
messenger for Noah, and when other Bible lines seemed to
say that God himself had to feed the raven fledglings, since
their parents did not do so, the failure to return to the Ark
was taken as proof that a raven has no care for mate or young.

Anyone who watched ravens would soon learn that these
birds are loyal and considerate mates and devoted parents.
You also learn that young raven nestlings squawk for food
with louder and longer cries than almost any other species you
could name, so they were the example that came immediately
to mind when the writers of Job 38:41 and Psalm 147:7–9
wanted to call up a reminder of how God the Father provides
for all small wildlings, giving each its food—not with his own

hand but by providing parent ravens—as he does almost all wild parents, beast or bird—with the instincts to choose the food best suited to infant needs, to bring such food again and again as long as the opened beaks and lifted voices reveal hunger's need. The newer translations that ask who provides the raven with its prey or quarry (rather than with its food, as in the King James Bible) give a clearer idea of God's role. Because young ravens cry with such persistent demand, parent ravens bring more and more food, often too much even for growing youngsters that consume their own weight in food each day—as most nestlings of all kinds do in order to reach full growth in such a brief span. Consequently, unneeded food is sometimes left untouched on the nest rim, or even pushed off to the ground below where some other hungry meat-eater may seize it for a welcome meal.

Certain scholars have suggested that the prophet Elijah was thus fed on the ravens' surplus provender, not by birds that brought meat directly to his hand at the command of God (1 Kings 17:4–6). Other scholars claim that the "orebim" involved in this rescue mission were nor ravens at all but citizens of the nearby town of Orbo, who would, of course, have had an almost duplicate name. Still other scholars who refuse to see a miracle in this passage suggest that traveling pack peddlers fed the prophet, for peddlers were called "ravens" and both birds and peddlers were called "thieves" in the jargon of the times. Whatever the truth in the matter, the ravens and most other meat-eating birds do sometimes bring more food to their nests than their young ones can eat —or perhaps more than they can handle at the moment, so that a fresh-caught rabbit or fish or quail is pushed over the nest rim by squabbling youngsters. Not too long ago newspapers carried the story of hikers lost in the woods without weapons who managed to subsist on just such fare from a hawk's nest.

But firm belief that the ravens brought both bread and meat to Elijah at God's command has remained a part of Judeo-Christian teaching, restoring some of the good name that this bird of blackness lost as Noah's unreturning messenger. And the lines from Job and the Psalms, declaring that God himself made feeding the ravens his special charge, were remembered all the more by Christians who read the Gospel according to St. Luke, finding in 12:24 this forthright command to observe these black-feathered birds and learn their ways, which were also the ways of the Lord:

Consider the ravens: for they neither sow nor reap; which have neither storehouse nor barn; and God feedeth them: how much more are ye better than the fowls?

In Matthew 6:26 the same scene is described, but with Jesus asking his followers to look at all birds and so learn of a Heavenly Father's care, not just at ravens. It seems possible that Jesus spoke with both wordings. We can almost see him there on the mountainside, the gray craggy rocks behind him rising up like a throne against the blue sky, his voice low, but clear and vibrant with the earnestness of his message.

"Behold the birds," he might have begun. "Look at the birds." And then—perhaps—a familiar black shadow came soaring into view, catching his eye for more specific example so that he said, "Consider the raven. . . ."

In the early Christian centuries these words gave ravens a special significance among devout believers, so that watching ravens and watching over them, feeding them, became a chosen way of life for hermits striving to live their lives as Christ commanded. Today we almost have to be hermits ourselves to see a raven, for relentless hunting and wanton destruction have driven these birds deeper and deeper into their mountain retreats. However, the word is getting around that ravens give good scavenger service and should be protected, and gradually they are returning to some of their old haunts, even in eastern states where they were so long absent.

Ravens have learned that they are safe in certain areas where hunting them is forbidden, and they have also learned that speeding cars on the highways leave many mangled bodies of small woods creatures that will serve them well as food. So now ravens follow the cars—instead of bears or hunters with bow and arrow or priests with meat for the altar—and consequently any national highway through wooded hill country is the place to look for a raven: Blue Ridge Parkway . . . Skyline Drive . . . Rocky Mountain passes . . . the highway west along the Columbia River, through Idaho, Washington, Oregon.

A raven is a raven is a raven. There are white-necked ravens in our southwest, just as there are fan-tailed ravens in Israel, but "the" raven is *Corvus corax,* the same species here as in Bible lands and lines.

Ravenous Birds

HEBREW: *ayit,* bird of prey. Isaiah 46:11; Ezekiel 39:4

See also the many references to the birds that raven (tear and eat) human flesh: *Old Testament,* Genesis 40:19; Deuteronomy 28:26; 1 Samuel 17:44–46; 2 Samuel 21:8–10; 1 Kings 14:11; 16:4; 21:24; Psalm 79:2; Isaiah 18:1–6; Jeremiah 7:33; 15:3; 16:4; 19:7; 34:20; Ezekiel 29:5; 31:13; 32:4. *Apocrypha,* 2 Maccabees 9:15; 15:33. *New Testament,* Revelation 18:2.

The ravenous birds mentioned in the Bible are not raven-like except in their feasting on meat and carrion. The English word "raven" comes from Anglo-Saxon and Nordic roots when it is the name of the harsh-voiced bird. When it means to tear at flesh, to seize and carry off things, it comes from the Latin words for thief, greediness, to plunder and loot—and it is only an accident that these words from two different sources are spelled alike in modern English. So "ravenous" birds are the predator species, all predators and scavengers, not just ravens.

According to tradition, the "ravenous bird from the East" in Isaiah 46:11 is supposed to be a figure of speech, a picturesque way of naming an enemy army massed for attack or for the leader of that army, supposedly Cyrus of Persia.

Ravens of the Valley

HEBREW: *orebim anahal.* Proverbs 30:17 (*see* Birds of Abomination: No. 6, oreb)

Since ravens are birds of the hills and crags or upland mesa, not the valleys, it seems logical to mark this name for one of raven kindred, not *Corvus corax,* "the" oreb and chieftain of the clan. The fan-tailed raven might qualify. So might the hooded crow, always found in lowland farming country rather than in lonely hills, and so might the magpie and the jay. In Israel today it seems to name the magpie more often than other species, but there is no real proof that watchers of Old Testament times were as precise in using one name for just one species. Perhaps magpie, jay, crow, rook, and jackdaw were all included.

Certainly all these species do exactly what the lines declare—pick out the eye of whatever carrion or kill they feed upon and eat it first, before they eat any other part of the carcass. All predator and scavenger birds do likewise much of the time, and the verse serves as a reminder that the valley orebim are not alone in this matter, for the beni-nesher also eat the eyes of their prey.

Most Bible texts translate *beni-nesher* as "young eagles" (or sometimes "young vultures") but the word *beni* means kindred, as well as offspring, grown sons and daughters as well as children. This same misunderstanding of the meaning of *beni* led to calling the Israelites led by Moses the "Children of Israel"—as if there weren't an adult in the entire band. Young birds may be especially likely to eat the eyes first, since their beaks may not be strong enough to tear out other portions of a carcass, but this "eyes-first" rule is not limited to young birds by any means. All of eagle kindred—all meat-eating eagles, hawks, and vultures; all predator birds—have this custom.

Even ants seem to attack the eyes first, and if you find a dead bird on the lawn—killed, perhaps by flying into the deceptive reflection of sky and greenery in a picture window —you will often find that only the eye has been devoured. A much more vivid reminder of this verse from Proverbs came to me one day on the South Carolina island called Hilton Head, when my birding companion and I saw a huge sea turtle washed ashore—dead or half-dead—and a gathering of black vultures, turkey vultures, and fish crows from all up and down the beach. We hurried to give what aid we could to the poor sea creature, but by the time we got there death had provided its own mercy, and all we could do was stare in wonder at the empty eye sockets. Even in that little time they had been picked clean.

Superstitious folk of olden times believed that eating the eyes gave the birds unusually keen vision. Some even said that being kind to ravens would help a blind person regain his own lost sight—as if the bird had vision to spare and could bestow it at will on others less fortunate. Still others said that vision could be restored only by eating a raven's heart burned to ashes in certain ceremonial rites.

The real explanation of the custom may be that any part of the carcass is edible from the predator's viewpoint, and the eye is easiest to eat and therefore first. Also, it may only be easy to pry out in the first moments of death. Also possible is the suggestion that the eye is taken first and quickly so that the dying creature cannot see its despoilers and fight back. Certainly it is true that a blinded bird loses its will to fight, more often than not—that is why men who set decoys put out the eyes or sew them shut, and hunters who train hawks and falcons also used to sew shut the eyelids with fine thread that could later be removed. The hoods worn by hunting falcons when not in pursuit of game serve the same purpose, more humanely, and the ancient falconers who first devised this trick may have taken their hint from watching kindred of oreb the raven and nesher the eagle.

Ring Dove (*see* Dove and Pigeon)

Ringtail
HEBREW: *da'ah* (*see* Birds of Abomination: No. 4, da'ah)

"Ringtail" is a nickname given to any bird with a dark band or ring across the end of its tail, or perhaps several bands, dark against lighter color. The female marsh hawk has such markings of brown-on-buff, seen much more clearly than any markings on the smaller gray male; and the immature golden eagle has an even more striking pattern of white tail feathers tipped in dark brown or black. The white changes to dark as the bird matures, and adult eagles were often mistaken for a different species from their ring-tailed young—even by expert birders like Alexander Wilson. Male and female marsh hawks were mistaken for two species, also. Probably the marsh hawk, a bird that has much of the kite's gliding flight pattern, was intended here by the ringtail name.

Sand-partridge
HEBREW: *kippoz*. Isaiah 34:15
See Birds of Doom; Darter; Partridge

The word *kippoz* is translated "sand-partridge" only in the New English Bible. Translators of the New American Bible, the Revised Standard Version, and the King James Bible all thought it was some kind of owl. Authors of the Jewish Holy Scriptures and the American Standard Version thought it was a kind of snake, and this combination suggests the snakebird, *Anhinga rufa,* a denizen of just such lonely places as the lines portray.

Since "sand-partridge" is not the official name of any species, the bird named here may be either the desert partridge or the sandgrouse, another desert bird with sand-colored camouflage plumage. There are four species of sandgrouse in Israel and all of them, like the partridge, gather at water holes each morning and evening. Colonel Richard Meinertzhagen, who has written so much about birds of this region, describes how the parent birds bring back water to their nestlings, both in their bills and on their dampened breast feathers. Watchers also tell how the sandgrouse can drink without lifting their heads, as most other birds must do, and this ability is one of the reasons that the sandgrouse family, Pteroclidae, is classified in the Order Columbiformes with doves and pigeons, which have the same skill.

Neither the sandgrouse nor the desert partridge is known by kippoz name in Israel today. But both *kore* for partridge and *katah* for sandgrouse are written with three Hebrew characters that look much like the letters of *kippoz,* and readers might reasonably assume that any one of the three names might be miscopied for the other.

There are no members of the sandgrouse family in North America, and if this is indeed a Bible bird we will have to match it on our birdwalk by watching the drinking technique of doves and pigeons. North American grouse are in a completely different family and order—Family Tetraonidae, Order Galliformes—and along with the other members of this chicken-like group drink by tilting back their heads to let the water run down their throats.

Sea Gull, Sea Mew (*see* Birds of Abomination: No. 9, shahaf)

Singing of Birds, Songbirds
HEBREW: *zippor, zipporim,* the chirper(s), birds. Psalm 104:12; Ecclesiastes 12:4

    banoth-shir, daughters of music (singing). Ecclesiastes 12:4

    zamir, singing of birds, nightingale. Song of Songs 2:12
APOCRYPHA: Wisdom 17:18

Bird song as the symbol of springtime marks one of the most quoted Bible passages, Song of Songs 2:12:

For, lo, the winter is past, the rain is over and gone; the flowers appear on the earth; the time of the singing of birds is come, and the voice of the turtledove is heard in our land.

But *zamir,* the word for singing, changes with only one different letter to mean "pruning of vines," and the New American Bible, among others, has this reading. Certain Hebrew scholars, however, not only keep the echo of bird song, but say that zamir names one singer in particular, the nightingale, the bird that has always been the symbol for heavenly music in Old World lore and legend.

Two birds in the Holy Land share the name: the true nightingale, *Luscinia megarhynchos,* and the thrush-nightingale, *Luscinia luscinia,* both much alike in thrush-toned brown plumage and in lyric springtime song. During the rest of the year their vocalizing is largely limited to chips and churks, making the fluting trills of their courting song sound all the more ecstatic, and such a heavenly song from birds so humbly dressed has always caught the poetic fancy of listeners. It is quite possible that the bulbul, another modestly feathered bird famous for lilting spring song, also shared the zamir name, even though it belongs to a different family. Also sharing the name, at least in folk speech, was surely the little bluethroat, *Luscinia svecica* (listed by some authors as *Cyanosylvia svecica*), a close relative of both nightingales and having much the same lyric spring-song.

Of all these springtime carolers, only the bluethroat comes to North America, and it has nested here only in Alaska. But a pair of red-whiskered bulbuls, close cousins of the bulbul of Israel, escaped from a bird-dealer's cage in Florida in 1962 and raised a family in the wild, and their offspring have been making themselves at home ever since.

If neither Florida bulbuls nor Alaska bluethroats cross your bird-walk trail, you can always find a stand-in among their thrush cousins. And the mockingbird, though not a nightingale relative, does share its custom of moonlight serenade. There is something so ethereal about bird song amid night stillness that you wonder if the "songs in the night" of Job 35:10 and Psalm 42:8 echo nightingale music, too.

Zippor echoes a twittering voice, not nightingale ecstasy, but chirping songsters were nevertheless counted as something to be thankful for, one of the many gifts from God to man, and the lines of Psalm 104 rejoice in the sun on the water, white clouds in the sky, the touch of a Presence like brushing wings and an echo of bird song from the cedar's sheltering branches.

Ecclesiastes 12:4 may carry an appreciation of bird music, too, for the lines could picture a household hushed at twilight for the homecoming of a man of wealth and importance, too harried now after a busy day even to want to hear the entertainment his professional musicians usually provide, waving away the men with flute and lyre, the bevy of young girl singers. Yet suddenly there comes a ripple of birdsong outside the window—a nightingale, a lark, or a thrush—and now he sits upright in listening wonder, hushing the others to silence with imperious gesture, not wanting to miss a note of the ethereal carol. And the girls listen with him, humbly. Daughters of music—devotees of music—though they are, they cannot sing like these birds and they know it. "All the daughters of music shall be brought low," as the King James Version phrases their humbling.

However, the recent translation by the Jewish Publication Society interprets the whole scene as a picture of the infirmities of old age—an old man's voice as shrill as a bird's and his hearing so poor that flute and lyre and singing voices all seem mere whispers.

The scene is also changed in the newer Christian translations. In both the New English and the New American Bibles the reading seems to be a prediction of the time when there will be no more singing birds, no chirping sparrows, and "daughters of music" becomes a picturesque name for songbirds, rather than the trained girl singers that were often part of wealthy households in olden times. Remember your Creator now, the lines give warning, before the time of troubles comes—and the next lines echo with the grim forecast of polluted air and water and sky, pestilence and death

and dearth, when even the sparrows can scarce be heard and
no birds sing (*see* No More Birds).

The places where you can no longer hear bird song are
all too numerous and there is no need to cite them here. But
if you are among those who do not listen in vain, who still
"rise up at the voice of a bird," and count it among your
blessings, then surely you have a special memory to mark the
lines. For me it came on a June evening, while I climbed an
Oregon hillside at the back door of the house that had just
become our home after years of wanderings, and was suddenly
caught spellbound as the chimes from the golden throat of a
Swainson's thrush soared skyward from the hawthorn tree beside me—and Heaven seemed very close.

Perhaps it will be the song of the meadowlark that brings
Heaven close to you in the voice of a bird, as it has done for
many prairie folk when drought and dust and despair made
the world seem dark. The skylark filled the same role for Old
World people, and you think of the look of hope on the face
of the girl in the painting by Jules Breton named "Song of
the Lark." Or it could be a hermit thrush, a wood thrush, a
mockingbird; the *cheer-up-cheeralie* of the robin, the *cher-
ami* of the redwinged blackbirds—who certainly have no ex-
cuse to sing in French even if "dear friend" is their message.
Perhaps, since they are native to North America only, they are
singing *Cher-o-kee* and bringing us wistful reminder of long-
gone days with Indian campfires and tepees and soft mocca-
sin feet on the Cherokee Trail.

There's a magic in bird song that makes its own pictures,
its own words. The white-crowned sparrow seems to tune up
with the opening bars of the loved hymn, "My Faith Looks
up to Thee. . . ." And while the white-throated sparrow, its
sweet-voiced cousin, may seem to chime "Goodnight, fishermen" to listeners with rod and reel, and mourn for "Old Sam
Peabody" to certain New Englanders, those who hear it on
Bible bird walk may find the voice an echo of medieval choir
boys and the words: "Deo! Gloria! Gloria! Gloria!" sung to
notes of:

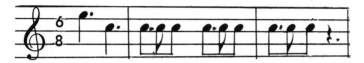

Sparrow

HEBREW: *zippor, zipporim,* chirper(s), bird(s). Translated as "sparrows" in some versions of Psalms 84:3; 102:7; Proverbs 26:2; Ecclesiastes 12:4; Hosea 11:11

APOCRYPHA: Tobit 2:10–11 (*or* swallows, birds)

GREEK: *struthion,* sturdy-legged. Matthew 10:29–31; Luke 12:6–7

No matter what the word *zipporim* may mean in other lines—small birds, songbirds, birds of any kind and size—in some lines the name seems to fit the sparrows best of all, the little ground birds of brown feathering that seem drab or humble and unassuming, giving no claim to glamour or beauty.

The watcher who really knows sparrows will deny that drab coloring denotes drab character, but then too many people never give a sparrow a second glance—let alone a second chance to prove its worth. The song sparrows who make our yard their home are the cockiest birds in the garden, driving away robins and towhees from the bird bath near their nest, even attacking a 15-inch snake. They are also the "singingest" birds in sight, giving forth with their happy melody any day of the year, any hour of the day—and sometimes even in the night, waking up with sleepy whisper-song or full trill and then falling back to sudden silence.

Yet sparrows undeniably look drab, no matter how they act, in spite of an occasional handsome frill of black bib or silver or golden crown or rosy cap, and they are—above all— ground birds, scratching for seeds and crumbs in dust and dirt and fallen leaves or even city gutters. When the poet looks for contrast to the free-flying swallows, always on the wing, glinting in the sunlight as they dip and dive and swoop, the bird for opposite behavior has to be the sparrow. The sparrow "wanders" or merely "flutters" in Proverbs 26:2, while the swallow "flies" or "flits" or "darts."

Sparrows are also gregarious, for the most part, as if trying to live up to the saying that misery loves company. Therefore, a sparrow suddenly left alone on the housetop—because of a broken wing, perhaps—would surely be as sad and solitary a spectacle as any comparison that could be made. So, in Psalm 102 when the mourner has already compared his loneliness to the hermit ways of the marabou and the desert owl, he adds with telling picture:

I watch, and am as a sparrow alone upon the house top.

You can see it there, alone, fluttering a useless wing, watching the others of its kind fly off, calling out with the piping plea of the nestling, often used by adult birds in distress, or with the high-pitched distress cry that is recognized by all species, no matter which kind of bird does the calling.

Or perhaps a fledgling cowbird, no longer being fed by its bewildered and exhausted foster-parent, may give you an echo of this "sparrow"—this "least one"—alone on the housetop. Birds do not have human emotions; they cannot project their sorrow of the moment into a mental picture of the lonely days ahead, the coming hunger, the certainty of death; but they can respond to the sensation as it happens—hunger, cold, fear, illness, pain, thirst—and also to the inability to follow the flock as instinct bids them, if flocking is the way of their kind. So the abandoned cowbird cries with sharper and sharper voice, echoing the sad tones heard by the psalmist long ago in Jerusalem.

Instead of being crippled, the bird left alone by its companions might have been a fledgling just orphaned by a slingshot, a stone tossed with evil purpose or even idle carelessness, or by a prowling predator. The saddest bird cries I have ever heard came from a baby goldfinch, left in just this fix. One moment it had been at the roadside begging its parents for another bite, and the next moment a speeding car had swerved off the pavement into the gravel—for reasons unknown—leaving only one bewildered and frightened and still-hungry baby. Some house sparrows settled down for a moment and then whirred off and away, looking for better gleaning among the breadcrumbs scattered in our yard, and the goldfinch managed to flutter after them on wobbly wings. There on the grass it piped eagerly, hopping from sparrow to sparrow with open beak, the piping getting louder and more plaintive with each rejection. It piped so pleadingly that at last a female house sparrow—busily gathering crumbs for her own nestlings—turned to ram a beakful down the open mouth that was far too small to accept such bounty. She tried again, failed again, and flew off, but when she returned a few moments later for another beakful, the pleading piper ran to her in recognition and this time she had just started her gathering and had an offering that was goldfinch size. A few times more she stopped her marketing to feed the orphan, but there were long waits between times and during one of them the baby managed to nibble a crumb for itself. But until this skill came to the rescue at instinct's bidding, all it could do was wait and pipe and pipe again with the loneliest cry a heart could know. Surely the psalmist made no mistake when he chose a little rooftop bird for simile, a bird of sociable flocking habits like the finch and sparrow.

The house sparrow, *Passer domesticus,* is one of the birds you can look for on Bible bird walk and know that this very species will also be seen in almost any street or roadway in Bible lands. Here in America it is most commonly called "English sparrow"—because the first birds of this species imported here in 1850 had come from England—but it is native to many places besides England, including much of Europe and Asia and parts of North Africa. Ornithologists classify it as a finch—a weaver finch, to be exact—and not a true sparrow at all. But "sparrow" has long been the folk name for all small brown birds, and *Passer domesticus* qualifies in color, if not in anatomy.

The weaver finch and its close kin are all natives to the

Old World and are listed in the Family Ploceidae. True sparrows and other finches, buntings, and grosbeaks are all in the Family Fringillidae—a large group with many subdivisions. Among those seen in both Israel and North America are the red crossbill of northern forests; the brambling, an occasional visitor on both coasts; the hawfinch, another straggler, and the European goldfinch, *Carduelis carduelis,* introduced a century ago in places here and there across the North American continent from Oregon to Long Island and on down to Bermuda. Most of these imports soon vanished, but once there was such a thriving colony near Massapequa, Long Island, that anyone who wanted to see this bird of Old World legend could simply take a car or a bicycle or horse and buggy and go there, as you'd go to a duck pond in the park. But a housing development in the mid 1950's took away the nesting site, so the birds had to move elsewhere, and it seems that many of them never found a suitable place, never nested again.

Nevertheless, reports of European goldfinches keep turning up—from Westtown, Pennsylvania, in 1962 . . . Cleveland, Ohio, in 1966 . . . Marshfield, Massachusetts, in 1969 . . . Bound Brook, New Jersey, in 1970. . . . Some of these may be escaped cage birds, of course, rather than survivors from old plantings or Massapequa refugees, but however they got here, it's good to know that some of us on Bible bird walk may see this bird with gold-black-and-white feathering and a blood-red visor that gave it a role in the legends of the Cross.

Three other birds share this legend—the barn swallow, the robin, and the red crossbill—all because they have red feathers like the goldfinch. Long ago some unknown storyteller started the tale of how the birds came to the dying Saviour on the Cross, trying to ease his pain by pulling out the nails and thorns. The more they tugged, the faster the blood flowed, staining their feathers—even twisting the tips of the crossbill's beak—and legend-weavers declared that the red stain and the crossed bill were given the birds as badges of honor on that very day, so that all who saw the birds forever after would remember the One they had tried to comfort.

Other legends said that the robin had received its first red stain by singeing its feathers as it hovered close to the brazier fire in the stable at Bethlehem, trying to fan the dying embers back to warmth, lest the newborn Child grow cold. And they pictured the goldfinch with the Baby Jesus, too, saying that it had been just a lifeless toy of yellow clay—a present from some village lad—till the Christ Child took pity on it and clapped his hands to bid it come to life and fly away. And the legends said, too, that the Boy Jesus always fed the robins and goldfinches and sparrows when they came to his door, feeling for them and for the gentle doves a special fondness. Artists who heard the stories often added these birds to their paintings of the Christ Child, letting the blood-stained feathers give the silent message that his death on the cross was ordained from the beginning. So if you cannot find a European goldfinch on a walk by field and stream, you can find one in a painting of Madonna and Child and bird by artists as famous as Raphael, Tiepolo, Benozzo Gozzoli, and Aretino, or by artists whose names remain unknown. You will find an owl in other paintings—always the symbol of death —and a peacock in others for the symbol of eternal life; and still in other portraits of Mother and Child the small bird will be the robin or swallow.

But whatever role other small ground birds may have had in fact or legend, the name of "sparrow" was always given the lowest rank, the symbol for least, last, and most worthless. Even as food they did not count for much, and the vendors in market used to pluck them and dip them in spicy sauce, crowding two or three of them together on a stick—or even four or five—so that they'd make a decent mouthful for a hungry man when they were browned over the brazier coals.

So Jesus must have seen them, and knew that his disciples had seen them, too, knew how little they cost, how everyone said, "Oh, just sparrows"—counting them next to nothing.

And so when he wanted a phrase to picture God's infinite care for all living things and for mankind most of all, "sparrows" was the word that came to mind. The translations of Matthew 10:29–31 and Luke 12:6–7 remind readers how sparrows are sold two for a farthing . . . two for a penny . . . five for a mere two cents—or whatever coin seems smallest—and then reach right for your heart with assurance that God sees and knows and cares what happens to these least ones—and cares even more for what happens to all of us.

"His eye is on the sparrow," an old hymn echoes with soaring note, "and I know He watches me. . . ."

Speckled Bird (of Prey)

HEBREW: *ayit-tsabua,* speckled, streaked (*tsabua*) bird of prey (*ayit*). Jeremiah 12:9

The King James Version of this puzzling passage reads:

Mine heritage is unto me as a speckled bird, the birds round about are against her. . . .

and we cannot help wondering why a bird should be abused merely for spotted, speckled, or streaked plumage.

Yet the prophets of old spoke with picturesque imagery, using simile and metaphor, making comparison to homely things that listeners would understand, not fanciful ideas beyond common experience. So we know that the ayit-tsabua, the speckled bird of Jeremiah's message, must have been a bird that the Israelites knew well, both by name and nature.

Unfortunately, the words do not bring the same instant recognition to us today. Checking back to find that the Hebrew word is *ayit*—bird of prey—not just a bird of any kind, clears the way a little. But some scholars feel that it wasn't *ayit* in the original script, but *hayyah,* the word for wild beasts, and that this spotted beast was the hyena. The hyena does fit the scene, in a way, for both hyenas and vultures vie

for feeding rights at a carcass, one turning against the other
as the lines describe.

But if the word is *ayit*, there is a bird that fits the scene
even better—the hawk-eagle of the Holy Land, also called
Bonelli's eagle, measuring a little more than the larger hawks
but still short of the largest eagles by a good 10 inches in
length. In Israel today it is still called ayit, although the full
name in common use seems to be "eagle-like" ayit, rather
than "speckled."

That speckling—or spotting or streaking—is a recognizable trademark, however, for this bird's Latin label is *Hieraëtus fasciatus*—and *fasciatus* means streaked, striped, banded.
All the larger eagles of the Holy Land have solid-toned breast
feathering, mottled, perhaps, with individual feathers shading
from buff to brown, but not striped or streaked—except
among a few juveniles not yet in full feather. But Bonelli's
eagle is streaked of breast, and so are all the hawks and falcons that share its preference for dining on smaller birds
rather than on rodents—the peregrine, the goshawk, the sparrow hawk (*Accipiter badius*, much larger than our bird of the
same name, more like our Cooper's hawk), and their very
menu ensures that all the birds roundabout would be turned
against them, as Jeremiah pictured his streak-fronted predator. In Jeremiah's own day, and for many centuries thereafter, hawks were common sights, birds that everyone knew
by reputation if not by individual name, and "streak-fronted
ayit" might well have served as a special name for Bonelli's
eagle and a group name for all the *Accipiter* hawks and falcons, too.

Bonelli's eagle, for all its size, has a falcon-like manner
of swooping and diving in among bush and bramble in dash-
dart raiding, snatching a startled turtledove from its perch, a
robin from its nest. Off it goes with its prize and more often
than not it is pursued by the victim's angry mate, even an
entire flock, all shrieking invective that doesn't need to be
translated to be understood.

No Bonelli's eagle will be seen on an American bird walk to illustrate Jeremiah's lines, but any *Accipiter* hawk will take the same role, swooping down to snatch up egg or nestling or full-grown robin or sparrow or lark, and then dashing off so swiftly that only the streaked breast can be noted for a remembered clue to the robber's identity. The Cooper's hawk that haunts our hill chanced one day to make off with some prize that the neighborhood crows considered their own property, and I was called to the window by the irate chorus of cawing "Stop, thief!" cries. The hawk went calmly on her way at even-beat wing stroke, not even turning her head to notice the three black figures in pursuit as they circled and recircled about her, now above, now below her wide wings. Now she found the spire of a tall Douglas fir in her path and settled into its branches without fuss or flurry, staring straight ahead—or seeming to do so, although the wide-angle vision granted all hawks must have given her full view.

Round and round the black-winged protesters swooped and squawked, keeping well out of range of her hooked beak with last-minute wing-over and body-roll maneuver, yet coming closer and closer with each circuit. Now the hawk admitted their presence—and the havoc a crow's beak could wreak upon her always vulnerable eyes—and she hunched up one shoulder for eye guard each time they passed, turning her head from left to right and back again in wary watching.

Each time she turned, the streaked breast showed plainly, and there was the speckled bird of prey from Jeremiah, with all the birds roundabout—or at least three very angry crows —all turned against her. At just the right moment she launched herself up and away, ending the scene, and the weary-winged crows did not follow.

Stork

HEBREW: *hasidah,* bird of kindness. Leviticus 11:19; Deuteronomy 14:18; Job 39:13 (misreading for *haserah; see* Ostrich); Psalm 104:17 (*see* Nests); Jeremiah 8:7 (*see* Migrating Birds); Zechariah 5:9, stork-winged women.

See also Birds of Abomination: No. 17, hasidah

Swallow

HEBREW: *deror,* bird of freedom. Psalm 84:3; Proverbs 26:2
  sis, echoic. Isaiah 38:14; Jeremiah 8:7
APOCRYPHA: Tobit 2:10–11 (*or* sparrows, birds); Baruch
  6:21, 22

The word "swallow" in our own bird books has come
to be the label only for species of the Family Hirundinidae,
with the barn swallow, *Hirundo rustica,* its best-loved member, known all around the globe. The barn swallow's deeply
forked tail gave us the phrase "swallow-tailed" for use in describing other things of similar chevron pattern, and beginning birders are sometimes surprised to find that all swallows
do not have this trademark, making do with only a small
notch.

But one feature all swallows share is the ability to wing
aloft hour after hour, eating insects as they go, and no need
to alight at all, except to build a nest and rear their young or
perhaps pause for a few minutes of sociable gathering on a
wire or branch. This talent gave them the name *deror,* bird
of freedom, not bound to earth by any need to scratch for
daily weed or worm, and *deror* is used in contrast to *zippor,*
the little ground birds of Psalm 84:3 and Proverbs 26:2.

In the passages of Isaiah and Jeremiah that mark the
swallow as one of the migrating birds who well know the
regular time of coming and going, the word is either *sis* or
agar (*see* Migrating Birds). Either fits the swallow, since *sis*
could be counted an echoic duplication—like the word "swallow"—of its lisping cry, while *agar* means "gatherers," and
swallows do gather for migration in flocks of incredible size.
In Israel today they are known by another word that means
the same thing—*synunah*—while *sis* has become the name for
the swifts.

If you have a bird book to tell you that swifts have
curved wings like a sickle or a new moon, while swallows have

straight-line wings, and you also have binoculars to get both birds in close view, then you can easily tell the difference between them and use a different name for each. Seeing that difference was not so easy in olden times, and most people of bygone days let one word serve for both. Whatever name was used for swallows was also given to other free-flying sky-rovers too small to be hawks or falcons. Terns are still called "sea swallows" in many places, and petrels and gannets have also shared this name. The nightjars were "night swallows." The little iridescent sunbirds—much like our hummingbirds —also shared the swallow name, for they are the very opposite of groundlings. The pratincole, a plover-like bird, is the "meadow swallow," known by its deeply forked tail. The forked tails on the bee-eaters probably gave them swallow names, too, and the misnomer is supported by the bee-eater custom of eating insects on the wing, swallow-style. Also, it nests in a hole in a river bank—as does the bank swallow— but the two would never be confused, for the bank swallow is a drab camouflage brown, while the bee-eater is one of the most beautiful birds in the realm, feathered in jewel tones of gold and turquoise, amber, bronze, jet.

Neither bee-eater nor pratincole comes to North America, but we have both swifts and swallows to look for on Bible bird walk. Of the three species of Israeli swifts, only one has been seen here—*Apus apus,* the common swift—and that has come only as a rare straggler to Alaska's offshore islands. But of the five swallows still found in the Holy Land, two species are as much at home here as there—the bank swallow, *Riparia riparia,* and the barn swallow. In addition we have several New World swallows—cliff swallow, cave swallow, rough-winged swallow, tree swallow, violet-green swallow, Bahama swallow, and the purple martin.

A few Old World swallows are called "martins" too— from the martial way they defend their nests. And it is interesting to note that words very much like the swallow's Hebrew name of *sis* also have a warlike overtone, used as the name for a war horse or stallion and for a wild and ferocious beast. Perhaps there is something more than just an echo of a swallow's lisping voice in that name after all, and if it isn't of warlike origin, it may mean "long-flying."

The meaning of the words is something you can argue about, but the birds themselves call only for wonder and watching.

Swan

HEBREW: *tinshemeth* (*see* Birds of Abomination: No. 14, tinshemeth)

Both the mute swan and the whooper swan are winter visitors in the Holy Land, though the whooper is rare now and even the mute swan not so abundant as it was in earlier times. The whooper has made only very occasional visits to North America, but has turned up a time or two both in Alaska and on the Atlantic coast as far south as Maine. The mute swan was brought here long ago as a park bird, for it is easier to tame, and escaped birds have set up their own feral colonies in several places—perhaps somewhere near you.

Two North American swans will give you the same graceful picture, either wing-borne against the sky or floating across the dark waters of a northern lake. The whistling swan is far more common than the larger trumpeter swan, but both species have been overhunted in past years, and it may take a special trek to swan country to find them. The national parks in the northwestern states have their swan-holds, and the birds winter wherever the water is free of ice, always going north to nest in Alaska or Canada, though the feral mute swans tend to stay the year around in whatever lake or slough they have claimed a wild home.

The swans do not really belong among Bible birds, since they were named among the Birds of Abomination only by translator's error, but the mistake was a very lucky one for us on Bible bird walk. My first glimpse of wild white swans, floating in airy grace among the drifting ice floes on a Minnesota lake, gave me one of the most beautiful scenes in all my treasured store of birdlore memories.

Swift (*see* Swallow)

Symbolic Birds

In the early years of Christian persecution, when any open affirmation of faith might get the speaker tossed to the lions, the followers of Jesus learned to give their testimony to each other in an exchange of symbols that only Christians understood. One of the first of these was the Greek letter *chi*—written like an X—the initial letter of the name of Christ. The second letter—*rho,* written like a P—was sometimes added in a monogram, the two letters placed one atop the other. Another symbol was the Greek word for fish—*icthys*—for its letters, taken one by one in sequence, form the initial letters of an acrostic of the Greek words meaning "Jesus Christ, Son of God, Saviour." And since a fish can live only in water, the little outline drawing of a fish was a reminder that Jesus began his mission as converts begin the Christian life—with baptism in water.

Birds were soon added to these secret symbols. Any bird that flies was counted the sign of the crucifixion, for birds make the sign of the cross with opened wings each time they take to the air. Also, the dove, especially a white dove, represented the presence of God, since he had appeared in this form at his Son's baptism. Both the phoenix and the peacock became symbols of the Resurrection, for the jewel-feathered bird from India was thought to be immortal, no more subject to death than the legendary phoenix of older superstitions. Using these symbols did not mean that the Christians shared these pagan superstitions—it was belief in the Risen Lord that mattered—but the birds expressed that belief without need for words, a silent sermon.

So, peacock, phoenix, and dove were chalked on walls,

embroidered on kerchiefs and shawls, engraved on signet rings. And the weathervane cock bespoke a silent "Christ is born!" while a picture of a hen gathering her chicks under sheltering wings was a reminder of words that Christ himself had spoken, yearning to bring all Jerusalem to his side with the same loving tenderness. Other words of Jesus were recalled with small birds perched amid a twisting grape arbor, for he had said, "I am the vine; ye are the branches . . ." (John 15:5), and some thought that the comparison was to birds, instead, since the words for birds and branches are much alike, in both Hebrew and the Aramaic dialect that Jesus spoke.

The eagle was one of the secret symbols, too, the wings of the Lord from Old Testament lines and seen at God's throne in a mystic vision that came to John of Patmos (Revelation 4:7–8; 8:13; 12:14).

All of these birds became so much a part of Christian expression that they were used in church murals, stained-glass windows, embroidered altar cloths, carved woodwork for chancel and choirloft, carved stonework for cathedral façade long after the need for secrecy had passed—and we can see them still on many artworks that have survived the years. The famous fourth-century silver chalice of Antioch shows songbirds among the grape vines. The wooden casket for seventh-century Pope Theodore is carved with a peacock. A twelfth-century Danish ballad told about a crowing cock in King Herod's palace, and a sixteenth-century English carol by William Austin gives the crowing cock at Bethlehem talent to tell the world the joyous news. Medieval knights were wont to take their oath on a peacock feather as if it were the Bible, and the pelican—symbol of Christ's atonement for mortal sin—was emblazoned for heraldic emblem.

The Second Commandment (Exodus 20:1–6) forbidding graven images would seem to prohibit such representation, but many of the early Christian leaders—though not all of them—interpreted these lines as a ban against idols, against images to be worshiped, not image and likeness carved or painted to show the beautiful creatures God had created. And when someone challenged this broader interpretation, he was reminded that God himself had ordered that the likeness of winged cherubim be carved on both the sacred Ark and the tabernacle, saying that these and the priests' robes and the holy vessels should be designed "for glory and for beauty" (Exodus 28:40). In later years when Jehovah spoke to David and to Solomon of the building of the temple in Jerusalem, he directed that cherubim be a part of its glory and beauty also, and so it was done.

From the fourth century on through the next two or three hundred years, both Hebrews and Christians seemed to accept this broader interpretation of the Second Commandment, and synagogues of this era, as well as Christian churches, had lifelike designs of birds and beasts on altars and candlesticks and in the mosaic tiles of wall and floor. Among those that have been preserved—at least in part—are the sixth-century mosaics from the synagogues at Beth Alpha and Beth Shean, both with realistic bird designs. Most elaborate of all is the birdlore scene from the fourth-century chapel at Tabgha near the shores of Galilee, not far from Capernaum, designed for the floor of the north transept by artisans who must surely have studied living birds as earnestly as they studied their craft of making pictures with bright-hued squares of limestone tiles.

Part of these tiles were chipped and broken, even destroyed entirely during the centuries when armies of many nations and many faiths warred on Galilean shores; and the Tabgha mosaics were covered over with dirt and debris and forgotten until they were finally rediscovered in the 1930s and the slow work of restoration begun. But they are once more clean and shining and are surely one of the treasures to look for if ever your bird walk with the Bible should take you to the Holy Land—or to keep in pictured likeness if your journey is only in mind and heart.

Thrush (*see* Migrating Birds)

Turtle, Turtledove (*see* Dove and Pigeon)

Visions of Birds and Winged Creatures

OLD TESTAMENT: Genesis 40:17–19; 2 Samuel 22:11; Isaiah 6:2–7; 8:8; Ezekiel 1:5–25; 3:12–14; 10:1–22; 11:22; 17:3–23; Daniel 4:10–33; 7:4–6; Zechariah 5:1–9; Malachi 4:2

NEW TESTAMENT: Matthew 3:16; Mark 1:10; Luke 3:22; John 1:32; Acts 10:9–15; 11:6–10; Revelation 4:7–8; 5:13; 8:13; 9:9; 12:14; 18:2; 19:17–21

The birds seen by pharaoh's baker in the dream interpreted by Joseph, then his fellow prisoner in Egypt, were real enough, even if they came as a vision. They behaved as real birds do, helping themselves to the food in the open basket, displaying the typical boldness of any hungry crow, kite, or raven or even sparrows. And when Joseph foretold that the baker would soon be a dangling corpse, with birds feeding on his flesh, that was in keeping with actuality, too, for vultures, kites, hawks, and eagles all feed on human flesh as they do on other meat when occasion offers, and a similar incident is described in 2 Samuel 21:8–10 (*see also* Ravenous Birds). Only the dream itself had mystical meaning.

But in other dreams and visions of Bible lines, the birdlike creatures themselves are supernatural beings—winged lions and leopards; a winged calf; women with wings of an eagle or of a stork; winged ones with the faces of eagle, lion, ox, or human; a king appearing with eagle feathers and eagle talons. Also of mystical vision were the six-winged seraphim shown to Isaiah (6:2) and the cherubim described to Moses (Exodus 25:18–20; 26:1,31) and to David and Solomon (1 Kings 6:23–35; 7:29; 8:6–7; 1 Chronicles 28:18; 2 Chronicles 3:7–14; 5:7–8).

Vulture

HEBREW: *nesher*, vulture, griffon, eagle (*see* Eagle)

peres, bearded vulture (*see* Birds of Abomination: No. 2, peres)

ozniyyah, great (black) vultures (*see* Birds of Abomination: No. 3, ozniyyah)
rahama, Egyptian vulture (*see* Birds of Abomination: No. 16, rahama)
da'ah, dayyah, kites, vultures (*see* Birds of Abomination: No. 4, da'ah)
dayyah, vultures. Psalm 74:19
dayyoth, vultures. Isaiah 34:15
reshef, vulture, fire, pestilence. Habakkuk 3:5
See Firebird; Phoenix.
APOCRYPHA: Sirach (Ecclesiasticus) 43:14; 2 Maccabees 9:15
GREEK: *ornea,* unclean and hateful birds. Revelation 18:2
See also Birds of Doom; Birds of Prey; Buzzard; Ravenous Birds

There are five kinds of vultures still seen in the Holy Land today as there were in Bible times. Two of them are quite distinct and easily identified—the bearded vulture, *Gypaëtus barbatus,* with full-feathered head and black mustache-feathers; and the Egyptian vulture, *Neophron percnopterus,* a much smaller bird with white feathers on head and body and white wings trimmed in black. The remaining three are all large and black, with little head covering; and all are called "black" vultures in addition to the names of cinereous vulture, *Aegypius monachus;* and griffon vulture, *Gyps fulvus;* and eared (lappet-faced) vulture, *Torgos (Aegypius) tracheliotus.*

The abundance of vultures in Bible times is well marked by the number of times that Scripture lines tell of a threat to leave bodies dead by the roadside for the birds to devour. The scavenger birds gleaned their flesh even in city streets and most often of all on the battlefield. Unless we have lived in tropical lands, we have no picture of our own to match the grisly scene, the inevitable silhouette of the lone vulture circling high overhead, the sudden drop from sky-hook watch tower when a dead or dying animal is sighted, the quick gathering of other circlers from near and far, the row of patient watchers with half-open beaks.

The picture painted by the prophets of these birds descending to feed on human flesh is gruesome beyond the telling, yet it did not bring the repentance that was asked.

Vulture of the Wilderness (see Pelican of the Wilderness)

Wagtail

The wagtail is not mentioned in Bible translations, but in 6:22 of the Apocryphal Book of Baruch there is a scene of bats and swallows and cats roosting on the heads of pagan idols. Since birds and cats would scarcely be roosting there at the same time, some readers have suggested that the Latin word *cattae* did not mean cats at all but was an old folk name for the wagtails. The more common word for "cat" is *felis,* another case in point, and *catus*—meaning "tom cat" —is a masculine word of the second declension, not having the "ae" ending, except by copyist's error.

Since Baruch was a Hebrew, serving as scribe for the prophet Jeremiah, he must have originally written in Hebrew, but the oldest texts known so far are in Greek and Latin, making the tracing of this word difficult.

Whether the wagtails belong in the story or not, they are found in Israel—three different species—and all three (the yellow, the white, and the gray wagtails) now come to Alaska as summer nesters. The yellow wagtail is the most common, spreading now into the Yukon, with further wandering perhaps an event of the near future.

Wandering Birds

Isaiah 16:2 compares outcasts from Moab to "wandering birds cast out of the nest," and the same idea of homeless roaming is applied to the sparrow, the little ground bird, of Proverbs 26:2. The swallow goes on swift wing, the sparrow by sturdy hopping or walking or running, the lines seem to say, but neither goes without reason and cause, even though each takes its own way.

Many young birds, on their own for the first time in the days of late summer, do take to wandering, not seeming to follow the set southbound route of northern-hemisphere birds on winter migration. Water birds are especially likely to do so, turning up even by a cattail pool in the middle of a city golf course. They wander of their own choice—or because of hunger and thirst—not because the parents cast them out of the nest; but watchers do not always give the right interpretation to the behavior of birds and beasts, and the yearlings, or even adult wanderers, roaming where they do not nest, may well have seemed outcasts.

Any of the fruit or seed-eating birds that feed in great flocks may be habitual wanderers, also, for the flock quickly depletes the food supply in one area and off they must go to find another. Among the flocking wanderers of the Holy Land also seen in this country are the red crossbills and the common starling, the meadow pipit, the red-throated pipit and the water pipit, the cattle egret—which actually introduced itself to North America by "wandering" all the way across the Atlantic Ocean, probably aided by storm winds. The first ones were seen in British Guiana in 1930, in Florida in 1942, and by a decade later they were moving both north and west, reaching Texas in 1955, Oregon in 1965, and this wanderer is now found coast to coast, Canada to the Caribbean. The glossy ibis, another self-inducted citizen, was first recorded in 1817, with no nesting colonies until 1909.

Water Hen (*see* Birds of Abomination: No. 14, tinshemeth)

Wings
HEBREW: *kanaf*. Genesis 1:21; Exodus 19:4; 25:20; 37:9; Leviticus 1:17; Deuteronomy 4:17; 32:11; Ruth 2:12; 2 Samuel 22:11; 1 Kings 6:24, 27; 8:6–7; 2 Chronicles 3:11–13; 5:7–8; Job 39:13, 18, 26; Psalms 17:8; 18:10;

36:7; 57:1; 61:4; 63:7; 68:13; 91:4; 104:3; 139:9; Proverbs 1:17; 23:5; Ecclesiastes 10:20; Isaiah 6:2; 8:8; 10:14; 18:1; Jeremiah 48:40, 49:22; Ezekiel 1:6–25; 3:13; 10:5–21; 11:22; 17:3–23; Hosea 4:19; Zechariah 5:9; Malachi 4:2

eber. Psalm 55:6; Isaiah 40:31

ebrah. Deuteronomy 32:11; Job 39:13

gaf. Daniel 7:4, 6

tsits. Jeremiah 48:9

APOCRYPHA: 2 Esdras 1:30 (omitted in some texts); Wisdom 5:11

GREEK: *pteron:* Matthew 23:37; Luke 13:34; Revelation 4:7–8; 5:13; 9:9

See also Visions of Birds and Winged Creatures. *See* Eagle, Exodus 19:4, etc., for Wings of the Lord.

The wings of the eagle, the sheltering, strength-giving wings of any parent bird caring for its young, are likened to the shelter and strength of God the Father throughout the Bible, but most of all in the Psalms. Those who wrote these lines and those who read them or heard them chanted must have felt heart-lift and hope each time the word-picture brought a remembered scene of hovering wings:

Hide me under the shadow of Thy wings. . . . The children of men put their trust under the shadow of Thy wings. . . . For my soul trusteth in Thee, yea, in the shadow of Thy wings will I take my refuge. . . . Because Thou hast been my help, therefore in the shadow of Thy wings will I rejoice. . . . In the Lord put I my trust: how say ye to my soul, Flee, as a bird, to your mountain?

Wren
HEBREW: *zippor.* Psalm 84:3

The word *zippor,* translated so many ways—bird, songbird, fowl, poultry, sparrow—becomes a wren in one version

of the lines that picture both little ground birds and the
airborne swallow nesting near each other under the eaves
of the temple or on its windowsills, even beside the altar.

Naming the wren here is quite reasonable, for wrens do
build their nests in a crevice or a niche. Also they are little
and brown-feathered, like the sparrows, and so make an equal
match for the "least ones" meaning that the word *zippor*
holds, along with its echo of twitter and chirp.

The English word "wren" had the same "smallest birds"
connotation in its Anglo-Saxon, Old Norse, and German
roots. It belonged first of all to the little 4-inch songster we
call the winter wren, *Troglodytes troglodytes,* the only true
wren found in the Old World. But the wren name was also
applied in common speech to any birds of the same small
size, especially to the little goldcrest, close cousin to our
golden-crowned and ruby-crowned kinglets. In fact, when
Audubon painted these cousins for his famous folio of American birds, he called them golden-crowned and ruby-crowned
wrens, not kinglets. Four other small birds found in the Holy
Land—all in the genus *Phylloscopus* of the Family Sylviidae,
the Old World warblers—are also called wrens as well as
warblers: willow wren, wood wren, Bonelli's wren, and the
chiffchaff.

So although there is only one true wren that might have
been seen nesting on temple eaves in old Jerusalem, there
are six small birds that shared this name. The true wren is a
worldwide roamer and can be found on Bible bird walk almost anywhere in North America, at least as a winter visitor
or migrant, if not as a nesting neighbor. Of the other five,
only one—the willow warbler, *Phylloscopus trochilus*—
comes to this continent, and it is seen only in Alaska on
"accidental" visit.

But there are 10 different wrens in North America to
show you the smallness and perky friendliness of this "least
one," and our two kinglets will add to the tally of stand-ins.
The Old World kinglet, the goldcrest, was undoubtedly the

"wren" of European legends that matched its wits against eagle wings to see which could reach the greatest height and so be crowned king of all the birds. Up, up the two went, so the story goes, and when a cloud hid them from the watching birds below, the wren slyly climbed aboard the eagle's back, getting a free and effortless sky ride. Up and up the eagle still soared, but then seeing no sign of its rival, started to descend, thinking it had won the kingship, but the little wren fluttered up from its feathery perch and winged a few feet higher—as all the birds below could clearly see—and claimed the crown, the title and the right to rule.

The title it has, for it is called kinglet, and it also has the golden crown—a bright crest of gold-toned feathers—but the birds refused to serve one who had won by trickery, and each has gone its own way ever since, so the legend ends.

Incidentally, an old Greek word for small ground birds, *trochilos,* was usually used in the Middle Ages only for the very smallest ones, the same ones called wrens. But in the eighteenth century when the Swedish classifier, Carl Linnaeus, found that the hummingbirds from America were even smaller than the wrens, he gave them the family label of Trochilidae, and it has been the hummingbird name for scientific rosters ever since. If you translate it by its original Greek meaning, it doesn't fit them at all, for *trochilos* came from the word for "wheel" and implied having sturdy legs that could run over the ground as readily as a wheel could roll. Hummingbird legs are about as poorly built for running as any in the entire bird world, but by the time Linnaeus gave them this name it had lost its original meaning of "little runner" and only meant "little." Much the same turnabout twisting must have surely happened to many Hebrew bird names, too, and we are reminded once again to look at the birds themselves to interpret Bible birdlore passages, not just the words.

A wren, a sparrow, or any other small ground bird nesting near the swallows on some church windowsill or wall cranny will be your match for the psalmist's lines on Bible bird walk.

Wryneck
HEBREW: *agar* (*see* Migrating Birds)

Young Birds
HEBREW: *gozal, gozalaw,* young bird(s). Genesis 15:9; Deuteronomy 32:11
  efrochim, young of birds or animals. Deuteronomy 22:6–7; Job 39:30; Psalm 84:3
  yeled, young of birds or animals. Job 38:41
  beni, sons, young (*see* Dove and Pigeon; Eagle; Firebird; Raven)
  bath, banoth, daughter(s) (*see* Ostrich; Singing of Birds, Songbirds)
APOCRYPHA: 2 Esdras 1:30 (omitted in some texts)
GREEK: *neossos,* new ones, young (pigeon). Luke 2:24
  nossion, young domesticated birds, chickens, brood. Matthew 23:37; Luke 13:34

The first young bird to be pointed out by name in the Old Testament is the one that Abraham offered for sacrifice when God had promised him an heir. Two birds were required of him—as well as heifer, she-goat, and ram—and the two named are *tor* and *gozal*. The *tor* is the turtledove, of course—no one ever suggests a substitute for that translation, except the short-cut "dove." And *gozal* is the word for any young bird, any nestling or fledgling whose flesh would be more tender—and therefore more prized—than that of an older bird.

But in most Bibles the birds are named as turtledove and young pigeon, for elsewhere when the laws for sacrifice are given (Leviticus 1:14; 12:6, 8; 14:22, 30; 15:14, 29) the wording is *tor* and *beni-yonah*—clearly implying that birds of kinship with yonah, the rock dove, are to be used. In our time, the common word for birds like the yonah is "pigeon," and whether or not the phrase becomes "young pigeon" seems to be the translator's choice.

Gozal, the word for Abraham's young bird, is used again in Deuteronomy to name the young eagles, so there is no doubt but that it had a broader use, naming any nestling. Our word "fledgling" names a slightly older bird—one having feathers enough to fly—though most people do not always make careful distinction between fledgling and nestling in everyday conversation, or even in written accounts. People of Bible times might have been less than precise in their use of words for young birds of various ages, too, so that *gozal, yeled,* and *efrochim* might all have named nestlings in pinfeathers in one passage and full-fledged youngsters just trying their wings in another. For the young ravens that cry and the young eaglets that are still in the nest beneath their mother's sheltering wings, the precise fixing of age does not matter, for the message lies in the picture of the parent birds' loving care.

Loving care is the theme, too, for the young birds that are pictured by the words of Jesus in Matthew and Luke. The translations show new-hatched chicks of the barnyard and a clucking mother hen gathering them under her wings when danger threatens or a cold wind blows, but any wild mother bird shelters her chicks, too. A robin in her nest on the windowsill, a hen pheasant and her brood in the woods, a nesting eagle on the crags, swallows and sparrows under the eaves of shed or barn, a mallard duck by the pond—even owl and hawk and vulture—all stretch sheltering wings for their young with the strength and tenderness and selfless devotion that have given birds their cherishing in Bible lands and Bible lines and on this bird walk with the Book of Books.

Praise ye the Lord . . . for he commanded and they were created. . . . Fire and hail; snow and vapours; stormy wind fulfilling his word: Mountains, and all hills; fruitful trees and all cedars: Beasts, and all cattle; creeping things, and flying birds. . . . Praise ye the Lord (Psalm 148:1–13).

PART THREE

Lists and Tables

APPENDIX 1

Hebrew Designations of Birds

agar, crane
ahf, bird(s)
anafah, heron and flamingo
atalaf, bat
ayit, bird(s) of prey
ayit-harim, birds of prey of the mountains
ayit-tsabua, speckled bird of prey
ayyah, falcon
ba'al kanaf, bird (possessor of a wing)
banoth-shir, songbirds (daughters of music) (sing. *bath*)
barburim abusim, fattened fowl
bath-ya'annah, ostrich and/or bustard (pl. *ye'enim*)
beni-reshef, bird, firebird, eagle (sons of glowing coals)
da'ah, kite (pl. *dayyoth*)
dayyah, kite (vulture) (or misspelling for *da'ah*)
deror, swallow and/or swift
dukifath, hoopoe
gozal, young bird (pl. *gozalaw*)
harab, bustard (error for *oreb*?)
haserah, ostrich
hasidah, stork
hoglah, partridge (used only as a place name)
hol, phoenix (or sand or palm tree)
ka'ath, pelican and marabou and cormorant, possibly snake-
    bird

ka'ath midbar, marabou (pelican of the wilderness)
kanahath, bird (winged ones)
kippod, bittern
kippoz, snakebird
kol, blue roller
kore, partridge
kos, little owl
kos aharboth, owl of the desert
lilith, barn owl
nesher, beni-nesher, eagle and all of eagle kind
nez, hawk
oahim, owls
oreb, beni-oreb, raven and all of raven kind (pl. *orebim*)
oreb anahal, raven of the valley (or magpie)
ozniyyah, great vultures
peres, bearded vulture
ra'ah (probable error for *da'ah*)
rahama, Egyptian vulture
renanim, peacocks (or ostriches, error for *ye'enim*)
sekvi, cock
selav, quail
shahaf, gull
shalak, owl (tawny owl or barn owl) or cormorant
sis, swallow and swift
tachmas, nightjar (or night heron or skimmer)
tinshemeth, great crested grebe (or barn owl)
tor, turtledove
tuhoth, cock
tukkiyim, peacocks
yanshof, ibis (or miscopy for *yanshuf*)
yanshuf, eagle owl
yonah, beni-yonah, dove and pigeon (pl. *yonim*)
yonim gai, doves of the rocky gorge (rock doves)
zamir, song-bird (or nightingale)
zarzir mothnayim, cock, peacock, marabou
zippor, bird or songbird (pl. *zipporim*)

Greek Designations of Birds

aetos, eagle
alektor, cock
korax, raven
neossos, young birds
nossion, young birds or chickens
ornea, bird of prey
ornis, hen (no counterpart in Hebrew)
peristera, dove, pigeon
peteina, bird
struthion, sparrow
trugon, turtledove

Latin Designation, in Apocrypha

cattae, wagtails

APPENDIX 2

Bible Birdlore Passages—Old Testament (203 Passages)

Reference	Hebrew	King James Version	Variants
GENESIS			
1:20–22	ahf, kanaf	fowl, winged	birds
:26	ahf		
:28	ahf		
:30	ahf		
2:19–20	ahf		
6:7	ahf		
:19–20	ahf		
7:2–3	ahf		
:8–9	ahf		
:14	ahf, zippor	fowl, bird	
:21–23	ahf		
8:7	oreb	raven	
:8–12	yonah	dove	
:17–19	ahf	fowl	
:20	ahf		
9:1–7	ahf		
:8–17	ahf		
15:9	tor, gozal	turtledove, young pigeon	fledgling
:10	zipporim	birds	
:11	ayit	fowls	birds of prey
40:17	ahf		
:19	ahf		

Reference	Hebrew	King James Version	Variants
Exodus			
16:13	selav	quail	
19:4	nesher, kanaf	eagle, wings	
Leviticus			
1:14–17	kanaf, notsah	wings, feathers	
	ahf, tor	fowls, turtledoves	birds
	beni-yonah	young pigeons	
5:7–13	tor, beni-yonah	turtledove, young pigeon	bird
7:26	ahf	fowl	
11:13–20	nesher, peres, ozniyyah, daʾah, ayyah, oreb, bath-yaʿannah, shalak, yanshuf, tinshemeth, kaʾath, rahama, hasidah, anafah, namts = The Birds of Abomination; see p. 38–39 for translations.)	tachmas, shahaf, nez, kos, dukifath, atalaf (20	
11:46	ahf	fowl	
12:6	tor, beni-yonah	turtledove, young pigeon	
:8	tor, beni-yonah	turtles, young pigeons	
14:4–7	zipporim	birds	
:22,30	tor, beni-yonah	turtledoves, young pigeon	
:49–53	zipporim	birds	
15:14	tor, beni-yonah	turtledoves, young pigeons	
:29	tor, beni-yonah	turtles, young pigeons	
17:13	ahf	fowl	birds
20:25	ahf	fowl	birds

Numbers		
6:10	tor, beni-yonah	turtledove, young pigeon
11:31–32	selav	quail
24:21	kinnim	nests
Deuteronomy		
4:15–18	zippor, kanaf	birds, wings
14:11–20	nesher, peres, ozniyyah, ra[>]ah, ayyah, dayyah, oreb, bath-ya^cannah, tachmas, shahaf, nez, kos, yanshuf, tinshemeth, ka[>]ath, rahama, shalak, hasidah, anafah, dukifath, atalaf (21 names = **Birds of Abomination**; see p. 40–41 for translations.)	
22:6–7	zippor, ama, efrochim, betsim	bird, dam, young, eggs
28:26	ahf	fowl
:49	nesher	eagle
32:11–12	nesher, gozalaw, kanaf	eagle, young, wing
Ruth		
2:12	kanaf	wing
1 Samuel		
17:44–46	ahf	fowl
26:20	kore	partridge
2 Samuel		
1:23	nesher	eagle
21:8–10	ahf	birds

The "vulture" appears aligned with the 14:11–20 block on the far right.

Reference	Hebrew	King James Version	Variants
1 Kings			
4:23	barburim	fatted fowl	guinea fowl, cuckoos
:33	ahf	fowl	
10:22	tukkiyim	peacocks	monkeys
14:11	ahf	fowl	
16:4	ahf		
17:4–6	orebim	ravens	
21:24	ahf	fowl	
2 Kings			
6:25	hariyonim	dove's dung	locust beans, onions
2 Chronicles			
9:21	tukkiyim	peacocks	monkeys
Nehemiah			
5:18	zipporim	fowl	
Job			
5:6–7	beni-reshef	sparks	wild bird, eagle
6:6	challamuth	white of egg	juice of mallows
9:26	nesher	eagles	vultures
12:7–9	ahf	fowls	
28:7–10	ayit, ayyah	fowl, vulture	bird of prey, falcon, hawk
:20–21	ahf	fowl	
29:18	hol	sand	phoenix
30:29	ya'annah	owls	ostriches
35:10–11	ahf	fowls	

Reference	Hebrew	Meaning	Note
38:36	tuhoth, sekvi	inward parts, heart	cock, ibis, mists
:41	orebim, yeled	ravens, young ones	
39:13	kanaf	wings	
	renanim	peacock	ostrich
	ebrah	wings	
	notsah	feathers	
	haserah	ostrich	
:18	tamara	lifteth up	hawk
:26	nez, kanaf	hawk, wings	stork, heron
:27–30	nesher, efrochim	eagle, young	struts like a cock
41:5	zippor	bird	songbird
(40:29 in some texts)			
PSALMS			
8:4–8	zippor	fowl	
11:1–2	zippor		birds
17:8	kanaf	wings	
36:7	kanaf	wings	
50:11	ayit	birds of the mountains	of hills
55:6	yonah, eber	dove, wings	
57:1	kanaf	wings	
61:4	kanaf	wings	
63:7	kanaf	wings	
68:13	yonah, kanaf, ebrah	dove, wings, feathers	
74:19	tor, dayyah	turtledove, wicked	tor = soul / dayyah = vulture
78:26–29	kanaf	feathered fowl	
79:2	ahf	fowl	

Reference	Hebrew	King James Version	Variants
84:3	zippor, deror, efrochim	sparrow, swallow, young	
91:3	yakosh	fowler	
:4	kanaf, ebrah	wings, feathers	
102:6	kaʾath midbar	pelican of the wilderness	desert owl
	kos aharboth	owl of the desert	owl of ruins
:7	zippor	sparrow	
103:5	nesher	eagle	
104:10–12	zipporim	fowls	
:16–17	zipporim, hasidah	birds, stork	
105:40	selav	quail	
124:7	zippor, yakosh	bird, fowler	
147:7–9	beni-oreb	young ravens	
148:5–13	zipporim	fowl	
PROVERBS			
1:17	baʿal kanaf	bird	
6:5	zippor, yakosh	bird, fowler	
7:23	zippor	bird	
23:5	nesher, kanaf	eagle, wings	
26:2	zippor, deror	bird, swallow	sparrow, swallow
27:8	zippor	bird	
30:17	oreb anahal	raven of the valley	
	beni-nesher	young eagles	
:18–19	nesher	eagle	vulture
:31	zarzir mothnayim	greyhound	strutting cock
ECCLESIASTES			
9:12	zippor	birds	
10:20	zippor, kanahath	bird, hath wings	winged messenger

12:4	zippor	bird	sparrow
	banoth-shir	daughters of music	songbirds
SONG OF SONGS			
1:15	yonah	dove	
2:11–12	zippor or zamir?	birds	vines
	tor	turtle	
:13	yonah?	dove	
:14	yonah	dove	
4:1	yonah	dove	
5:2	yonah	dove	
:11	oreb	raven	
:12	yonah	dove	
6:9	yonah	dove	
ISAIAH			
8:8	kanaf	wings	
10:14	ken, betsim, kanaf	nest, eggs, wing	
13:21	oahim	doleful creatures	owls
	yaʿannah	owls	ostriches
14:22–23	kippod	bittern	bustard, porcupine, hoot owl
16:2	zippor	bird	
18:1	kanaf	wings	
:6	ayit-harim	fowls of mountains	bird of prey on hills
31:5	zippor	birds	
34:11–16	kaʾath, kippod	cormorant, bittern	owls, bustard
	yanshof, oreb	owl, raven	screech owl
:13	yaʿannah	owls	ostrich
:14	lilith	screech owl	nightjar
:15	kippoz, dayyoth	great owl, vultures	sand-partridge, kites

Reference	Hebrew	King James Version	Variants
ISAIAH (cont.)			
38:14	sis, agar, yonah	crane, swallow, dove	swallow, crane
40:31	nesher, eber	eagles, wing	
43:20	ya꜄annah	owls	ostrich
46:11	ayit	ravenous bird	bird of prey
59:11	yonim	doves	
60:8	yonim, arubah	doves, window	
JEREMIAH			
4:13	nesher	eagle	
:19,23–25	ahf	birds	
5:26–27	ahf	birds	
7:33	ahf	fowls	
8:7	hasidah, tor, sis, agar	stork, turtle, crane, swallow	stork, dove, swift, wryneck, swallow, thrush
9:10	ahf	fowl	
12:4	ahf	birds	
:9	ayit tsabua	speckled bird	speckled bird of prey, hyena vultures
15:3	ahf (da꜄ah?)	birds	
16:4	ahf	fowls	
17:11	kore, betsim	partridge, eggs	
19:7	ahf	fowls	
22:23	ken	nest	
34:20	ahf	fowls	
48:9	tsits	wings	feathers
:28	yonah	dove	
:40	nesher, kanaf	eagle, wing	vulture

Reference	Hebrew		
49:16	nesher		vulture
:22	nesher, kanaf		
50:39	ya‘annah	owls	ostriches
LAMENTATIONS			
3:52	zippor	bird	
4:3	ye‘enim	ostriches	
:19	nesher	eagles	vultures
EZEKIEL			
1:10	nesher	eagle	
7:16	yonim gai	doves of the valley	
10:14	nesher	eagle	
17:3–7	nesher, notsah	eagle, feathers	
:22–23	ahf	fowl of every wing	birds of every kind
29:5	ahf	fowl	
31:6	ahf	fowl	
:13	ahf		
32:4	ahf		
38:19–20	ahf		
39:4	ayit	ravenous birds	bird of prey
:17	ahf	fowl	
44:29–31	ahf		
DANIEL			
2:38	ahf	fowl	
3:80 (Apocr.)	ahf		
4:12, 14, 20–21	zipporim	fowls	
:33	nesher, zephar	eagle, claws	
7:4	nesher	eagle	
:6	gaf	wings	

Reference	Hebrew	King James Version	Variants
HOSEA			
2:18	ahf	fowls	
4:1–3	ahf		
7:11	yonah	dove	pigeon
:12	ahf	fowl	
8:1	nesher	eagle	vulture
9:8	yakosh	fowler	
:11	ahf	bird	
11:11	zippor, yonah	bird, dove	pigeon
AMOS			
3:5	zippor	bird	
OBADIAH			
1:4	nesher	eagle	vulture
MICAH			
1:8	yaᶜannah	owls	ostriches, desert owl
:16	nesher	eagle	vulture
NAHUM			
2:7	yonim	doves	
HABAKKUK			
1:8	nesher	eagle	vulture
2:9	ken	nest	
3:5	reshef	burning coals	birds, plague, vultures

ZEPHANIAH			
1:2–3	ahf	fowls	
2:14	ka²ath	cormorant	pelican, bittern, owl, vulture
	kippod	bittern	porcupine, hedgehog, owl
	kol	voice	owl, bustard
	oreb (harab)	raven	bustard, desolation
ZECHARIAH			
5:9	hasidah, kanaf	stork, wings	
MALACHI			
4:2	kanaf	wings	rays

Bible Birdlore Passages—Apocrypha (23 Passages)

Reference	King James Version	Variants
2 ESDRAS		
1:15	quail	omitted
:30	hen, chickens	omitted
TOBIT		
2:10–11	sparrows	birds, swallows
8:18	cockcrow	morning, dawn
11:13	egg	omitted
JUDITH		
11:17	fowls	birds, or omitted
WISDOM		
5:11	bird	
16:2	quail	
17:18	birds	
19:11–12	new generation of fowls . . . quail	new sort (kind) of bird
SIRACH (Ecclesiasticus)		
11:30	partridge	bird
17:4	fowl	bird
22:20	birds	
27:9	birds will resort unto their like	nest with their own kind
43:14	fowl	birds, vultures
:17	birds	

BARUCH			
3:9–17		fowls	birds
6:21–22		bats, swallows, birds . . . cats (in Latin = *cattae*, formerly a vernacular term for the species of bird known as wagtails)	
:54		crows	
:69–70		scarecrow, birds	
SONG OF THE THREE			
1:58 (*or* DANIEL 3:80)		fowls	
2 MACCABEES			
9:15		fowls	birds, vultures
15:33		fowls	birds

Bible Birdlore Passages—New Testament (47 Passages)

Reference	Greek	King James Version	Variants
MATTHEW			
3:16	peristera	dove	
6:26	peteinon	fowl	birds
8:20	peteinon	fowl	
10:16	peristera	doves	
:29–31	struthion	sparrows	
18:3–4	peteinon	fowl	birds
:31–32	peristera	doves	
21:12	peristera	doves	pigeons
23:37	ornis, nossion, pteron	hen, chickens, wing	mother bird, young
24:28	aetos	eagles	vultures
26:34	alektor	cock	
:74–75	alektor	cock	
MARK			
1:10	peristera	dove	
4:4	peteina	fowls	birds
:31–32	peteinon		
11:15	peristera	doves	pigeons
13:35	alektor	cock	
14:30	alektor		
:38–72	alektor		

	Greek	English	
LUKE			
2:24	trugon, neossos	turtledove, young pigeon	
3:22	peristera	dove	
8:5	peteinon	fowls	birds
9:58	peteinon, kataskenosis	birds, nest	
11:11–13	oon	egg	
12:6–7	struthion	sparrows	
:24	korax	ravens	
13:19	peteinon	fowls	birds
:34	ornis, nossia, pteron	hen, brood, wing	mother bird, young
17:37	aetos	eagles	vultures
22:34	alektor	cock	
:60–61	alektor	cock	
JOHN			
1:32	peristera	dove	
2:14–16	peristera	dove	pigeons
13:38	alektor	cock	
18:27	alektor	cock	
ACTS			
10:9–16	peteinon	fowls	
11:4–10	petomai	things that fly	
ROMANS			
1:22–25	peteinon	birds	
1 CORINTHIANS			
15:38–39	ptenon	birds	

Reference	Greek	King James Version	Variants
JAMES			
3:7–8	peteinon	birds	
REVELATION			
4:7–8	aetos, pteron	eagle, wing	
8:13	aetos	angel	eagle
9:9	pteron	wing	
12:14	aetos, pteron	eagle, wing	
18:2	ornea	unclean birds	vile, etc.
19:17	peteinon	fowls	
:21	peteinon		

APPENDIX 3

Check-list of Birds of Bible Lands

The asterisk * indicates an Order, Family, or Species named in one or more Bible versions or in this book.

The dagger † indicates an Order, Family, or Species also listed in *The A.O.U. Check-list of North American Birds* or in *American Birds* (formerly *Audubon Field Notes,* published by the National Audubon Society) as appearing regularly or fairly often in some part of North America.

The double dagger ‡ indicates an occasional or isolated sighting somewhere in North America. Check your bird books for possible local occurrence. You may encircle each † or ‡ to show which species you have seen on your own Bible bird walk. All Orders and Families and most of the Israeli Species are described and pictured in *Birds of the World* by Oliver Austin or in *A Field Guide to the Birds of Britain and Europe* by Peterson, Mountfort, and Hollom. Species found in North America are in *Birds of North America* by Robbins, Bruun, and Zim. Alternate terminology in frequent use is indicated in parentheses.

The letters following each species indicate present status in Israel: R = resident, S = summer nester, W = winter visitor, M = migrant, U = uncommon, X = extinct, I = introduced for domestication.

*ORDER STRUTHIONIFORMES—Flightless Walker
  *Family Struthionidae
    Struthio camelus, ostrich X
†*ORDER PODICIPEDIFORMES (*or* Podicipitiformes)—Lobate-toed Divers
  †*Family Podicipedidae (*or* Podicipitidae, Colymbidae)
    †*Podiceps grisegena,* red-necked grebe U
    †*Podiceps auritus,* horned grebe U
    †*Podiceps caspicus,* eared grebe W
    Podiceps cristatus, great crested grebe R
    Podiceps ruficollis, little grebe S
    Podiceps nigricollis, black-necked grebe W

†*ORDER PROCELLARIIFORMES—Tube-nosed Swimmers
 †*Family Procellariidae
      †*Puffinus puffinus,* Manx shearwater   W
       Puffinus kuhli, Mediterranean shearwater   W

†*ORDER PELECANIFORMES—Webfooted Pouch-wearers
 †*Family Pelecanidae
      **Pelecanus onocratalus,* Eurasian white pelican   M
      **Pelecanus crispus,* Dalmatian pelican   U
      **Pelecanus rufescens,* pink-backed pelican   U
  †Family Sulidae
      †*Morus (Sula) bassanus,* gannet   W
 †*Family Phalacrocoracidae
      †**Phalacrocorax carbo,* European (great) cormorant   W
      **Phalacrocorax pygmaeus,* pygmy cormorant   W
      **Phalacrocorax aristotelis,* shag   U
 †*Family Anhingidae
      **Anhinga rufa,* African darter   W

†*ORDER CICONIIFORMES—Long-billed Waders
 †*Family Ardeidae
      ‡**Ardea cinerea,* gray heron   S, M
      **Ardea goliath,* Goliath heron   U
      **Ardea purpurea,* purple heron   R
      †**Bubulcus (Ardeola) ibis,* cattle egret   R
      **Ardeola ralloides,* squacco heron   M
      ‡**Egretta garzetta,* little egret   W, M
      †**Egretta (Casmerodius) alba,* common egret   W, M
      **Egretta gularis,* African reef heron   R
      **Butorides striatus,* green-backed heron   U
      †**Nycticorax nycticorax,* night heron   R
      **Ixobrychus minutus,* little bittern   S, M
      **Botaurus stellaris,* Eurasian bittern   W, M
 †*Family Ciconiidae
      **Ciconia ciconia,* white stork   R, M
      **Ciconia negra,* black stork   M
      **Leptoptilus crumeniferus,* marabou   U
 †*Family Threskiornithidae (*or* Plataleidae, Order Phoenicopter-
      iformes)
       Platalea leucorodia, spoonbill   W, M
      †**Plegadis falcinellus,* glossy ibis   M
 †*Family Phoenicopteridae (*or* Order Phoenicopteriformes—Big-
      billed Waders)
      †**Phoenicopterus ruber,* flamingo   W, M

†*Order Anseriformes—Broad-billed Webfoots
  †*Family Anatidae
    †**Cygnus olor,* mute swan   W
    ‡**Cygnus (Olor) cygnus,* whooper swan   U
    †*Anser albifrons,* white-fronted goose   W
    ‡*Anser anser,* graylag goose   M
    ‡*Anser fabalis,* bean goose   U
     Anser erythropus, lesser white-fronted goose   U
    ‡*Tadorna tadorna,* shelduck   W
    ‡*Tadorna (Casarca) ferruginea,* ruddy shelduck   W
    †*Anas platyrhynchos,* mallard   W, M
    †*Anas strepera,* gadwall   W, M
    †*Anas acuta,* pintail   W, M
    †*Anas (Mareca) penelope,* European widgeon   W, M
    †*Anas crecca,* teal   W, M
    ‡*Anas querquedula,* garganey   M
     Anas angustirostris, marbled teal   R
    †*Anas (Spatula) clypeata,* shoveler   W, M
    ‡*Netta rufina,* red-crested pochard   U
    ‡*Aythya ferina,* pochard   M
    †*Aythya marila,* greater scaup   U
    ‡*Aythya fuligula,* tufted duck   W, M
     Aythya nyroca, ferruginous duck   W, M
     Oxyura leucocephala, white-headed duck   U
    †*Mergus merganser,* American merganser (goosander)   U
    †*Mergus serrator,* red-breasted merganser   U
    ‡*Mergus albellus,* smew   W

†*Order Falconiformes—Daylight Predators
  †*Family Accipitridae
    **Gyps fulvus,* griffon vulture   R
    **Aegypius monachus,* cinereous (black) vulture   R
    **Torgos (Aegypius) tracheliotus,* eared (lappet) vulture   R
    **Gypaetus barbatus,* bearded vulture (lammergeyer)   R
    **Neophron percnopterus,* Egyptian vulture   R
    **Milvus milvus,* red kite   W, R
    **Milvus migrans,* black kite   R
    **Pernis apivorus,* honey buzzard   M
    †**Accipiter gentilis,* goshawk   U
    **Accipiter badius,* shikra (Levant sparrow hawk)   M
    * *Accipiter nisus,* Eurasian sparrow hawk   W, M
    **Buteo buteo,* common buzzard (hawk)   W, M
    **Buteo ferox,* long-legged buzzard (hawk)   R

*Hieraëtus pennatus, booted eagle   M
*Hieraëtus fasciatus, Bonelli's eagle   R
†*Aquila chrysaëtos, golden eagle   U, R
*Aquila rapax, tawny eagle   W, M
*Aquila clanga, spotted eagle   W, M
*Aquila pomarina, lesser spotted eagle   W, M
*Aquila heliaca, imperial eagle   W, M
*Aquila verreauxi, Verreaux's eagle   U
‡*Haleaetus albicilla, white-tailed (gray) sea eagle   R
*Circaëtus gallicus, short-toed (serpent) eagle   S, M
†*Circus cyaneus, marsh hawk (hen harrier)   M
*Circus pygargus, Montagu's harrier   W, M
*Circus aeruginosus, marsh harrier   W, M, S
†*Family Pandionidae (or Family Accipitridae)
†*Pandion haliaëtus, osprey   W, M
†*Family Falconidae
†*Falco peregrinus, peregrine (duck hawk)   M
†*Falco columbarius, pigeon hawk (merlin)   W, M
‡*Falco tinnunculus, kestrel   R
*Falco naumanni, lesser kestrel   R
*Falco cherrug, saker falcon   W, M
*Falco biarmicus, lanner falcon   R
*Falco vespertinus, red-legged falcon   M
*Falco concolor, sooty falcon   R
*Falco subbuteo, hobby falcon   S

†*ORDER GALLIFORMES—Chicken-like Birds
†*Family Phasianidae
†*Alectoris graeca, rock partridge (chukar)   R
*Ammoperdix heyi, Hey's desert partridge   R
*Coturnix coturnix, Old World quail   M
*Francolinus francolinus, black partridge   R
(†*Gallus gallus, red jungle fowl   I)
(†*Pavo cristatus, peafowl   I)

†*ORDER GRUIFORMES—Prairie and Marsh Birds
†*Family Gruidae
‡*Grus grus, common crane   W, M
*Anthropoides virgo, demoiselle crane   M
†*Family Rallidae
Rallus aquaticus, water rail   W, M
Porzana porzana, spotted crake   W, M
Porzana parva, little crake   W, M
Porzana pusilla, Baillon's crake   W, M

†*Crex crex*, corn crake   M
†**Gallinula* *chloropus*, moorhen (water hen, gallinule)   S, W
   Porphyrio porphyrio, Eurasian purple gallinule   W
   ‡*Fulica atra*, Eurasian coot   S, W, M
*Family Otididae
   **Otis tarda*, great bustard   W
   **Otis tetrax*, little bustard   W
   **Chlamydotis undulata*, houbara bustard   R

†*ORDER CHARADRIIFORMES—Shorebirds
   †Family Haematopodidae
      Haematopus ostralegus, Eurasian oystercatcher   U
   †*Family Charadriidae
      †**Vanellus vanellus*, lapwing   W
      ‡*Vanellus spinosus*, spur-winged plover   R
         Vanellus leucura, white-tailed plover   U
      †*Charadrius hiaticula*, ringed plover   W, M
      ‡*Charadrius dubius*, little ringed plover   W, M
      †*Charadrius alexandrinus*, snowy (Kentish) plover   W, M
         Charadrius leschenaultii, greater sand plover   W, M
      †*Charadrius mongolus*, Mongolian plover   W, M
      †*Eudromias (Charadrius) morinellus*, dotterel   W
      ‡*Pluvialis apricaria*, Eurasian golden plover   W, M
      †*Pluvialis (Squatarola) squatarola*, black-bellied (gray) plover   M
      †*Arenaria interpres*, ruddy turnstone   M
   †Family Scolopacidae
      ‡*Scolopax rusticola*, European woodcock   W
      †*Gallinago (Capella) gallinago*, common snipe   W, M
         Gallinago (Capella) media, great snipe   M
      ‡*Lymnocryptes minima*, European jacksnipe   W
      ‡*Numenius arquata*, Eurasian curlew   W, M
      ‡*Tringa glareola*, wood sandpiper   W, M
         Tringa stagnatilis, marsh sandpiper   W, M
         Tringa ochropus, green sandpiper   W, M
      ‡*Tringa hypoleucos, common sandpiper*   W, M
      ‡*Tringa (Totanus) erythropus*, spotted redshank   W, M
      ‡*Tringa (Totanus) nebularia*, greenshank   W, M
      ‡*Tringa (Totanus) totanus*, redshank   W, M
         Calidris minuta, little stint   W, M
         Calidris temmincki, Temminck's stint   W, M
         Calidris (Erolia) testacea, curlew sandpiper   W, M
      †*Calidris (Erolia) alpina*, dunlin   W, M
      †*Calidris (Crocethia) alba*, sanderling   W, M
      †*Limosa lapponica*, bar-tailed godwit   U

‡*Limosa limosa*, black-tailed godwit   W, M
†*Philomachus pugnax*, ruff   M
†*Family Recurvirostridae
 Recurvirostra avosetta, Eurasian avocet   W, M
 Himanotopus himanotopus, black-winged stilt   S
Family Burhinidae
 Burhinus oedicnemus, stone curlew   R, M
Family Glareolidae
 Cursorius cursor, cream-colored courser   S
 Glareola pratincola, pratincole   S, M
†*Family Stercorariidae (*or* Order Lariformes—Gulls and Allies)
 †*Stercorarius parasiticus*, parasitic jaeger (skua)   W, M
†*Family Laridae (*or* Order Lariformes)
 †*Larus fuscus*, lesser black-backed gull   W
 †*Larus marinus*, greater black-backed gull   U
 †*Larus argentatus*, herring gull   W, S, M
 †*Larus canus*, mew gull   W, M
 †*Larus ridibundus*, black-headed gull   W
 †*Larus minutus*, little gull   W
 Larus genei, slender-billed gull   W, M
 Larus leucopthalmus, white-eyed gull   W
 †*Larus (Xema) sabini*, Sabine's gull   U
 †*Rissa tridactyla*, black-legged kittiwake   W
 †*Gelochelidon nilotica*, gull-billed tern   U
 †*Sterna hirundo*, swallow tern   S
 †*Sterna albifrons*, least tern   S, M
 †*Hydroprogne caspia*, Caspian tern   U
 †*Chlidonias niger*, black tern   S, M
 ‡*Chlidonias leucopterus*, white-winged tern   M
 Chlidonias hybrida, hybrid tern   M
†*Family Rhynchopidae (*or* Order Lariformes)
 Rhynchops flavirostris, red-billed skimmer   U

†*ORDER COLUMBIFORMES—Dovelike Birds
 †*Family Columbidae
  †*Columba livia*, rock dove (common pigeon)   R
  Columba palumbus, wood pigeon   W
  Columba oenas, stock dove (pigeon)   W
  Streptopelia decaocto, collared dove   R
  Streptopelia senegalensis, palm dove   R
  Streptopelia turtur, turtledove   R
  †*Streptopelia risoria*, ringed turtledove (Barbary)   U
 *Family Pteroclidae
  Pterocles senegallus, spotted sandgrouse   R

Pterocles exustus, chestnut-bellied sandgrouse   U
Pterocles alchata, pin-tailed sandgrouse   M
Pterocles coronatus, coronetted sandgrouse   R

†*ORDER CUCULIFORMES—Reversible-yoke-toed Birds
 †*Family Cuculidae
  Cuculus canorus, Eurasian cuckoo   M, U
  Clamator glandarius, great spotted cuckoo   S

†*ORDER STRIGIFORMES—Nocturnal Predators
 †*Family Tytonidae
  †*Tyto alba*, barn owl (white, yellow owl)   R
 †*Family Strigidae
  Otus scops, scops owl   S, M
  Bubo bubo, eagle (great) owl   R
  Strix aluco, tawny owl   R
  Strix butleri, Hume's tawny owl   U
  †*Asio otus*, long-eared owl   W
  †*Asio flammeus*, short-eared owl   M
  Athene noctua, little owl   R
  Ketupa ceylonensis, brown fishing owl   U

†*ORDER CAPRIMULGIFORMES—Twilight Insect-feeders
 †*Family Caprimulgidae
  Caprimulgus europaeus, European nightjar   M
  Caprimulgus nubicus, Nubian nightjar   R

†*ORDER APODIFORMES—Weak-footed Fliers
 †*Family Apodidae
  ‡*Apus apus*, common swift   S, M
  Apus affinis, white-rumped swift   R
  Apus melba, Alpine swift   S

†*ORDER CORACIIFORMES—Split-toed Hole-nesters
 †*Family Alcedinidae
  Alcedo atthis, Eurasian kingfisher   W, M
  Ceryle rudis, pied kingfisher   R
  Halcyon smyrnensis, Smyrna kingfisher   R
 *Family Meropidae
  Merops apiaster, common bee-eater   S
  Merops orientalis, dwarf bee-eater   R
  Merops superciliosus, blue-cheeked bee-eater   S, M
 *Family Coraciidae
  Coracias garrulus, blue roller   S, M
 *Family Upupidae
  Upupa epops, hoopoe   S

†*Order Piciformes—Yoke-toed Hole-nesters
  †*Family Picidae
      Dendrocopos (Dryobates) syriacus, Syrian woodpecker   R
      ‡**Jynx torquilla,* wryneck   M

†*Order Passeriformes—Perching Birds
  †*Family Alaudidae
      ‡*Alauda arvensis,* skylark   W, M
      Alaemon alaudipes, hoopoe (bifasciated) lark   R
      Calandrella cinerea, short-toed lark   R
      Ammomanes deserti, desert lark   R
      †*Eremophilia alpestris,* horned (shore) lark   S
      Melanocorypha calandra, calandra lark   R
      Galerida cristata, crested lark   R
      Lullula arborea, wood lark   W
  †*Family Hirundinidae
      †**Riparia riparia,* bank swallow (sand martin)   M
      **Hirundo rupestris,* crag martin   R, M
      †**Hirundo rustica,* barn swallow   R, M
      **Hirundo daurica,* red-rumped swallow   S
      ‡**Delichon urbica,* house martin   M
      Family Oriolidae
      Oriolus oriolus, golden oriole   M
  †*Family Corvidae
      **Garrulus glandarius,* Eurasian jay   R
      †**Pica pica,* black-billed magpie   U
      †**Corvus corax,* raven   R
      ‡**Corvus monedula,* jackdaw   W, R
      ‡**Corvus frugilegus,* rook   M
      ‡**Corvus cornix,* hooded crow   R
      **Corvus corone,* carrion crow   M, R
      **Corvus rhipidurus,* fan-tailed raven   R
      †Family Paridae
      Parus major, great tit   R
      Parus ater, coal tit   W
      Remiz pendulinus, penduline tit   W
      †Family Certhiidae (or Sittidae)
      Tichodroma muraria, wall creeper   W
      Family Timaliidae
      Turdoides squamiceps, Arabian babbler   R
  ‡*Family Pycnonotidae
      **Pycnonotus capensis,* bulbul   R
  †*Family Troglodytidae
      †**Troglodytes troglodytes,* winter wren   R

†*Family Turdidae (*or* Muscicapidae)
 ‡*Turdus musicus,* redwing   W
 ‡*Turdus merula,* blackbird (merle)   R
 ‡*Turdus pilaris,* fieldfare   W
  Turdus philomelus, song thrush   W, M
  Turdus viscivorus, mistle thrush   W
 †*Oenanthe oenanthe,* wheatear   M
  Oenanthe deserti, desert wheatear   R
  Oenanthe finischii, Finsch's wheatear   W
  Oenanthe isabellina, Isabelline wheatear   R
  Oenanthe hispanica, black-eared wheatear   S, M
  Oenanthe pleschanka, pied wheatear   W
  Oenanthe leucopyga, white-rumped wheatear   R
  Oenanthe moesta, red-rumped wheatear   R
  Oenanthe monacha, hooded wheatear   R
  Oenanthe lugens, mourning chat   R
  Monticola saxatilis, rock thrush   M
  Monticola solitarius, blue rock thrush   R, M
  Cercomela melanura, black-tailed rock thrush (chat)   R
  Erithracus rubecula, Eurasian robin   W, M
 **Luscinia megarhynchos,* nightingale   M, S
 **Luscinia luscinia,* thrush nightingale   M
 †**Luscinia (Cyanosylvia) svecica,* bluethroat   W, M
 ‡*Saxicola rubetra,* whinchat   M
  Saxicola torquata, stonechat   W, M
  Phoenicurus phoenicurus, redstart   M
  Phoenicurus ochrurus, blackstart   W
‡Family Sylviidae (*or* Muscicapidae)
  Phylloscopus bonelli, Bonelli's warbler   M
  Phylloscopus inornatus, yellow-browed warbler   U
  Phylloscopus collybita, chiffchaff   W
  Phylloscopus sibilatrix, wood warbler   M
 ‡*Phylloscopus trochilus,* willow warbler   W, M
  Cettia cetti, Cetti's warbler   R
  Locustella luscinioides, Savi's warbler   R
  Lusciniola melanopogon, mustached warbler   R
  Acrocephalus arundinaceus, great reed warbler   S, M
  Acrocephalus scirpaceus, reed warbler   S, M
  Acrocephalus schoenobaenus, sedge warbler   W
  Acrocephalus stentoreus, clamorous reed warbler   R
  Erythopygia galactotes, rufous warbler   S
  Hippolais languida, Upcher's warbler   R
  Hippolais olivetorum, olive tree warbler   R
  Hippolais pallida, olivaceous warbler   S

Sylvia nisoria, barred warbler   M
Sylvia hortensis, orphean warbler   S
Sylvia borin, garden warbler   M
Sylvia atricapilla, blackcap   M
Sylvia communis, whitethroat   S, M
Sylvia curruca, lesser whitethroat   M
Sylvia ruppelli, Ruppell's warbler   M
Sylvia melanocephala, Sardinian warbler   S
Syliva cantillans, subalpine warbler   U
Sylvia conspicillata, spectacled warbler   R
Prinia gracilis, graceful warbler   R
Scotocerca inquieta, scrub warbler   R
Cisticola juncidis, fan-tailed warbler   R
†Family Regulidae (*or* Muscicapidae)
Regulus regulus, goldcrest   W
Family Muscicapidae
Muscicapa striata, spotted flycatcher   S, M
Muscicapa hypoleuca, pied flycatcher   M
Muscicapa albicollis, collared flycatcher   M
Muscicapa parva, red-breasted flycatcher   M
‡Family Prunellidae
Prunella collaris, alpine accentor   U
Prunella modularis, hedge accentor (dunnock)   W
†Family Motacillidae
†*Motacilla alba,* white wagtail   S, W, M
‡*Motacilla cinerea,* gray wagtail   W
†*Motacilla flava,* yellow wagtail   S, M
†*Anthus spinoletta,* water (rock) pipit   W
Anthus campestris, tawny pipit   W
Anthus trivialis, tree pipit   M
‡*Anthus pratensis,* meadow pipit   M
‡*Anthus cervinus,* red-throated pipit   W
Anthus similis, long-billed pipit   R
†*Family Laniidae
†*Lanius excubitor,* northern (great gray) shrike   R
Lanius collurio, red-backed shrike   S, M
Lanius nubicus, masked shrike   S, M
Lanius senator, woodchat shrike   S, M
Lanius minor, lesser gray shrike   M
†*Family Sturnidae
†*Sturnus vulgaris,* starling   M
Sturnus (Pastor) roseus, rose-colored starling   U
Onychognatus tristrami, Tristram's grackle   R

  Family Nectariniidae
    Cynnyris oseae, sunbird   R
†*Family Ploceidae
  †*_Passer domesticus,_ house sparrow   R
   *_Passer hispaniolensis,_ Spanish sparrow   R
   *_Passer moabiticus,_ Dead Sea sparrow   S
    Petronia petronia, rock sparrow   S
    Petronia brachydactyl, pale rock sparrow   W
†*Family Emberizidae (*or* subfamily under Fringillidae)
   *_Emberiza calandra,_ corn bunting   R
   *_Emberiza citrinella,_ yellowhammer   S, M
   *_Emberiza cia,_ rock bunting   M
   *_Emberiza cineracea,_ cinereous bunting   M
   *_Emberiza hortulana,_ ortolan   W
   *_Emberiza caesia,_ Cretzschmar's bunting   S, M
   *_Emberiza melanocephala,_ black-headed bunting   S
   *_Emberiza schoeniclus,_ reed bunting   W
   *_Emberiza striolata,_ house bunting   R
†*Family Fringillidae
  ‡*_Fringilla montifringilla,_ brambling   W
   *_Fringilla coelebs,_ chaffinch   W
   *_Serinus canarius,_ canary   W
   *_Carduelis (Chloris) chloris,_ greenfinch   W
   *_Carduelis spinus,_ European siskin   W
  ‡*_Carduelis carduelis,_ European goldfinch   R
   *_Acanthis (Carduelis) cannabina,_ linnet   R
   *_Rhodopechys (Erythospiza) githaginea,_ trumpeter bullfinch   R
   *_Erythrina sinoica,_ Sinai rosefinch   R
  ‡*_Coccothraustes coccothraustes,_ hawfinch   U
  †*_Loxia curvirostra,_ red crossbill   U
   *_Rhodospiza obsoleta,_ Isabelline finch   W

Summary

Number of Orders: 20, less 1 extinct, 2 optional = 17 to 19
Number of Families: 61, less 1 extinct, 5 optional = 55 to 60
Number of Species: 344, less 1 extinct, 2 introduced = 341 (+ 20–25
    more not listed here that may come as rare vagrants from Asia,
    Africa, or Europe)
Number of Israeli species seen in North America: = 124
    regularly or fairly often = 78
    as occasional visitors   = 46

SELECTED READINGS

For Bird-Walk Identification

Peterson, Roger Tory. *A Field Guide to the Birds* (eastern North America) and companion album, "A Field Guide to Bird Song." Boston: Houghton Mifflin, 1947.

———. *A Field Guide to Western Birds* and companion album, "A Field Guide to Western Bird Songs." Boston: Houghton Mifflin, 1961.

Peterson, Roger Tory; Guy Mountfort; P. A. D. Hollum. *A Field Guide to the Birds of Britain and Europe*. Boston: Houghton Mifflin, 1967.

Robbins, Chandler; Bertel Bruun; Herbert Zim. *Birds of North America*. New York: Golden Press, 1966.

For General Background

Alon, Azaria. *The Natural History of the Land of the Bible*. London: Hamlyn Publishers, 1969.

Arnold, Paula. *Birds of Israel*. Haifa: Shalit Publishers, 1962.

Austin, Oliver L. *Birds of the World*. New York: Golden Press, 1961.

Ferguson, Walter. "Wildlife of Sinai," *Audubon*, March 1970.

Gilliard, E. Thomas. *Living Birds of the World*. Garden City: Doubleday, 1958.

Grossman, Mary; John Hamlet. *Birds of Prey of the World*. New York: Clarkson Potter, 1964.

Kingsley, Charles. *The Hermits*. London: Macmillan, 1890.

Kitzinger, Ernst. *Israeli Mosaics*. New York: Unesco-Mentor, New American Library, 1965.

Meinertzhagen, Richard. *Birds of Arabia*. Edinburgh: Oliver & Boyd, 1954.

———. *Nicoll's Birds of Egypt*. London: Hugh & Rees, 1930.

———. *Pirates and Predators*. Edinburgh: Oliver & Boyd, 1959.

Miller, M. S. and J. L. *Encyclopedia of Bible Life*. New York: Harper, 1944.

Parmelee, Alice. *All the Birds of the Bible*. New York: Harper, 1959.

Stefereud, Alfred (ed.). *Birds in Our Lives*. Washington, D.C.: U.S. Government Printing Office, 1966.

Wetmore, Alexander. *Song and Garden Birds of North America*. Washington, D.C.: National Geographic Society, 1964 (includes song album).

———. *Water, Prey and Game Birds of North America*. Washington, D.C.: National Geographic Society, 1965 (includes song album).

For More Special Interests

American Ornithologists' Union. *The A.O.U. Check-list of North American Birds* (fifth edition, 1957).

Armstrong, Edward. *Folklore of Birds*. Boston: Houghton Mifflin, 1958.

Audubon, John James. *The Birds of America*. 7 vols. New York: Dover, 1967.

Avi-Yonah. *The Illustrated World of the Bible*. New York: McGraw-Hill, 1961.

Bent, A. C. *Life Histories of North American Birds*. 26 vols. New York: Dover, 1961–68.

Bodsworth, Fred. *Last of the Curlews*. New York: Dodd, Mead, 1954; Apollo, 1961.

Brewster, H. P. *Saints and Festivals*. Stokes, 1904.

Broun, Maurice. *Hawks Aloft*. New York: Dodd, Mead, 1949.

Buttrick, G. A. (ed.). *The Interpreter's Bible*. Nashville: Abingdon, 1962.

———. *The Interpreter's Bible Dictionary*. Nashville: Abingdon, 1962.

Carson, Rachel. *Silent Spring*. Boston: Houghton Mifflin, 1962.

Deuel, Leo. *Testaments of Life*. New York: Alfred A. Knopf, 1965.

Dorst, Jean. *South America*. New York: Random House: 1967 (pp. 28–31).

Etchecopar, R. D.; F. Hue. *Birds of North Africa*, Edinburgh: 1967.

Frederick II of Hohenstaufen. *The Art of Falconry* (translated by Wood and Fyfe). Stanford: Stanford University Press, 1943–61.

Hanzak, J. *The Pictorial Encyclopedia of Birds*. New York: Crown, 1967.

Hastings, James. *A Dictionary of the Bible.* New York: Scribner, 1963.

Ingersoll, Ernest. *Birds in Legend, Fable and Folklore.* New York: Longmans, 1923.

Jewish Publication Society of America, Philadelphia. *The Holy Scriptures* (1917); *The Torah* (1962); *The Five Megilloth and the Book of Jonah* (Ruth, Songs, Lamentations, Ecclesiastes, Esther, Jonah) (1971); *Notes on the New Translation of the Torah* (ed. Harry Orlinsky) (1968).

Lamsa, Georg. *The Holy Bible from the Ancients.* Philadelphia: Holman, 1933.

Ley, Willie. *Dawn of Zoology.* Englewood Cliffs, N.J.: Prentice-Hall, 1968.

Lorenz, Konrad. *King Solomon's Ring.* New York: Crowell, 1952; Apollo, 1961.

Mackworth-Praed, C. W.; C.H.B. Grant. *Birds of Eastern and Northern Africa.* London: Longmans, 1933.

Mathews, F. Schuyler. *Field Book of Wild Birds and Their Music.* New York: Dover, 1967.

Matthiessen, Peter. *Wildlife in America.* New York: Viking, 1959.

Moffatt, James. *The Bible, a New Translation.* New York: Harper, 1922.

Munthe, Axel. *Story of San Michele.* New York: Dutton, 1929.

Muses, C. A. (ed.). *Septuagint Bible,* (trans. Charles Thomson). Indian Hills, Colo.: Falcon Wing Press, 1954.

Peterson, Roger Tory. *Birds Over America.* New York: Dodd, Mead, 1964.

Peterson, Roger Tory; James Fisher. *The World of Birds.* Garden City: Doubleday, 1964.

Pettingill, Olin S. *Birdwatcher's America.* New York: McGraw-Hill, 1965.

———. *Guide to Bird Finding (East).* New York: Oxford, 1951.

———. *Guide to Bird Finding (West).* New York: Oxford, 1953.

Smith, J. M. P.; E. J. Goodspeed. *The Complete Bible: An American Translation.* Chicago: University of Chicago Press, 1925–48.

Soncino Books of the Bible (Hebrew and English texts in parallel). Surrey, England: Soncino Press, 1964.

Sparks, John; Tony Soper. *Owls.* New York: Taplinger, 1971.

Ticehurst, N. F. *The Mute Swan in England.* London: Cleaverhume Press, 1957.

Welker, Robert. *Birds and Men.* Cambridge, Mass.: Harvard University Press, 1935.

Welty, Joel. *The Life of Birds.* New York: Alfred A. Knopf, 1963.

White, T. H. *The Book of Beasts* (12th-century manuscript bestiary translated from the Latin). London: Cope, 1954.

Wood, J. G. *Bible Animals.* Philadelphia: Bradley, 1875.

Young, Robert. *Young's Analytical Concordance of the Bible.* New York: Funk and Wagnalls, 1965.

Periodicals

American Birds (formerly *Audubon Field Notes*). National Audubon Society, New York.
Audubon. National Audubon Society, New York.
Auk. American Ornithologists' Union, New York.
International Wildlife. National Wildlife Federation, Washington, D.C.
National Geographic. National Geographic Society, Washington, D.C.
National Wildlife. National Wildlife Federation, Washington, D.C.
Natural History. American Museum of Natural History, New York.
Smithsonian. Smithsonian Institution, Washington, D.C.

Film

Hareuveni, Nogah. "Ecology of the Bible" (film with printed text). Photographed in Israel by Neot Kedunim (Gardens of Israel) P.O. Box 299, Kiryat Ono, Israel.

A CATALOG OF SELECTED
DOVER BOOKS
IN ALL FIELDS OF INTEREST

A CATALOG OF SELECTED DOVER
BOOKS IN ALL FIELDS OF INTEREST

CONCERNING THE SPIRITUAL IN ART, Wassily Kandinsky. Pioneering work by father of abstract art. Thoughts on color theory, nature of art. Analysis of earlier masters. 12 illustrations. 80pp. of text. 5⅜ × 8½.   23411-8 Pa. $2.95

LEONARDO ON THE HUMAN BODY, Leonardo da Vinci. More than 1200 of Leonardo's anatomical drawings on 215 plates. Leonardo's text, which accompanies the drawings, has been translated into English. 506pp. 8⅜ × 11¾.
24483-0 Pa. $11.95

GOBLIN MARKET, Christina Rossetti. Best-known work by poet comparable to Emily Dickinson, Alfred Tennyson. With 46 delightfully grotesque illustrations by Laurence Housman. 64pp. 4 × 6¾.   24516-0 Pa. $2.50

THE HEART OF THOREAU'S JOURNALS, edited by Odell Shepard. Selections from *Journal*, ranging over full gamut of interests. 228pp. 5⅜ × 8½.
20741-2 Pa. $4.50

MR. LINCOLN'S CAMERA MAN: MATHEW B. BRADY, Roy Meredith. Over 300 Brady photos reproduced directly from original negatives, photos. Lively commentary. 368pp. 8⅜ × 11¼.   23021-X Pa. $14.95

PHOTOGRAPHIC VIEWS OF SHERMAN'S CAMPAIGN, George N. Barnard. Reprint of landmark 1866 volume with 61 plates: battlefield of New Hope Church, the Etawah Bridge, the capture of Atlanta, etc. 80pp. 9 × 12.   23445-2 Pa. $6.00

A SHORT HISTORY OF ANATOMY AND PHYSIOLOGY FROM THE GREEKS TO HARVEY, Dr. Charles Singer. Thoroughly engrossing nontechnical survey. 270 illustrations. 211pp. 5⅜ × 8½.   20389-1 Pa. $4.95

REDOUTE ROSES IRON-ON TRANSFER PATTERNS, Barbara Christopher. Redouté was botanical painter to the Empress Josephine; transfer his famous roses onto fabric with these 24 transfer patterns. 80pp. 8¼ × 10⅞.   24292-7 Pa. $3.50

THE FIVE BOOKS OF ARCHITECTURE, Sebastiano Serlio. Architectural milestone, first (1611) English translation of Renaissance classic. Unabridged reproduction of original edition includes over 300 woodcut illustrations. 416pp. 9⅜ × 12¼.   24349-4 Pa. $14.95

CARLSON'S GUIDE TO LANDSCAPE PAINTING, John F. Carlson. Authoritative, comprehensive guide covers, every aspect of landscape painting. 34 reproductions of paintings by author; 58 explanatory diagrams. 144pp. 8⅜ × 11.
22927-0 Pa. $5.95

101 PUZZLES IN THOUGHT AND LOGIC, C.R. Wylie, Jr. Solve murders, robberies, see which fishermen are liars—purely by reasoning! 107pp. 5⅜ × 8½.
20367-0 Pa. $2.00

TEST YOUR LOGIC, George J. Summers. 50 more truly new puzzles with new turns of thought, new subtleties of inference. 100pp. 5⅜ × 8½.   22877-0 Pa. $2.50

THE MURDER BOOK OF J.G. REEDER, Edgar Wallace. Eight suspenseful stories by bestselling mystery writer of 20s and 30s. Features the donnish Mr. J.G. Reeder of Public Prosecutor's Office. 128pp. 5⅜ × 8½.

24374-5 Pa. $3.95

ANNE ORR'S CHARTED DESIGNS, Anne Orr. Best designs by premier needlework designer, all on charts: flowers, borders, birds, children, alphabets, etc. Over 100 charts, 10 in color. Total of 40pp. 8¼ × 11.   23704-4 Pa. $2.50

BASIC CONSTRUCTION TECHNIQUES FOR HOUSES AND SMALL BUILDINGS SIMPLY EXPLAINED, U.S. Bureau of Naval Personnel. Grading, masonry, woodworking, floor and wall framing, roof framing, plastering, tile setting, much more. Over 675 illustrations. 568pp. 6½ × 9¼.   20242-9 Pa. $9.95

MATISSE LINE DRAWINGS AND PRINTS, Henri Matisse. Representative collection of female nudes, faces, still lifes, experimental works, etc., from 1898 to 1948. 50 illustrations. 48pp. 8⅜ × 11¼.   23877-6 Pa. $3.50

HOW TO PLAY THE CHESS OPENINGS, Eugene Znosko-Borovsky. Clear, profound examinations of just what each opening is intended to do and how opponent can counter. Many sample games. 147pp. 5⅜ × 8½.   22795-2 Pa. $3.50

DUPLICATE BRIDGE, Alfred Sheinwold. Clear, thorough, easily followed account: rules, etiquette, scoring, strategy, bidding; Goren's point-count system, Blackwood and Gerber conventions, etc. 158pp. 5⅜ × 8½.   22741-3 Pa. $3.50

SARGENT PORTRAIT DRAWINGS, J.S. Sargent. Collection of 42 portraits reveals technical skill and intuitive eye of noted American portrait painter, John Singer Sargent. 48pp. 8¼ × 11⅛.   24524-1 Pa. $3.50

ENTERTAINING SCIENCE EXPERIMENTS WITH EVERYDAY OBJECTS, Martin Gardner. Over 100 experiments for youngsters. Will amuse, astonish, teach, and entertain. Over 100 illustrations. 127pp. 5⅜ × 8½.   24201-3 Pa. $2.50

TEDDY BEAR PAPER DOLLS IN FULL COLOR: A Family of Four Bears and Their Costumes, Crystal Collins. A family of four Teddy Bear paper dolls and nearly 60 cut-out costumes. Full color, printed one side only. 32pp. 9¼ × 12¼.

24550-0 Pa. $3.50

NEW CALLIGRAPHIC ORNAMENTS AND FLOURISHES, Arthur Baker. Unusual, multi-useable material: arrows, pointing hands, brackets and frames, ovals, swirls, birds, etc. Nearly 700 illustrations. 80pp. 8⅜ × 11¼.

24095-9 Pa. $3.75

DINOSAUR DIORAMAS TO CUT & ASSEMBLE, M. Kalmenoff. Two complete three-dimensional scenes in full color, with 31 cut-out animals and plants. Excellent educational toy for youngsters. Instructions; 2 assembly diagrams. 32pp. 9¼ × 12¼.   24541-1 Pa. $4.50

SILHOUETTES: A PICTORIAL ARCHIVE OF VARIED ILLUSTRATIONS, edited by Carol Belanger Grafton. Over 600 silhouettes from the 18th to 20th centuries. Profiles and full figures of men, women, children, birds, animals, groups and scenes, nature, ships, an alphabet. 144pp. 8⅜ × 11¼.   23781-8 Pa. $5.95

25 KITES THAT FLY, Leslie Hunt. Full, easy-to-follow instructions for kites made from inexpensive materials. Many novelties. 70 illustrations. 110pp. 5⅜ × 8½.
22550-X Pa. $2.50

PIANO TUNING, J. Cree Fischer. Clearest, best book for beginner, amateur. Simple repairs, raising dropped notes, tuning by easy method of flattened fifths. No previous skills needed. 4 illustrations. 201pp. 5⅜ × 8½.
23267-0 Pa. $3.50

EARLY AMERICAN IRON-ON TRANSFER PATTERNS, edited by Rita Weiss. 75 designs, borders, alphabets, from traditional American sources. 48pp. 8¼ × 11.
23162-3 Pa. $1.95

CROCHETING EDGINGS, edited by Rita Weiss. Over 100 of the best designs for these lovely trims for a host of household items. Complete instructions, illustrations. 48pp. 8¼ × 11.
24031-2 Pa. $2.95

FINGER PLAYS FOR NURSERY AND KINDERGARTEN, Emilie Poulsson. 18 finger plays with music (voice and piano); entertaining, instructive. Counting, nature lore, etc. Victorian classic. 53 illustrations. 80pp. 6½ × 9¼. 22588-7 Pa. $2.25

BOSTON THEN AND NOW, Peter Vanderwarker. Here in 59 side-by-side views are photographic documentations of the city's past and present. 119 photographs. Full captions. 122pp. 8¼ × 11.
24312-5 Pa. $7.95

CROCHETING BEDSPREADS, edited by Rita Weiss. 22 patterns, originally published in three instruction books 1939-41. 39 photos, 8 charts. Instructions. 48pp. 8¼ × 11.
23610-2 Pa. $2.00

HAWTHORNE ON PAINTING, Charles W. Hawthorne. Collected from notes taken by students at famous Cape Cod School; hundreds of direct, personal *apercus,* ideas, suggestions. 91pp. 5⅜ × 8½.
20653-X Pa. $2.95

THERMODYNAMICS, Enrico Fermi. A classic of modern science. Clear, organized treatment of systems, first and second laws, entropy, thermodynamic potentials, etc. Calculus required. 160pp. 5⅜ × 8½.
60361-X Pa. $4.50

TEN BOOKS ON ARCHITECTURE, Vitruvius. The most important book ever written on architecture. Early Roman aesthetics, technology, classical orders, site selection, all other aspects. Morgan translation. 331pp. 5⅜ × 8½. 20645-9 Pa. $6.95

THE CORNELL BREAD BOOK, Clive M. McCay and Jeanette B. McCay. Famed high-protein recipe incorporated into breads, rolls, buns, coffee cakes, pizza, pie crusts, more. Nearly 50 illustrations. 48pp. 8¼ × 11.
23995-0 Pa. $2.00

THE CRAFTSMAN'S HANDBOOK, Cennino Cennini. 15th-century handbook, school of Giotto, explains applying gold, silver leaf; gesso; fresco painting, grinding pigments, etc. 142pp. 6⅛ × 9¼.
20054-X Pa. $3.95

FRANK LLOYD WRIGHT'S FALLINGWATER, Donald Hoffmann. Full story of Wright's masterwork at Bear Run, Pa. 100 photographs of site, construction, and details of completed structure. 112pp. 9¼ × 10.
23671-4 Pa. $7.95

OVAL STAINED GLASS PATTERN BOOK, C. Eaton. 60 new designs framed in shape of an oval. Greater complexity, challenge with sinuous cats, birds, mandalas framed in antique shape. 64pp. 8¼ × 11.
24519-5 Pa. $3.95

THE BOOK OF WOOD CARVING, Charles Marshall Sayers. Still finest book for beginning student. Fundamentals, technique; gives 34 designs, over 34 projects for panels, bookends, mirrors, etc. 33 photos. 118pp. 7¾ × 10⅝. 23654-4 Pa. $3.95

CARVING COUNTRY CHARACTERS, Bill Higginbotham. Expert advice for beginning, advanced carvers on materials, techniques for creating 18 projects—mirthful panorama of American characters. 105 illustrations. 80pp. 8⅜ × 11. 24135-1 Pa. $2.95

300 ART NOUVEAU DESIGNS AND MOTIFS IN FULL COLOR, C.B. Grafton. 44 full-page plates display swirling lines and muted colors typical of Art Nouveau. Borders, frames, panels, cartouches, dingbats, etc. 48pp. 9⅜ × 12¼. 24354-0 Pa. $6.95

SELF-WORKING CARD TRICKS, Karl Fulves. Editor of *Pallbearer* offers 72 tricks that work automatically through nature of card deck. No sleight of hand needed. Often spectacular. 42 illustrations. 113pp. 5⅜ × 8½. 23334-0 Pa. $3.50

CUT AND ASSEMBLE A WESTERN FRONTIER TOWN, Edmund V. Gillon, Jr. Ten authentic full-color buildings on heavy cardboard stock in H-O scale. Sheriff's Office and Jail, Saloon, Wells Fargo, Opera House, others. 48pp. 9¼ × 12¼. 23736-2 Pa. $4.95

CUT AND ASSEMBLE AN EARLY NEW ENGLAND VILLAGE, Edmund V. Gillon, Jr. Printed in full color on heavy cardboard stock. 12 authentic buildings in H-O scale: Adams home in Quincy, Mass., Oliver Wight house in Sturbridge, smithy, store, church, others. 48pp. 9¼ × 12¼. 23536-X Pa. $4.95

THE TALE OF TWO BAD MICE, Beatrix Potter. Tom Thumb and Hunca Munca squeeze out of their hole and go exploring. 27 full-color Potter illustrations. 59pp. 4¼ × 5½. (Available in U.S. only) 23065-1 Pa. $1.75

CARVING FIGURE CARICATURES IN THE OZARK STYLE, Harold L. Enlow. Instructions and illustrations for ten delightful projects, plus general carving instructions. 22 drawings and 47 photographs altogether. 39pp. 8⅜ × 11. 23151-8 Pa. $2.95

A TREASURY OF FLOWER DESIGNS FOR ARTISTS, EMBROIDERERS AND CRAFTSMEN, Susan Gaber. 100 garden favorites lushly rendered by artist for artists, craftsmen, needleworkers. Many form frames, borders. 80pp. 8¼ × 11. 24096-7 Pa. $3.95

CUT & ASSEMBLE A TOY THEATER/THE NUTCRACKER BALLET, Tom Tierney. Model of a complete, full-color production of Tchaikovsky's classic. 6 backdrops, dozens of characters, familiar dance sequences. 32pp. 9⅜ × 12¼. 24194-7 Pa. $4.50

ANIMALS: 1,419 COPYRIGHT-FREE ILLUSTRATIONS OF MAMMALS, BIRDS, FISH, INSECTS, ETC., edited by Jim Harter. Clear wood engravings present, in extremely lifelike poses, over 1,000 species of animals. 284pp. 9 × 12. 23766-4 Pa. $9.95

MORE HAND SHADOWS, Henry Bursill. For those at their 'finger ends," 16 more effects—Shakespeare, a hare, a squirrel, Mr. Punch, and twelve more—each explained by a full-page illustration. Considerable period charm. 30pp. 6½ × 9¼. 21384-6 Pa. $1.95

SURREAL STICKERS AND UNREAL STAMPS, William Rowe. 224 haunting, hilarious stamps on gummed, perforated stock, with images of elephants, geisha girls, George Washington, etc. 16pp. one side. 8¼ × 11.   24371-0 Pa. $3.50

GOURMET KITCHEN LABELS, Ed Sibbett, Jr. 112 full-color labels (4 copies each of 28 designs). Fruit, bread, other culinary motifs. Gummed and perforated. 16pp. 8¼ × 11.   24087-8 Pa. $2.95

PATTERNS AND INSTRUCTIONS FOR CARVING AUTHENTIC BIRDS, H.D. Green. Detailed instructions, 27 diagrams, 85 photographs for carving 15 species of birds so life-like, they'll seem ready to fly! 8¼ × 11.   24222-6 Pa. $3.00

FLATLAND, E.A. Abbott. Science-fiction classic explores life of 2-D being in 3-D world. 16 illustrations. 103pp. 5⅜ × 8.   20001-9 Pa. $2.00

DRIED FLOWERS, Sarah Whitlock and Martha Rankin. Concise, clear, practical guide to dehydration, glycerinizing, pressing plant material, and more. Covers use of silica gel. 12 drawings. 32pp. 5⅜ × 8½.   21802-3 Pa. $1.00

EASY-TO-MAKE CANDLES, Gary V. Guy. Learn how easy it is to make all kinds of decorative candles. Step-by-step instructions. 82 illustrations. 48pp. 8¼ × 11.
     23881-4 Pa. $2.95

SUPER STICKERS FOR KIDS, Carolyn Bracken. 128 gummed and perforated full-color stickers: GIRL WANTED, KEEP OUT, BORED OF EDUCATION, X-RATED, COMBAT ZONE, many others. 16pp. 8¼ × 11.   24092-4 Pa. $3.50

CUT AND COLOR PAPER MASKS, Michael Grater. Clowns, animals, funny faces...simply color them in, cut them out, and put them together, and you have 9 paper masks to play with and enjoy. 32pp. 8¼ × 11.   23171-2 Pa. $2.95

A CHRISTMAS CAROL: THE ORIGINAL MANUSCRIPT, Charles Dickens. Clear facsimile of Dickens manuscript, on facing pages with final printed text. 8 illustrations by John Leech, 4 in color on covers. 144pp. 8⅜ × 11¼.
     20980-6 Pa. $5.95

CARVING SHOREBIRDS, Harry V. Shourds & Anthony Hillman. 16 full-size patterns (all double-page spreads) for 19 North American shorebirds with step-by-step instructions. 72pp. 9¼ × 12¼.   24287-0 Pa. $5.95

THE GENTLE ART OF MATHEMATICS, Dan Pedoe. Mathematical games, probability, the question of infinity, topology, how the laws of algebra work, problems of irrational numbers, and more. 42 figures. 143pp. 5⅜ × 8½.
     22949-1 Pa. $3.50

READY-TO-USE DOLLHOUSE WALLPAPER, Katzenbach & Warren, Inc. Stripe, 2 floral stripes, 2 allover florals, polka dot; all in full color. 4 sheets (350 sq. in.) of each, enough for average room. 48pp. 8¼ × 11.   23495-9 Pa. $2.95

MINIATURE IRON-ON TRANSFER PATTERNS FOR DOLLHOUSES, DOLLS, AND SMALL PROJECTS, Rita Weiss and Frank Fontana. Over 100 miniature patterns: rugs, bedspreads, quilts, chair seats, etc. In standard dollhouse size. 48pp. 8¼ × 11.   23741-9 Pa. $1.95

THE DINOSAUR COLORING BOOK, Anthony Rao. 45 renderings of dinosaurs, fossil birds, turtles, other creatures of Mesozoic Era. Scientifically accurate. Captions. 48pp. 8¼ × 11.   24022-3 Pa. $2.50

JAPANESE DESIGN MOTIFS, Matsuya Co. Mon, or heraldic designs. Over 4000 typical, beautiful designs: birds, animals, flowers, swords, fans, geometrics; all beautifully stylized. 213pp. 11⅜ × 8¼. 22874-6 Pa. $7.95

THE TALE OF BENJAMIN BUNNY, Beatrix Potter. Peter Rabbit's cousin coaxes him back into Mr. McGregor's garden for a whole new set of adventures. All 27 full-color illustrations. 59pp. 4¼ × 5½. (Available in U.S. only) 21102-9 Pa. $1.75

THE TALE OF PETER RABBIT AND OTHER FAVORITE STORIES BOXED SET, Beatrix Potter. Seven of Beatrix Potter's best-loved tales including Peter Rabbit in a specially designed, durable boxed set. 4¼ × 5½. Total of 447pp. 158 color illustrations. (Available in U.S. only) 23903-9 Pa. $12.25

PRACTICAL MENTAL MAGIC, Theodore Annemann. Nearly 200 astonishing feats of mental magic revealed in step-by-step detail. Complete advice on staging, patter, etc. Illustrated. 320pp. 5⅜ × 8½. 24426-1 Pa. $5.95

CELEBRATED CASES OF JUDGE DEE (DEE GOONG AN), translated by Robert Van Gulik. Authentic 18th-century Chinese detective novel; Dee and associates solve three interlocked cases. Led to van Gulik's own stories with same characters. Extensive introduction. 9 illustrations. 237pp. 5⅜ × 8½. 23337-5 Pa. $4.95

CUT & FOLD EXTRATERRESTRIAL INVADERS THAT FLY, M. Grater. Stage your own lilliputian space battles.By following the step-by-step instructions and explanatory diagrams you can launch 22 full-color fliers into space. 36pp. 8¼ × 11. 24478-4 Pa. $2.95

CUT & ASSEMBLE VICTORIAN HOUSES, Edmund V. Gillon, Jr. Printed in full color on heavy cardboard stock, 4 authentic Victorian houses in H-O scale: Italian-style Villa, Octagon, Second Empire, Stick Style. 48pp. 9¼ × 12¼. 23849-0 Pa. $4.95

BEST SCIENCE FICTION STORIES OF H.G. WELLS, H.G. Wells. Full novel *The Invisible Man,* plus 17 short stories: "The Crystal Egg," "Aepyornis Island," "The Strange Orchid," etc. 303pp. 5⅜ × 8½. (Available in U.S. only) 21531-8 Pa. $4.95

TRADEMARK DESIGNS OF THE WORLD, Yusaku Kamekura. A lavish collection of nearly 700 trademarks, the work of Wright, Loewy, Klee, Binder, hundreds of others. 160pp. 8¾ × 8. (EJ) 24191-2 Pa. $5.95

THE ARTIST'S AND CRAFTSMAN'S GUIDE TO REDUCING, ENLARGING AND TRANSFERRING DESIGNS, Rita Weiss. Discover, reduce, enlarge, transfer designs from any objects to any craft project. 12pp. plus 16 sheets special graph paper. 8¼ × 11. 24142-4 Pa. $3.95

TREASURY OF JAPANESE DESIGNS AND MOTIFS FOR ARTISTS AND CRAFTSMEN, edited by Carol Belanger Grafton. Indispensable collection of 360 traditional Japanese designs and motifs redrawn in clean, crisp black-and-white, copyright-free illustrations. 96pp. 8¼ × 11. 24435-0 Pa. $4.50

CHANCERY CURSIVE STROKE BY STROKE, Arthur Baker. Instructions and illustrations for each stroke of each letter (upper and lower case) and numerals. 54 full-page plates. 64pp. 8¼ × 11. 24278-1 Pa. $2.50

THE ENJOYMENT AND USE OF COLOR, Walter Sargent. Color relationships, values, intensities; complementary colors, illumination, similar topics. Color in nature and art. 7 color plates, 29 illustrations. 274pp. 5⅜ × 8½. 20944-X Pa. $4.95

SCULPTURE PRINCIPLES AND PRACTICE, Louis Slobodkin. Step-by-step approach to clay, plaster, metals, stone; classical and modern. 253 drawings, photos. 255pp. 8⅛ × 11. 22960-2 Pa. $7.50

VICTORIAN FASHION PAPER DOLLS FROM HARPER'S BAZAR, 1867-1898, Theodore Menten. Four female dolls with 28 elegant high fashion costumes, printed in full color. 32pp. 9¼ × 12¼. 23453-3 Pa. $3.95

FLOPSY, MOPSY AND COTTONTAIL: A Little Book of Paper Dolls in Full Color, Susan LaBelle. Three dolls and 21 costumes (7 for each doll) show Peter Rabbit's siblings dressed for holidays, gardening, hiking, etc. Charming borders, captions. 48pp. 4¼ × 5½. (USCO) 24376-1 Pa. $2.50

NATIONAL LEAGUE BASEBALL CARD CLASSICS, Bert Randolph Sugar. 83 big-leaguers from 1909-69 on facsimile cards. Hubbell, Dean, Spahn, Brock plus advertising, info, no duplications. Perforated, detachable. 16pp. 8¼ × 11. 24308-7 Pa. $3.50

THE LOGICAL APPROACH TO CHESS, Dr. Max Euwe, et al. First-rate text of comprehensive strategy, tactics, theory for the amateur. No gambits to memorize, just a clear, logical approach. 224pp. 5⅜ × 8½. 24353-2 Pa. $4.50

MAGICK IN THEORY AND PRACTICE, Aleister Crowley. The summation of the thought and practice of the century's most famous necromancer, long hard to find. Crowley's best book. 436pp. 5⅜ × 8½. (Available in U.S. only) 23295-6 Pa. $6.95

THE HAUNTED HOTEL, Wilkie Collins. Collins' last great tale; doom and destiny in a Venetian palace. Praised by T.S. Eliot. 127pp. 5⅜ × 8½. 24333-8 Pa. $3.00

ART DECO DISPLAY ALPHABETS, Dan X. Solo. Wide variety of bold yet elegant lettering in handsome Art Deco styles. 100 complete fonts, with numerals, punctuation, more. 104pp. 8⅛ × 11. 24372-9 Pa. $4.50

CALLIGRAPHIC ALPHABETS, Arthur Baker. Nearly 150 complete alphabets by outstanding contemporary. Stimulating ideas; useful source for unique effects. 154 plates. 157pp. 8⅜ × 11¼. 21045-6 Pa. $5.95

ARTHUR BAKER'S HISTORIC CALLIGRAPHIC ALPHABETS, Arthur Baker. From monumental capitals of first-century Rome to humanistic cursive of 16th century, 33 alphabets in fresh interpretations. 88 plates. 96pp. 9 × 12. 24054-1 Pa. $4.50

LETTIE LANE PAPER DOLLS, Sheila Young. Genteel turn-of-the-century family very popular then and now. 24 paper dolls. 16 plates in full color. 32pp. 9¼ × 12¼. 24089-4 Pa. $3.95

KEYBOARD WORKS FOR SOLO INSTRUMENTS, G.F. Handel. 35 neglected works from Handel's vast oeuvre, originally jotted down as improvisations. Includes Eight Great Suites, others. New sequence. 174pp. 9⅜ × 12¼.
24338-9 Pa. $7.50

AMERICAN LEAGUE BASEBALL CARD CLASSICS, Bert Randolph Sugar. 82 stars from 1900s to 60s on facsimile cards. Ruth, Cobb, Mantle, Williams, plus advertising, info, no duplications. Perforated, detachable. 16pp. 8¼ × 11.
24286-2 Pa. $3.50

A TREASURY OF CHARTED DESIGNS FOR NEEDLEWORKERS, Georgia Gorham and Jeanne Warth. 141 charted designs: owl, cat with yarn, tulips, piano, spinning wheel, covered bridge, Victorian house and many others. 48pp. 8¼ × 11.
23558-0 Pa. $1.95

DANISH FLORAL CHARTED DESIGNS, Gerda Bengtsson. Exquisite collection of over 40 different florals: anemone, Iceland poppy, wild fruit, pansies, many others. 45 illustrations. 48pp. 8¼ × 11.
23957-8 Pa. $2.50

OLD PHILADELPHIA IN EARLY PHOTOGRAPHS 1839-1914, Robert F. Looney. 215 photographs: panoramas, street scenes, landmarks, President-elect Lincoln's visit, 1876 Centennial Exposition, much more. 230pp. 8⅜ × 11¾.
23345-6 Pa. $9.95

PRELUDE TO MATHEMATICS, W.W. Sawyer. Noted mathematician's lively, stimulating account of non-Euclidean geometry, matrices, determinants, group theory, other topics. Emphasis on novel, striking aspects. 224pp. 5⅜ × 8½.
24401-6 Pa. $4.50

ADVENTURES WITH A MICROSCOPE, Richard Headstrom. 59 adventures with clothing fibers, protozoa, ferns and lichens, roots and leaves, much more. 142 illustrations. 232pp. 5⅜ × 8½.
23471-1 Pa. $3.95

IDENTIFYING ANIMAL TRACKS: MAMMALS, BIRDS, AND OTHER ANIMALS OF THE EASTERN UNITED STATES, Richard Headstrom. For hunters, naturalists, scouts, nature-lovers. Diagrams of tracks, tips on identification. 128pp. 5⅜ × 8.
24442-3 Pa. $3.50

VICTORIAN FASHIONS AND COSTUMES FROM HARPER'S BAZAR, 1867-1898, edited by Stella Blum. Day costumes, evening wear, sports clothes, shoes, hats, other accessories in over 1,000 detailed engravings. 320pp. 9⅜ × 12¼.
22990-4 Pa. $10.95

EVERYDAY FASHIONS OF THE TWENTIES AS PICTURED IN SEARS AND OTHER CATALOGS, edited by Stella Blum. Actual dress of the Roaring Twenties, with text by Stella Blum. Over 750 illustrations, captions. 156pp. 9 × 12.
24134-3 Pa. $8.95

HALL OF FAME BASEBALL CARDS, edited by Bert Randolph Sugar. Cy Young, Ted Williams, Lou Gehrig, and many other Hall of Fame greats on 92 full-color, detachable reprints of early baseball cards. No duplication of cards with *Classic Baseball Cards*. 16pp. 8¼ × 11.
23624-2 Pa. $3.50

THE ART OF HAND LETTERING, Helm Wotzkow. Course in hand lettering, Roman, Gothic, Italic, Block, Script. Tools, proportions, optical aspects, individual variation. Very quality conscious. Hundreds of specimens. 320pp. 5⅜ × 8½.
21797-3 Pa. $5.95

HOW THE OTHER HALF LIVES, Jacob A. Riis. Journalistic record of filth, degradation, upward drive in New York immigrant slums, shops, around 1900. New edition includes 100 original Riis photos, monuments of early photography. 233pp. 10 × 7⅞. 22012-5 Pa. $9.95

CHINA AND ITS PEOPLE IN EARLY PHOTOGRAPHS, John Thomson. In 200 black-and-white photographs of exceptional quality photographic pioneer Thomson captures the mountains, dwellings, monuments and people of 19th-century China. 272pp. 9⅜ × 12¼. 24393-1 Pa. $13.95

GODEY COSTUME PLATES IN COLOR FOR DECOUPAGE AND FRAMING, edited by Eleanor Hasbrouk Rawlings. 24 full-color engravings depicting 19th-century Parisian haute couture. Printed on one side only. 56pp. 8¼ × 11. 23879-2 Pa. $3.95

ART NOUVEAU STAINED GLASS PATTERN BOOK, Ed Sibbett, Jr. 104 projects using well-known themes of Art Nouveau: swirling forms, florals, peacocks, and sensuous women. 60pp. 8¼ × 11. 23577-7 Pa. $3.95

QUICK AND EASY PATCHWORK ON THE SEWING MACHINE: Susan Aylsworth Murwin and Suzzy Payne. Instructions, diagrams show exactly how to machine sew 12 quilts. 48pp. of templates. 50 figures. 80pp. 8¼ × 11. 23770-2 Pa. $3.95

THE STANDARD BOOK OF QUILT MAKING AND COLLECTING, Marguerite Ickis. Full information, full-sized patterns for making 46 traditional quilts, also 150 other patterns. 483 illustrations. 273pp. 6⅞ × 9⅝. 20582-7 Pa. $5.95

LETTERING AND ALPHABETS, J. Albert Cavanagh. 85 complete alphabets lettered in various styles; instructions for spacing, roughs, brushwork. 121pp. 8¾ × 8. 20053-1 Pa. $3.95

LETTER FORMS: 110 COMPLETE ALPHABETS, Frederick Lambert. 110 sets of capital letters; 16 lower case alphabets; 70 sets of numbers and other symbols. 110pp. 8⅛ × 11. 22872-X Pa. $4.50

ORCHIDS AS HOUSE PLANTS, Rebecca Tyson Northen. Grow cattleyas and many other kinds of orchids—in a window, in a case, or under artificial light. 63 illustrations. 148pp. 5⅜ × 8½. 23261-1 Pa. $2.95

THE MUSHROOM HANDBOOK, Louis C.C. Krieger. Still the best popular handbook. Full descriptions of 259 species, extremely thorough text, poisons, folklore, etc. 32 color plates; 126 other illustrations. 560pp. 5⅜ × 8½. 21861-9 Pa. $8.50

THE DORÉ BIBLE ILLUSTRATIONS, Gustave Doré. All wonderful, detailed plates: Adam and Eve, Flood, Babylon, life of Jesus, etc. Brief King James text with each plate. 241 plates. 241pp. 9 × 12. 23004-X Pa. $8.95

THE BOOK OF KELLS: Selected Plates in Full Color, edited by Blanche Cirker. 32 full-page plates from greatest manuscript-icon of early Middle Ages. Fantastic, mysterious. Publisher's Note. Captions. 32pp. 9¾ × 12¼. 24345-1 Pa. $4.50

THE PERFECT WAGNERITE, George Bernard Shaw. Brilliant criticism of the Ring Cycle, with provocative interpretation of politics, economic theories behind the Ring. 136pp. 5⅜ × 8½. (EUK) 21707-8 Pa. $3.95

THE RIME OF THE ANCIENT MARINER, Gustave Doré, S.T. Coleridge. Doré's finest work, 34 plates capture moods, subtleties of poem. Full text. 77pp. 9¼ × 12. 22305-1 Pa. $4.95

SONGS OF INNOCENCE, William Blake. The first and most popular of Blake's famous "Illuminated Books," in a facsimile edition reproducing all 31 brightly colored plates. Additional printed text of each poem. 64pp. 5¼ × 7.
22764-2 Pa. $3.50

AN INTRODUCTION TO INFORMATION THEORY, J.R. Pierce. Second (1980) edition of most impressive non-technical account available. Encoding, entropy, noisy channel, related areas, etc. 320pp. 5⅜ × 8½. 24061-4 Pa. $5.95

THE DIVINE PROPORTION: A STUDY IN MATHEMATICAL BEAUTY, H.E. Huntley. "Divine proportion" or "golden ratio" in poetry, Pascal's triangle, philosophy, psychology, music, mathematical figures, etc. Excellent bridge between science and art. 58 figures. 185pp. 5⅜ × 8½. 22254-3 Pa. $4.50

THE DOVER NEW YORK WALKING GUIDE: From the Battery to Wall Street, Mary J. Shapiro. Superb inexpensive guide to historic buildings and locales in lower Manhattan: Trinity Church, Bowling Green, more. Complete Text; maps. 36 illustrations. 48pp. 3⅞ × 9¼. 24225-0 Pa. $2.50

NEW YORK THEN AND NOW, Edward B. Watson, Edmund V. Gillon, Jr. 83 important Manhattan sites: on facing pages early photographs (1875-1925) and 1976 photos by Gillon. 172 illustrations. 171pp. 9¼ × 10. 23361-8 Pa. $9.95

HISTORIC COSTUME IN PICTURES, Braun & Schneider. Over 1450 costumed figures from dawn of civilization to end of 19th century. English captions. 125 plates. 256pp. 8⅜ × 11¼. 23150-X Pa. $7.95

VICTORIAN AND EDWARDIAN FASHION: A Photographic Survey, Alison Gernsheim. First fashion history completely illustrated by contemporary photographs. Full text plus 235 photos, 1840-1914, in which many celebrities appear. 240pp. 6½ × 9¼. 24205-6 Pa. $6.00

CHARTED CHRISTMAS DESIGNS FOR COUNTED CROSS-STITCH AND OTHER NEEDLECRAFTS, Lindberg Press. Charted designs for 45 beautiful needlecraft projects with many yuletide and wintertime motifs. 48pp. 8¼ × 11.
(EDNS) 24356-7 Pa. $2.50

101 FOLK DESIGNS FOR COUNTED CROSS-STITCH AND OTHER NEEDLE-CRAFTS, Carter Houck. 101 authentic charted folk designs in a wide array of lovely representations with many suggestions for effective use. 48pp. 8¼ × 11.
24369-9 Pa. $2.25

FIVE ACRES AND INDEPENDENCE, Maurice G. Kains. Great back-to-the-land classic explains basics of self-sufficient farming. The one book to get. 95 illustrations. 397pp. 5⅜ × 8½. 20974-1 Pa. $6.50

A MODERN HERBAL, Margaret Grieve. Much the fullest, most exact, most useful compilation of herbal material. Gigantic alphabetical encyclopedia, from aconite to zedoary, gives botanical information, medical properties, folklore, economic uses, and much else. Indispensable to serious reader. 161 illustrations. 888pp. 6½ × 9¼. (Available in U.S. only) 22798-7, 22799-5 Pa., Two-vol. set $17.00

DECORATIVE NAPKIN FOLDING FOR BEGINNERS, Lillian Oppenheimer and Natalie Epstein. 22 different napkin folds in the shape of a heart, clown's hat, love knot, etc. 63 drawings. 48pp. 8¼ × 11. 23797-4 Pa. $2.25

DECORATIVE LABELS FOR HOME CANNING, PRESERVING, AND OTHER HOUSEHOLD AND GIFT USES, Theodore Menten. 128 gummed, perforated labels, beautifully printed in 2 colors. 12 versions. Adhere to metal, glass, wood, ceramics. 24pp. 8¼ × 11. 23219-0 Pa. $3.50

EARLY AMERICAN STENCILS ON WALLS AND FURNITURE, Janet Waring. Thorough coverage of 19th-century folk art: techniques, artifacts, surviving specimens. 166 illustrations, 7 in color. 147pp. of text. 7⅞ × 10¾. 21906-2 Pa. $9.95

AMERICAN ANTIQUE WEATHERVANES, A.B. & W.T. Westervelt. Extensively illustrated 1883 catalog exhibiting over 550 copper weathervanes and finials. Excellent primary source by one of the principal manufacturers. 104pp. 6⅛ × 9¼. 24396-6 Pa. $3.95

ART STUDENTS' ANATOMY, Edmond J. Farris. Long favorite in art schools. Basic elements, common positions, actions. Full text, 158 illustrations. 159pp. 5⅜ × 8½. 20744-7 Pa. $3.95

BRIDGMAN'S LIFE DRAWING, George B. Bridgman. More than 500 drawings and text teach you to abstract the body into its major masses. Also specific areas of anatomy. 192pp. 6½ × 9¼. 22710-3 Pa. $4.50

COMPLETE PRELUDES AND ETUDES FOR SOLO PIANO, Frederic Chopin. All 26 Preludes, all 27 Etudes by greatest composer of piano music. Authoritative Paderewski edition. 224pp. 9 × 12. (Available in U.S. only) 24052-5 Pa. $7.50

PIANO MUSIC 1888-1905, Claude Debussy. Deux Arabesques, Suite Bergamesque, Masques, 1st series of Images, etc. 9 others, in corrected editions. 175pp. 9⅜ × 12¼. 22771-5 Pa. $6.95

TEDDY BEAR IRON-ON TRANSFER PATTERNS, Ted Menten. 80 iron-on transfer patterns of male and female Teddys in a wide variety of activities, poses, sizes. 48pp. 8¼ × 11. 24596-9 Pa. $2.25

A PICTURE HISTORY OF THE BROOKLYN BRIDGE, M.J. Shapiro. Profusely illustrated account of greatest engineering achievement of 19th century. 167 rare photos & engravings recall construction, human drama. Extensive, detailed text. 122pp. 8¼ × 11. 24403-2 Pa. $7.95

NEW YORK IN THE THIRTIES, Berenice Abbott. Noted photographer's fascinating study shows new buildings that have become famous and old sights that have disappeared forever. 97 photographs. 97pp. 11⅜ × 10. 22967-X Pa. $7.50

MATHEMATICAL TABLES AND FORMULAS, Robert D. Carmichael and Edwin R. Smith. Logarithms, sines, tangents, trig functions, powers, roots, reciprocals, exponential and hyperbolic functions, formulas and theorems. 269pp. 5⅜ × 8½. 60111-0 Pa. $4.95

HANDBOOK OF MATHEMATICAL FUNCTIONS WITH FORMULAS, GRAPHS, AND MATHEMATICAL TABLES, edited by Milton Abramowitz and Irene A. Stegun. Vast compendium: 29 sets of tables, some to as high as 20 places. 1,046pp. 8 × 10½. 61272-4 Pa. $21.95

REASON IN ART, George Santayana. Renowned philosopher's provocative, seminal treatment of basis of art in instinct and experience. Volume Four of *The Life of Reason.* 230pp. 5⅜ × 8.   24358-3 Pa. $4.50

LANGUAGE, TRUTH AND LOGIC, Alfred J. Ayer. Famous, clear introduction to Vienna, Cambridge schools of Logical Positivism. Role of philosophy, elimination of metaphysics, nature of analysis, etc. 160pp. 5⅜ × 8½. (USCO)
20010-8 Pa. $2.95

BASIC ELECTRONICS, U.S. Bureau of Naval Personnel. Electron tubes, circuits, antennas, AM, FM, and CW transmission and receiving, etc. 560 illustrations. 567pp. 6½ × 9¼.   21076-6 Pa. $9.95

THE ART DECO STYLE, edited by Theodore Menten. Furniture, jewelry, metalwork, ceramics, fabrics, lighting fixtures, interior decors, exteriors, graphics from pure French sources. Over 400 photographs. 183pp. 8⅜ × 11¼.
22824-X Pa. $7.95

THE FOUR BOOKS OF ARCHITECTURE, Andrea Palladio. 16th-century classic covers classical architectural remains, Renaissance revivals, classical orders, etc. 1738 Ware English edition. 216 plates. 110pp. of text. 9½ × 12¾.
21308-0 Pa. $11.95

THE WIT AND HUMOR OF OSCAR WILDE, edited by Alvin Redman. More than 1000 ripostes, paradoxes, wisecracks: Work is the curse of the drinking classes, I can resist everything except temptations, etc. 258pp. 5⅜ × 8½.
20602-5 Pa. $4.50

THE DEVIL'S DICTIONARY, Ambrose Bierce. Barbed, bitter, brilliant witticisms in the form of a dictionary. Best, most ferocious satire America has produced. 145pp. 5⅜ × 8½.   20487-1 Pa. $2.95

ERTÉ'S FASHION DESIGNS, Erté. 210 black-and-white inventions from *Harper's Bazar,* 1918-32, plus 8pp. full-color covers. Captions. 88pp. 9 × 12.
24203-X Pa. $7.95

ERTÉ GRAPHICS, Erté. Collection of striking color graphics: *Seasons, Alphabet, Numerals, Aces* and *Precious Stones.* 50 plates, including 4 on covers. 48pp. 9⅜ × 12¼.   23580-7 Pa. $6.95

PAPER FOLDING FOR BEGINNERS, William D. Murray and Francis J. Rigney. Clearest book for making origami sail boats, roosters, frogs that move legs, etc. 40 projects. More than 275 illustrations. 94pp. 5⅜ × 8½.   20713-7 Pa. $2.50

ORIGAMI FOR THE ENTHUSIAST, John Montroll. Fish, ostrich, peacock, squirrel, rhinoceros, Pegasus, 19 other intricate subjects. Instructions. Diagrams. 128pp. 9 × 12.   23799-0 Pa. $5.95

CROCHETING NOVELTY POT HOLDERS, edited by Linda Macho. 64 useful, whimsical pot holders feature kitchen themes, animals, flowers, other novelties. Surprisingly easy to crochet. Complete instructions. 48pp. 8¼ × 11.
24296-X Pa. $1.95

CROCHETING DOILIES, edited by Rita Weiss. Irish Crochet, Jewel, Star Wheel, Vanity Fair and more. Also luncheon and console sets, runners and centerpieces. 51 illustrations. 48pp. 8¼ × 11.   23424-X Pa. $2.75

YUCATAN BEFORE AND AFTER THE CONQUEST, Diego de Landa. Only significant account of Yucatan written in the early post-Conquest era. Translated by William Gates. Over 120 illustrations. 162pp. 5⅜ × 8½. 23622-6 Pa. $3.95

ORNATE PICTORIAL CALLIGRAPHY, E.A. Lupfer. Complete instructions, over 150 examples help you create magnificent "flourishes" from which beautiful animals and objects gracefully emerge. 8⅛ × 11. 21957-7 Pa. $3.50

DOLLY DINGLE PAPER DOLLS, Grace Drayton. Cute chubby children by same artist who did Campbell Kids. Rare plates from 1910s. 30 paper dolls and over 100 outfits reproduced in full color. 32pp. 9¼ × 12¼. 23711-7 Pa. $3.50

CURIOUS GEORGE PAPER DOLLS IN FULL COLOR, H. A. Rey, Kathy Allert. Naughty little monkey-hero of children's books in two doll figures, plus 48 full-color costumes: pirate, Indian chief, fireman, more. 32pp. 9¼ × 12¼. 24386-9 Pa. $3.50

GERMAN: HOW TO SPEAK AND WRITE IT, Joseph Rosenberg. Like *French, How to Speak and Write It.* Very rich modern course, with a wealth of pictorial material. 330 illustrations. 384pp. 5⅜ × 8½. 20271-2 Pa. $4.95

CATS AND KITTENS: 24 Ready-to-Mail Color Photo Postcards, D. Holby. Handsome collection; feline in a variety of adorable poses. Identifications. 12pp. on postcard stock. 8¼ × 11. 24469-5 Pa. $2.95

MARILYN MONROE PAPER DOLLS, Tom Tierney. 31 full-color designs on heavy stock, from *The Asphalt Jungle, Gentlemen Prefer Blondes,* 22 others. 1 doll. 16 plates. 32pp. 9⅜ × 12¼. 23769-9 Pa. $3.95

FUNDAMENTALS OF LAYOUT, F.H. Wills. All phases of layout design discussed and illustrated in 121 illustrations. Indispensable as student's text or handbook for professional. 124pp. 8⅛ × 11. 21279-3 Pa. $4.50

FANTASTIC SUPER STICKERS, Ed Sibbett, Jr. 75 colorful pressure-sensitive stickers. Peel off and place for a touch of pizzazz: clowns, penguins, teddy bears, etc. Full color. 16pp. 8¼ × 11. 24471-7 Pa. $3.50

LABELS FOR ALL OCCASIONS, Ed Sibbett, Jr. 6 labels each of 16 different designs—baroque, art nouveau, art deco, Pennsylvania Dutch, etc.—in full color. 24pp. 8¼ × 11. 23688-9 Pa. $3.95

HOW TO CALCULATE QUICKLY: RAPID METHODS IN BASIC MATHEMATICS, Henry Sticker. Addition, subtraction, multiplication, division, checks, etc. More than 8000 problems, solutions. 185pp. 5 × 7¼. 20295-X Pa. $2.95

THE CAT COLORING BOOK, Karen Baldauski. Handsome, realistic renderings of 40 splendid felines, from American shorthair to exotic types. 44 plates. Captions. 48pp. 8¼ × 11. 24011-8 Pa. $2.50

THE TALE OF PETER RABBIT, Beatrix Potter. The inimitable Peter's terrifying adventure in Mr. McGregor's garden, with all 27 wonderful, full-color Potter illustrations. 55pp. 4¼ × 5½. (Available in U.S. only) 22827-4 Pa. $1.75

BASIC ELECTRICITY, U.S. Bureau of Naval Personnel. Batteries, circuits, conductors, AC and DC, inductance and capacitance, generators, motors, transformers, amplifiers, etc. 349 illustrations. 448pp. 6½ × 9¼. 20973-3 Pa. $7.95

CATALOG OF DOVER BOOKS

SOURCE BOOK OF MEDICAL HISTORY, edited by Logan Clendening, M.D. Original accounts ranging from Ancient Egypt and Greece to discovery of X-rays: Galen, Pasteur, Lavoisier, Harvey, Parkinson, others. 685pp. 5⅜ × 8½.

20621-1 Pa. $11.95

THE ROSE AND THE KEY, J.S. Lefanu. Superb mystery novel from Irish master. Dark doings among an ancient and aristocratic English family. Well-drawn characters; capital suspense. Introduction by N. Donaldson. 448pp. 5⅜ × 8½.

24377-X Pa. $6.95

SOUTH WIND, Norman Douglas. Witty, elegant novel of ideas set on languorous Meditterranean island of Nepenthe. Elegant prose, glittering epigrams, mordant satire. 1917 masterpiece. 416pp. 5⅜ × 8½. (Available in U.S. only)

24361-3 Pa. $5.95

RUSSELL'S CIVIL WAR PHOTOGRAPHS, Capt. A.J. Russell. 116 rare Civil War Photos: Bull Run, Virginia campaigns, bridges, railroads, Richmond, Lincoln's funeral car. Many never seen before. Captions. 128pp. 9⅜ × 12¼.

24283-8 Pa. $7.95

PHOTOGRAPHS BY MAN RAY: 105 Works, 1920-1934. Nudes, still lifes, landscapes, women's faces, celebrity portraits (Dali, Matisse, Picasso, others), rayographs. Reprinted from rare gravure edition. 128pp. 9⅜ × 12¼.

23842-3 Pa. $8.95

STAR NAMES: THEIR LORE AND MEANING, Richard H. Allen. Star names, the zodiac, constellations: folklore and literature associated with heavens. The basic book of its field, fascinating reading. 563pp. 5⅜ × 8½. 21079-0 Pa. $7.95

BURNHAM'S CELESTIAL HANDBOOK, Robert Burnham, Jr. Thorough guide to the stars beyond our solar system. Exhaustive treatment. Alphabetical by constellation: Andromeda to Cetus in Vol. 1; Chamaeleon to Orion in Vol. 2; and Pavo to Vulpecula in Vol. 3. Hundreds of illustrations. Index in Vol. 3. 2000pp. 6⅛ × 9¼.

23567-X, 23568-8, 23673-0 Pa. Three-vol. set $37.85

THE ART NOUVEAU STYLE BOOK OF ALPHONSE MUCHA, Alphonse Mucha. All 72 plates from *Documents Decoratifs* in original color. Stunning, essential work of Art Nouveau. 80pp. 9⅜ × 12¼. 24044-4 Pa. $8.95

DESIGNS BY ERTE; FASHION DRAWINGS AND ILLUSTRATIONS FROM "HARPER'S BAZAR," Erte. 310 fabulous line drawings and 14 *Harper's Bazar* covers, 8 in full color. Erte's exotic temptresses with tassels, fur muffs, long trains, coifs, more. 129pp. 9⅜ × 12¼. 23397-9 Pa. $8.95

HISTORY OF STRENGTH OF MATERIALS, Stephen P. Timoshenko. Excellent historical survey of the strength of materials with many references to the theories of elasticity and structure. 245 figures. 452pp. 5⅜ × 8½. 61187-6 Pa. $9.95

Prices subject to change without notice.

Available at your book dealer or write for free catalog to Dept. GI, Dover Publications, Inc., 31 East 2nd St. Mineola, N.Y. 11501. Dover publishes more than 175 books each year on science, elementary and advanced mathematics, biology, music, art, literary history, social sciences and other areas.